AQA AS Economics

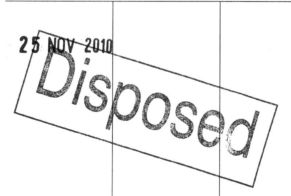

Heinemann

Heinemann is an imprint of Pearson Education Limited, a company incorporated in England and Wales, having its registered office at Edinburgh Gate, Harlow, Essex, CM20 2JE. Registered company number: 872828

www.heinemann.co.uk

Heinemann is a registered trademark of Pearson Education Limited

All text with the exception of Exam cafés © Chris Vidler 2008
Exam cafés © Pearson Education Ltd 2008

First published 2008

12 11 10 09 08
10 9 8 7 6 5 4 3 2 1

British Library Cataloguing in Publication Data is available from the British Library on request.

ISBN 978 0 435692 22 3

Edited by Bill MacKeith
Designed by Tek-Art
Typeset by Tek-Art
Original illustrations © Pearson Education Ltd 2008
Illustrated by Tek-Art
Cover design by Philippa Baile
Picture research by Sally Claxton
Cover photo © Corbis/Thomas Brummett
Printed in the UK by Scotprint

Websites

There are links to relevant websites in this book. In order to ensure that the links are up-to-date, that the links work, and that the sites are not inadvertently linked to sites that could be considered offensive, we have made the links available on the Heinemann website at www.heinemann.co.uk/hotlinks. When you access the site, the express code is 2223P.

Contents

About the authors

Charles Smith is one of the most experienced examiners of economics in the country. A founding fellow of the Chartered Institute of Educational Assessors and a former chief examiner, he is currently a principal examiner for a major A Level awarding body.

Dr Smith taught for 20 years in secondary and further education and is now a senior lecturer at Swansea Metropolitan University.

He broadcasts regularly on economic matters and has served as an adviser to the Welsh Assembly Government on skills, training and employment. He regularly addresses conferences attended by teachers and students of economics, and as a teacher trainer has run workshops for economics teachers and taken part in curriculum development projects in nearly 20 countries covering all five continents.

Chris Vidler is a highly experienced teacher, trainer, inspector and author of economics texts. He has taught in both schools and colleges for more years than he cares to reveal but has always remained an enthusiastic teacher who believes that learning economics helps students have a better understanding of the world and its problems. He has worked as an examiner and moderator for a number of awarding bodies.

Chris has always encouraged his students to look critically at what they read, what they hear, and what others say about economic issues. He is particularly interested in environmental and development economics and believes that all of us have a role in tackling global issues of inequality and climate change. Ten per cent of his royalties from writing this book will be donated to Oxfam to support their work in fighting global poverty.*

*Oxfam is a registered charity. The views expressed in this book are those of the author and should not be taken to represent those of Oxfam.

Acknowledgements

The author and publisher would like to thank the following individuals and organisations for permission to reproduce photographs:

Alamy / All Over Photography / TPH p 84; Alamy / Classic Image p 13; Alamy / Kevin Foy p 59; Alamy / David Levenson p 147; Alamy / Ian Miles-Flashpoint Pictures p 62; Alamy / Christopher Pillitz p 108; Alamy / The Print Collector p 50; Alamy / Alex Segre p 67; Alamy / Adrian Sherratt p 53; Alamy / John Sturrock p 113; Alamy / Keren Su / China Span p 49; Alamy / Peter Webb p 92; Associated Press / Walter Bieri p 35; Corbis / Bettmann pp 145, 150; Corbis / Tibor Bognár p 110; Corbis / For Picture / Stephane Reix p 41; Corbis / Andrew Holbrooke p 74; Corbis / Hulton-Deutsch Collection p 124; Corbis / Barry Lewis p 29; Corbis / Maurice McDonald / Pool / Reuters p 120; Corbis / MC PHERSON COLIN / CORBIS SYGMA p 128; Corbis / SABA / Gustavo Gilabert p 9; Corbis / Ramin Talaie p 165; Pearson Education Ltd / Arnos Design p 7; Getty Images / AFP / ALEXANDER NEMENOV p 130; Getty Images / Axiom Photographic Agency / Toby Adamson p 136; Getty Images / Tom Stoddart p 168; PA Photos / PA Archive pp 153, 162.

Every effort has been made to contact copyright holders of material reproduced in this book. Any omissions will be rectified in subsequent printings if notice is given to the publishers.

General introduction

Welcome to *Heinemann Economics AS for AQA*. This book has been specially written for students taking the AQA course. This means that it:

- follows the AQA specification very closely

- has been written to ensure that all concepts are clearly explained in terms understandable by students taking this subject for the first time

- includes lots of advice written by examiners to help you get the best possible grade.

The introduction is divided into three parts. First, you will be reminded that you probably already know something about a subject which is not usually taught before AS level. This is followed by a more formal description of how your course is organised, and finally you will be introduced to the features of this book, which have been designed to take as much of the pain out of learning as possible.

Taking economics as an AS

Well done – you have made a good decision. Economics will be different from most other subjects you have done before. One of the best things about economics is that it will help you have a better understanding of the things that shape your life. You will be able to make better sense of the news, current affairs and politics.

Another good thing about economics is that the subject is highly regarded by both universities and employers. They like to recruit people who can think for themselves, be critical and develop logical arguments. Studying economics will help you develop these skills.

Finally, studying economics is valuable to anyone thinking of any sort of career in the business world, dealing with finance, or tackling major issues such as global warming and world poverty.

For many of you this will be the first time that you have studied economics for a formal qualification. Don't let this put you off. Lack of formal study does not mean that you don't know anything about the subject. Most of us have a basic understanding of many of the concepts that, when put together, make up economics. Economics is divided up into two broad areas of study:

- microeconomics

- macroeconomics.

Microeconomics is about how individual **markets** might work. It is about how prices of goods and services are determined … what causes them to change. It is also about market failure, which is a term used to describe factors which might be socially undesirable, such as pollution and drug taking. Finally, microeconomics involves understanding what governments might try to do to improve how markets work, and how they sometimes fail in the attempt.

DEFINITIONS

Microeconomics: focuses on how individual markets work and fail.

Macroeconomics: is concerned with issues such as unemployment, inflation and growth – concepts which affect the whole economy.

Market: a notional place where buyers and sellers of goods and services meet.

Macroeconomics is about the bigger picture and is concerned with how whole economies might work. It is about what makes economies grow and change and includes major topics such as inflation and unemployment as well as an understanding of international trade. As with microeconomics, considerable attention is paid to looking at what governments can do and where they might fail in trying to improve the state of the economy.

You probably all know something about these topics, but one of the things that makes economics special and different is that it has a technical vocabulary all its own. As will be repeated often in this book and by your teachers, economists are very precise in the way they use particular terms. This can be quite a challenge to students new to the subject; one of the main things that is tested in your AS examination is your knowledge and understanding of basic economic terms.

Getting to grips with economics

We all learn things in different ways, so it is hard to be too prescriptive about the best ways of getting to grips with economics. The special technical vocabulary just mentioned can be a big barrier to some people. Sometimes economics can appear to be really confusing, especially when different meanings are given to words that we commonly use. Or students can be put off by the diagrams and simple maths which can be involved in understanding some economics concepts. Finally, nothing in economics is black and white. Some students may find it difficult to deal with these different shades of grey.

On the plus side, economics is about issues that confront all of us. Studying economics will help you understand the world as we know it and it can involve lots of argument and debate.

Starting off is usually the hardest stage. Once you get over the initial 'differentness' of the subject, it can be fun and really useful. Economics should help you think and argue more logically, and these skills are really valued in the employment marketplace. So hang in there even when it seems tough – it will be worth it in the end. Incidentally, economics has one of the highest progression rates from AS to A2 – in other words, a large majority of students who take AS go on to take the full A Level. That must say something for the subject.

The AQA Economics AS specification

To get your AS you have to take two examination papers known as units. Although these can be taught in different ways, most students will start on Unit 1, which is called 'Markets and market failure'. This is an introduction to microeconomics. As the title implies, you will be required to develop an understanding of how markets work and why they might fail. Central to understanding this module is learning about demand and supply. This involves the use of diagrams and building up logical arguments, which are often about controversial topics such as whether or not the government should charge motorists or whether or not large firms force us to pay more for goods than we should.

The second module is an introduction to macroeconomics and is called 'The national economy'. This involves learning more about inflation, the standard of living and the causes of unemployment. Again, diagrams are used to help you analyse the possible economic effects of events such rising energy prices, or changes in taxation. As with the first module, there should be lots of chances for debate and discussion and you should end up with a much better understanding of things in the news.

Your responses to both units are assessed by examinations which are structured in similar ways. They include a number of multiple choice questions and a choice from two stimulus response questions designed to test your ability to apply the economics you have learned to particular problems.

How to use this book

This book is divided into two parts to reflect the structure of the specification outlined above. Part 1 is devoted to microeconomics – markets and market failure, and Part 2 is about the national economy or macroeconomics.

Each part is divided into chapters devoted to the key material you have to learn. These are designed to follow the specification very closely. You will find it easy to locate the various concepts which you need to learn about.

Each chapter includes:

● a summary of *learning objectives*

● the main text, designed to explain the key concepts featured in the chapter

- clear *diagrams* which you need to be able to draw from memory

- *definitions* in **bold** type of key terms where they first appear in the text: you must learn these

- *learning tips* on how to improve your learning

- *'Economics in context' case studies* of economic issues

- *activities* designed to consolidate your learning and develop your research skills.

At the end of each part there is a list of Further reading and an Exam Café designed to help you get the best possible grade when it comes to sitting the Unit 1 and 2 examinations. The Exam Café is divided into three sections:

- Relax and prepare – designed to get you into the right frame of mind for the examination

- Refresh – revision activities to ensure that you know your stuff

- Get the result – test practice with tips and advice from an examiner.

Finally, there is a *Glossary* that brings together all the key terms defined in the text. (In the main text, where a term is used again later after the definition at its first appearance, the existence of a glossary definition may be indicated by the term being in *italics*.)

We hope that this book will develop your understanding and interest in economics. Our aims are to help you gain a high AS grade and to promote your enjoyment of the subject. Good luck!

PART 1

Markets and Market Failure

INTRODUCTION

The first five chapters are devoted to helping you understand microeconomics. In order to do well, you need to understand how individual markets work, the strengths and weaknesses of freely operating markets, and how and why governments might intervene to either improve markets or produce other desirable outcomes.

Chapter 1 provides an introduction to what economics is all about. It is designed to ensure that you have a good understanding of what is called 'the economic problem': all societies have to find ways of deciding how limited resources are used to satisfy unlimited wants. Exploring how this problem might be resolved is what economics is all about. The first chapter also encourages you to understand the behaviour of 'economic agents', those whose decisions are important in economics. It introduces graphical analysis and warns you of the problems of distinguishing between normative and positive economics.

The market system is the focus of Chapter 2. You will learn how the forces of demand and supply are brought together in markets, which provide a means of sorting out how resources might be allocated. Developing this understanding requires you to have a good grasp of exactly what economists mean when they talk about demand and supply. It involves extensive use of diagrams, and requires you to apply what you have learned to the markets for:

- commodities like oil
- agriculture
- health care
- housing
- sport and leisure.

The third chapter is about two important economic concepts, production and efficiency. In order to understand these you will need to learn about specialisation and the division of labour, short and long-run costs of production, and what economists call economies and diseconomies of scale.

Market failure is dealt with in Chapter 4. This is a broad topic which economists use to describe situations in which markets do not allocate resources in ways which are socially desirable. The content of this chapter is crucial to understanding major economic issues such as global warming, the funding of the National Health Service and the power of monopolies.

Finally, Chapter 5 considers how governments might intervene in markets in an effort to produce outcomes that are socially acceptable. This involves understanding about how a range of different policy measures might work and applying this understanding to healthcare, housing, agriculture, transport and the environment. You will also learn that sometimes intervention results in government failure. In other words, efforts by governments to improve how markets work can actually make things worse.

At the end of Chapter 5 there is an Exam Café section to help you prepare for the Unit 1 examination.

1 The economic problem

On completion of this chapter, you should be able to:

- know what economics is about
- understand how economists classify resources
- recognise that individuals, firms and governments may have different economic objectives
- understand why the scarcity of resources means that we have to make choices
- use production possibility diagrams to illustrate economic problems
- distinguish between value and normative judgements.

The nature and purpose of economic activity

'Economics is the science which studies human behavior as a relationship between ends and scarce means which have alternative uses.'

–Lionel Robbins, *Essay on the Nature and Significance of Economic Science (1932)*

This 75-year-old definition of economics is still widely accepted by economists, and provides a good summary of what the subject is all about. Its essence is very simple and once it is grasped you will see the world in a different light. Economic activity takes place because we live in a world in which resources are limited. There are not endless supplies of energy, minerals, foodstuffs and so on. Yet even though these resources are finite, many people aspire to improving their lifestyles by having more and better and newer and nicer things. Relatively speaking, most people living in the UK are well off, but most people aspire to a better lifestyle. Most people in the world are not as well off as we are. One third of the world's population does not get enough to eat. In short, people, both rich and poor, have unlimited **wants**.

These wants outstrip the means of satisfying them. There is not enough to go round. Some people starve while others enjoy fantastic luxury. This is not a morality tale. Rather, it is a description of the world in

which we live. Economists use this image to explain what economic activity is all about.

DEFINITION

Wants: the goods and services which we would like to purchase without taking into account our ability to buy them, which is usually determined by our income.

MAKING CHOICES

As people have virtually unlimited wants, and as resources are finite, all societies need economic mechanisms to resolve three major problems:

- *What* to produce? – It is perhaps obvious, but different societies produce different combinations of different goods and services. The same raw materials can be used to produce different things, and the economic problem is about actually deciding what is going to be produced.

- *How* to produce? – Goods and services can be produced in different ways. We may decide to do work on our homes but we could employ tradespeople. Some objects are produced by machines while others are hand crafted. Again, all societies are faced with choices about production.

● *For whom* to produce? In other words, who gets what? No society is totally fair in the way that resources are finally distributed. But every society needs to resolve the problem of who gets what. Crucially, all societies have to have a means of deciding how those goods and services that are produced are actually distributed.

ECONOMICS IN CONTEXT

THE STARK INEQUALITIES OF CONSUMPTION

Today's consumption is undermining the environmental resource base. It is exacerbating inequalities. And the dynamics of the consumption-poverty-inequality-environment nexus are accelerating. If the trends continue without change – not redistributing from high-income to low-income consumers, not shifting from polluting to cleaner goods and production technologies, not promoting goods that empower poor producers, not shifting priority from consumption for conspicuous display to meeting basic needs – today's problems of consumption and human development will worsen.

…The real issue is not consumption itself but its patterns and effects.

…Inequalities in consumption are stark. **Globally, 20% of the world's people in the highest-income countries account for 86% of total private consumption expenditures – the poorest 20% a minuscule 1.3%.** More specifically, the richest fifth:

● consume 45% of all meat and fish, the poorest fifth 5%
● consume 58% of total energy, the poorest fifth less than 4%
● have 74% of all telephone lines, the poorest fifth 1.5%
● consume 84% of all paper, the poorest fifth 1.1%
● own 87% of the world's vehicle fleet, the poorest fifth less than 1%.

Runaway growth in consumption in the past 50 years is putting strains on the environment never before seen.

Source: United Nations, *Human Development Report 1998: Overview*, pp. 1–2. By permission of Oxford University Press, Inc.

ACTIVITY ┅┅⟐

Investigate who gets what on a global scale by answering the following questions.

(a) Why do the inequalities identified in the above extract exist?
(b) Can they be justified?
(c) Why do the authors claim that these inequalities place strains on the environment?
(d) If you have the opportunity, find out what others in your class think about issues of global inequalities.

Unravelling and understanding these types of issues is what economics is all about, and learning about the subject gives a better understanding of the forces that have shaped and will continue to shape our lives.

INCENTIVES

At this stage it is useful to consider some psychological factors which might influence these major questions of what is produced, how it is produced and how these **outputs** are distributed. Most people modify their behaviour according to the pull or push of different **incentives**. These differ in different societies and cultures. Religion and expectations of others can have an influence, as can tradition, and the power of the state or government. In most 'developed' (industrialised, richer) societies

DEFINITIONS

Outputs: actual goods and services produced by firms in an economy.

Incentive: usually regarded as a financial factor that motivates an economic agent to behave in a particular way. Thus, a retail assistant might work harder to make sales if s/he receives a commission on each sale.

the acquisition of income and wealth are motivators, and these can provide incentives which help determine the what, the why and the for whom? How far financial incentives shape the behaviour of individuals is a major issue central to understanding how economic systems might or might not work.

ACTIVITY ⋯⋗

Undertake a survey designed to assess the importance of money as a motivator. You could do this by posing questions like: How much would you have to be paid to undertake a range of attractive and less attractive jobs?

Economic resources

One way of looking at economics is that it is concerned with a study of how wealth is created. The creation of wealth involves taking resources and transforming them into products or services that can then be consumed or used in some other way. This process, illustrated in Figure 1.1, captures a wide range of issues and concepts important to economists.

Figure 1.1 Simple input/output model

The diagram consists of three related elements:

● **inputs,** the raw materials of production drawn from the world's renewable and finite resources.

● **production,** concerned with how resources are transformed into a form that can be consumed by final users. Business studies students call this process *adding value*. It can include complex processes involving the use of sophisticated technology, or the more straightforward harvesting and packaging of an agricultural crop.

● *outputs,* the combination of goods and services that are actually produced and consumed at some time.

DEFINITIONS

Inputs: resources required to produce goods and services.

Production: the processes involved in transforming inputs to outputs.

TYPES OF RESOURCES

The simple input/output model shown in Figure 1.1 can be expanded to identify and classify different types of resources (see Figure 1.2).

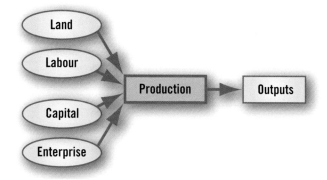

Figure 1.2 Factors of production

Economists call these resources **factors of production**, and all products and services that are produced will be made up of some mix of these different resources. In other words, it is not possible to produce a factor or service which does not include some element of each factor. Moreover, it is usually possible to produce the same good or service by using different

DEFINITION

Factors of production: land, labour, capital and enterprise – the four inputs required to produce a good or service. Nothing can be produced without some element of each, and a good or service can usually be produced with different amounts of each.

combinations of different factors. The four factors of production are:

- land
- labour
- capital
- enterprise.

Land

Land includes everything that is locked up in the Earth's surface – not just land in the sense of farmland, building and factory sites, but also what we call 'natural resources' such as minerals, fossil fuels and timber, and what can be grown and harvested. Land includes:

- the products of the seas
- the content of our atmosphere, and
- (by implication) what has yet to be discovered in space.

> **DEFINITION**
>
> **Land:** one of the four *factors of production* representing the primary resources involved in production.

Labour

Labour is a similar 'catch-all' concept to land, and includes what we as people bring to the production process, such as:

- personal attributes (for example, strength or manual dexterity)
- individual aptitudes
- skills and capabilities that we can learn.

> **DEFINITION**
>
> **Labour:** the factor of production representing human effort and work in transforming *inputs to outputs*.

Capital

Economists refer to **capital** as those assets used to produce goods or services – including the factories, machinery and equipment used to transform 'land' into some particular form of output. The term 'capital' is used in everyday conversation to describe money that is used to set up a business and keep it going, and savings in shares and so on.

All these uses are linked directly or indirectly to the actual production process, but economists use the term 'capital' in a more restricted sense. You might say they are not interested in money as such, but in the uses to which it can be put (especially uses that result in economic activity).

> **DEFINITION**
>
> **Capital:** machinery and plant that are used to help transform resources into production.

Enterprise

This is often described as the fourth factor of production. Economic activity involves the combination of particular quantities of land, labour and capital to produce something. **Enterprise** is the process of managing and deciding how factors should be combined and to what end. Being enterprising may also involve taking risks and guessing what goods or services are likely to be in demand. Economists consider enterprise as a separate factor of production as it emphasises the importance of decision making within the economy.

> **DEFINITION**
>
> **Enterprise:** decision making and risk taking in terms of combining the (other) factors of production to produce particular goods or services.

ACTIVITY ⋯⟡

Use the input–output model to identify examples of each of the four factors of production used in the production of

(a) crisps

(b) hairdressing

(c) designer clothing.

Are all factors of production equally important in the production of each good and service? Justify your answer.

PRODUCTION

So who decides what is produced, how it is produced and for whom it is produced? In most societies these crucial economic decisions are taken by three different types of institutions:

● privately owned organisations – known as the private sector

● national and local governments – known as the public sector

● a range of not-for-profit organisations (mainly but not exclusively charities) – known as the voluntary sector.

Economies such as this are called **mixed economies.** A minority of societies do not conform to this model. The government of North Korea, for example, is called a **command economy** because all economic decisions about what is produced, how it is produced and for whom it is produced are taken by the government. Many former communist states were run as command economies but even many of these had some elements of private sector activity.

DEFINITIONS

Mixed economy: an economy in which decisions are taken by the state, by privately owned companies and by voluntary organisations.

Command economy: an economy in which all economic decisions are taken by the state.

In theory, there is a third type of economy in which there is no government intervention and no voluntary sector. In such a case all economic decisions are taken by the private sector. This kind of economy is also called a **free market economy** and although many governments have aspired and do aspire to leaving all economic decisions to be resolved in this way, pure free market economies do not exist.

DEFINITION

Free market economy: an economy in which all economic decisions are made by the private sector.

In the UK, and in almost all other countries, economic decisions are taken by:

● private sector organisations which are primarily motivated to make a financial profit

● the public sector which uses taxation to provide services such as health care and education

● the voluntary sector including sports, help and advice and charitable work for which profit is less important.

These descriptions are simplifications (as your further study of economics will show), but they do provide a starting point.

Although, as noted earlier, most economies are mixed economies, the relative importance of the three sectors can be very different. Thus, the USA is often regarded, not necessarily accurately, as an example of an economy in which more decisions are left to the market and fewer taken by the state; whereas in France the role of the state is perceived to be more significant. One of the key questions which economists consider is the extent to which economic decisions are best taken by the private or public sectors.

Economic objectives

Even at this stage in your study of economics you will be aware that economic activity involves a huge set of relationships which link those who consume and

High street consumers are economic agents

those who produce goods and services. Economic activity is global and decisions that you might make as a consumer will affect many other individuals across the globe. Much of this we take for granted but economists are used to trying dig beneath the surface of these interactions. One way of doing so is by focusing on the actions of **economic agents.** This is an emerging and developing area of economic thinking which will be picked up in the sections on market failure in Chapter 4, but at this stage it is useful to identify three groups of economic agents whose decisions will impact on each other, and, in so doing help determine the kind of economic activity that will take place. They are:

- consumers
- firms
- governments.

> ### DEFINITION
>
> **Economic agent:** an economic decision maker who or which recognises that different factors motivate and influence different groups.

CONSUMERS

Individuals within an economy play a variety of economic roles, and each is motivated by different psychological factors. However, it is possible to make some generalisations about the role of individuals within the economy. We can look at individuals as consumers – those who finally consume, and hopefully enjoy, the products and services that are produced. It is probably reasonable to assume that as consumers we seek to spend whatever we have in such a way to maximise our satisfaction. In other words, how we spend our income provides economists with information about individual preferences. This is not rocket science – if you prefer dance music to rock you are more likely to spend money on the former rather than the latter. Also it is reasonable to assume that as consumers most of us would prefer more to less. Some would argue that

we are inherently selfish – it is possible to develop this line of reasoning further but at this stage it is enough to be able to recognise that as consumers we are likely to behave in particular ways and have economic objectives which impact on others.

> ### ACTIVITY ····
>
> Some kind person gives you £1,000 – how would you spend it?
>
> How might your spending decision be different in 10 years' time?
>
> What factors are likely to influence these two sets of decisions?
>
> Are your motivations different or similar to those of others in your class?

FIRMS

Economists define firms as those economic agents whose prime function is to transform the factors of production into goods and services which individuals can consume. As noted earlier, firms can be in the private, public or voluntary sectors.

Why should any of these agents be motivated to produce goods and services? As ever, there is no one clear answer. Oxfam exists to alleviate world poverty, Chelsea to win the Champions League, Tesco to dominate supermarket sales in the UK. All firms, however, will have one economic objective in common. They will all be aware in accounting terms of their bottom line – profitability. They need to be making enough in terms of revenue to more than meet the costs which they have incurred in transforming factors of production into goods and services. In other words, profit making is a prime objective of firms. Most economists will agree that profits are important to firms but there is less consensus on the relative importance of profits compared to other objectives, especially when considering the public and voluntary sectors.

ACTIVITY ┅┅┅

Use the Internet to access the annual accounts of three different firms. What do they say about the economic motives of each firm? Sometimes these are referred to in 'mission statements'.

GOVERNMENTS

The third economic agent to be considered at this stage is the government. It is easy to be cynical as to what motivates politicians, but this should not stop us from trying to take an objective view of the government. One way of looking at the role of government in terms of economic activity is to see the government as providing the rules which regulate how individuals and firms relate to each other. Thus, all **developed economies** have established laws of contract, hold records of land ownership, and provide particular services such as the police and armed forces. It can be argued that these institutions are necessary to regulate the relationships between firms and individuals.

DEFINITION

Developed economies: economies with higher levels of national income that tend to have more highly developed service sectors.

Most governments also have a wider range of objectives that are linked to their powers to raise and spend taxes. These can change according to the political objectives of those in government. In western democracies, conservative or right-wing governments often try to cut taxes and reduce the degree to which governments intervene in the economy, while socialist or left-wing governments are more likely to want to try to redistribute wealth from the rich to the poor. It is, therefore, easy to see how the actions of governments as economic agents can affect both individuals and firms and the contexts in which they interact.

ACTIVITY ┅┅┅

Choose and explain three examples of differences between the UK's Conservative and Labour parties in respect to economic priorities.

Scarcity, choice and the allocation of resources

The phrase 'scarcity, choice and the allocation of resources' is another way of framing the issue that economics is about – deciding what is to be produced, how it is to be produced and for whom it is to be produced. Scarcity refers to limited resources and, because there are many competing demands, all societies have to make choices as to how these resources are used and allocated. Understanding how in a market-based system economic agents interact to transform scarce resources into goods and services, which are then consumed by some members of society, is one of the main areas of study within microeconomics.

One way of understanding how scarce resources are allocated in a market based system is by analogy, by comparing economic activity with something else. In this case we can treat each individual consumer as a voter. In a totally fair society each individual could be allocated say 100 votes. Each would be free to cast these votes according to their individual tastes or preferences. We could add up the total value of individual votes for a good or service and this would indicate something of the priorities in terms of a particular society. If this were confined to food, we might find that the biggest single vote-winner was cheap meat. The outcome of this voting would be that the largest amounts of land, labour, capital and enterprise would be devoted to producing cheap meat. But this carries an **opportunity cost**: if the bulk of land were given over to producing cheap meat, there would be little land left to meet the demands of the second priority revealed by the people's vote. Suppose the second biggest vote-winner was organic vegetables. From the producer's point of view, the number of votes given to the production of meat and organic vegetables provides signals and incentives as to what should be produced. In this case there would be less incentive to produce organic vegetables and far fewer factors of production would be devoted to their production. If the people's vote were to change, and because resources are finite, the only way of producing more organic vegetables would be to produce less cheap meat. The analogy can be developed by altering how votes are allocated – in this case those with more votes would have more influence on which scarce resources would be used to produce which goods and services. This might explain the statement on page 3 that '20 per cent of the world's people in the highest-income countries account for 86 per cent of total private consumption expenditures'.

DEFINITION

Opportunity cost: the value of what has to be given up in order to produce or consume more of something.

Studying and understanding economics has probably never been more important at a time when we are becoming increasingly aware that the environment we live in is a scarce resource. The atmosphere, oceans, rivers and forest were, in former times, regarded as free goods to be used and consumed without any thought for the future. We now understand differently but this does not mean we have found ways to make better use of our global environment.

One of the classic contemporary examples of this is the impact of economic and human development on tropical rain forests. This is illustrated in the following extract.

ECONOMICS IN CONTEXT

WHY IS THE BRAZILIAN AMAZON BEING DESTROYED?

In many tropical countries, the majority of deforestation results from the actions of poor subsistence cultivators. However, in Brazil only about one-third of recent deforestation can be linked to 'shifted' cultivators. A large portion of deforestation in Brazil can be attributed to land clearing for pastureland by commercial and speculative interests, misguided government policies, inappropriate World Bank projects, and commercial exploitation of forest resources. For effective action it is imperative that these issues be addressed. Focusing solely on the promotion of sustainable use by local people would neglect the most important forces behind deforestation in Brazil.

Brazilian deforestation is strongly correlated to the economic health of the country: the decline in deforestation from 1988-1991 nicely matched the economic slowdown during the same period, while the rocketing rate of deforestation from 1993-1998 paralleled Brazil's period of rapid economic growth. During lean times, ranchers and developers do not have the cash to rapidly expand their pasturelands and operations, while the government lacks funds to sponsor highways and colonisation programmes and grant tax breaks and subsidies to forest exploiters.

A relatively small percentage of large landowners clear vast sections of the Amazon for cattle pastureland. Large tracts of forest are cleared and sometimes planted with African savannah grasses for cattle feeding. In many cases, especially during periods of high inflation, land is simply cleared for investment purposes. When pastureland prices exceed forest land prices (a condition made possible by tax incentives that favour pastureland over natural forest), forest clearing is a good hedge against inflation.

Such favourable taxation policies, combined with government subsidised agriculture and colonisation programmes, encourage the destruction of the Amazon. The practice of low taxes on income derived from agriculture and tax rates that favour pasture over forest overvalues agriculture and pastureland and makes it profitable to convert natural forest for these purposes when it normally would not be so.

Source: mongabay.com

ACTIVITY ⋯⋗

Use the Internet to add to the information contained in the extract above to:

(a) identify the economic pressures leading to the destruction of the Amazonian rain forest

(b) explain whether or not you believe that the destruction of the Amazonian rain forest can be limited.

Production possibility diagrams

Your understanding of what economics is all about can be further developed by using production possibility diagrams. These are a simplified model of economic activity which is illustrated using diagrams. They are easy to understand and should provide you with a way of organising how you describe and analyse economic activity. They can be used to illustrate:

● opportunity cost

● changes in the standard of living

● under-use and full use of economic resources

● trade-offs and conflicting objectives.

learning tip

Be prepared – lots of students see learning economics in terms of diagrams – they are right, up to a point. Diagrams can be really useful in helping you answer examination questions and dealing with issues logically. This is the first economics style graph that you are going to come across. When reading diagrams, always be logical and always ensure that you know what is measured on each axis and check that you understand each stage of the accompanying explanation by referring back to the diagram.

OPPORTUNITY COST

In Figure 1.3, it is assumed that an economy is capable of producing just two goods: handbags and shoes. If this economy were to use all its available factors of production to produce handbags, it would produce *C*. Alternatively, if all resources were devoted to making shoes, *B* would be made. The line between *C* and *B* is called a **production possibility curve**, because it shows all the different combinations of handbags and shoes that could be produced if all factors of production are being fully used.

This diagram can be used to illustrate *opportunity cost* – that is, what has to be given up as the result of a particular decision. We have considered the significance of scarce resources and unlimited wants. The concept of opportunity cost is a powerful way of illustrating this important economic concept. Everything we choose to do has a cost. Staying on into the sixth form or going to college costs you in terms of the lost income you would have if you were to work full time. Using the cleared Amazonian rainforest to produce soya beans means that that land cannot be used to produce timber, or beef, or to provide a habitat to different flora and fauna.

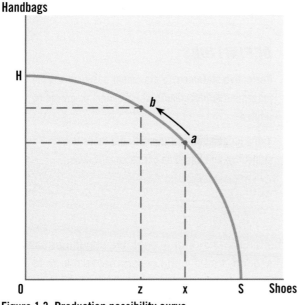

Figure 1.3 Production possibility curve

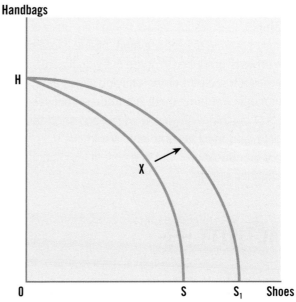

Figure 1.4 Increasing standard of living

Production possibility curves provide another way of illustrating opportunity cost diagrammatically. The movement from *a* to *b* on the production possibility curve would indicate an increase in the production of handbags but if all resources are being used, this can only be achieved by cutting the production of shoes from *x* to *z*. This represents the opportunity cost of increasing the output of handbags.

Other kinds of changes can be illustrated on a production possibility curve. For example, if a new technique were discovered that meant more shoes could be produced with the same amount of resources, there would be a movement in the curve from *HS* to HS_1 (see Figure 1.4).

This new production possibility curve indicates a higher possible standard of living. The fact that it is now possible to produce both more shoes and more handbags could be said to mean that people living in this society would be better off. This society could now produce both more handbags and shoes, using the same amount of resources.

UNEMPLOYMENT
Production possibility curves can also be used to illustrate both the full employment and underemployment of economic resources. Any point on the production possibility curve (PPC), by definition, shows that all resources are being used in an economy. Any point to the right of the PPC is unobtainable, whereas any point to the left (for example, point *x* on Figure 1.4) of the PPC indicates an economy that is not making full use of all its resources. Both more handbags and more shoes could be produced. This failure to use all resources can be described as unemployment of resources.

TRADE-OFFS AND CONFLICTING OBJECTIVES
Production possibility curves illustrate the economic choices that we all have to make as consumers, producers and the government. Objectives often

conflict with one another. In the handbag and shoe example, if all resources are being fully utilised, it is only possible to produce more of one if less of the other is produced. For the individual consumer there is a trade-off between buying shoes and handbags. For firms there is a trade-off between the level of customer service provided and short-term profits, and most governments would like to spend more on education – but at a cost of less spending on fighting crime?

ACTIVITY ····⟩

Use production possibility curves to model the impact of:

(a) spending more of a nation's resources on fighting AIDS rather than on more arms

(b) finding ways of producing anti-viral drugs more cheaply

(c) Cutting government expenditure on the armed forces.

Normative and positive economics

By now, you should be starting to think like an economist. We all know something about a range of economic issues. We are all consumers and producers. We have an idea how markets work and although you might not have used the term opportunity cost you are probably aware of the principle. All of us argue, knowingly and unknowingly, about economic issues. People have views about immigration, the destruction of rain forests or restrictions on tobacco advertising. However, it is really important to be able to distinguish between two different types of economics, namely:

● normative, and

● positive.

NORMATIVE ECONOMICS

Normative economics involves attempting to describe what *ought to be*. For example, I could argue that the government ought to do more to reduce inequality in the UK. This is a **normative statement** which is based on two **value judgements**. First, that there is

something wrong or unacceptable about inequality, and second, that it is the government's role to tackle such issues as inequality. Some of you will agree with my view and many will not. Your response, like mine, will be determined by your values, your sense of right or wrong.

Saying that immigration should be halted or that the destruction of the rainforests is desirable are also value judgements. They reflect the values of the person making that judgement. Because value judgements reflect the values of the individual, it is not logically possible to say whether they are right or wrong.

For a long time economics was called 'political economy', and many early economists developed theories and concepts because they wanted to bring about changes in society. They were concerned with how things ought to be.

POSITIVE ECONOMICS

The approach to economics started to change in the 19th century, when scientific methods and approaches developed first in the physical sciences were then applied to social sciences like economics. **Positive economics** seeks to be more objective than normative economics and much greater attention is paid to adopting scientific approaches as recognised by the inclusion of 'science' in Robbins' definition given at the start of this chapter. Positive economics involves using:

● evidence

● key economic theories and concepts

● a specialist technical vocabulary.

Evidence

Economics is classed as a social science, and this means that it has much in common with subjects like sociology and psychology. Economists strive to be objective, to avoid value judgements and to rely on evidence to support or contradict theories about economic behaviour. But, as with other social sciences, it is neither ethical nor possible to subject people to experimentation under strict laboratory conditions. Theories and concepts should still be based on the careful collection of evidence. This means that numerical data is very important, as is the development of a logical and ordered argument. The development of hypothesis to explain economic events is a key element of positive economics. A hypothesis is a possible explanation of events or relationships which can then be tested against evidence. Thus, if I were to argue that income inequality would be reduced if the government increased inheritance tax, it would be possible to search and collect evidence that both supported and challenged this view. The hypothesis is a **positive statement** which can be tested empirically, that is, by searching out evidence. In this example, I could investigate the possible relationship between levels of inheritance tax in different countries and measures of income inequality. I could search for data from the UK which would allow me to explore the possible correlation between these two variables.

Theories and concepts

Economics, as we know it today, has developed over the last 400 years. Some would argue that its origins are much older, but recent developments in economics are linked with industrialisation and the development of capitalism. Adam Smith, who wrote *The Wealth of Nations* in 1776, is often described as the first economist.

As with other disciplines, the subject has continually evolved and successive generations of economists have argued and debated each other's work. In this way, a body of knowledge and understanding associated with economics has developed.

Technical vocabulary

Economics is different from familiar subjects like history and English, because only a minority of students study economics before they are 16 years old. As with all disciplines, economics has its own technical vocabulary. Economists are also very precise in their use of particular terms. This precise use of particular terms takes some getting used to, but it is important – especially as you will need to clearly communicate your understanding of the subject and develop economic analysis and argument.

DEFINITIONS

Positive economics: an approach that seeks to be more objective than normative economics and to pay much greater attention to adopting a scientific approach.

Normative economics: economics that may include value judgements and lack scientific objectivity.

Positive statement: a statement that can be proved or disproved by reference to evidence.

Adam Smith (1723–1790)

NORMATIVE VS. POSITIVE ECONOMICS

Normative economics lacks the objectivity of positive economics. It incorporates our values and views, which makes it more subjective. It is claimed that positive economics is more objective. The truth is that it is often hard to distinguish between normative and positive economics. Some argue that even the choice of issues or topics which economists investigate reflects value judgements and that the distinction between normative and positive economics becomes blurred once the divide between economics and politics is crossed. When economists actually recommend policies, when they argue for a particular point of view, their economics becomes normative. Similarly politicians often have to make economic decisions and make judgements about economic priorities. This is when economics becomes normative.

Finally, economics is about choices. It is often about controversial issues. Economic arguments are often used by politicians to support particular ideas. In fact, economics and argument go hand in hand. Often there are no right or wrong answers, and no clear-cut solutions to economic issues. Governments and political parties often disagree about economic issues. This means that economics often appeals to those who enjoy argument and debate, and also take an interest in current affairs and politics.

ACTIVITY ···‹›

Use the Internet to identify the leading five current issues in the news. Which ones can be seen as economic, that is, about scarcity and choice and the allocation of resources, and why?

ACTIVITY ···‹›

Which of the following statements are normative and which positive?

(a) Immigrants make a positive contribution to the economy.

(b) Immigrants are an extra burden on the National Health Service.

(c) Immigration should be controlled.

(d) Immigrants take jobs from those born in this country.

2 The allocation of resources in competitive markets

On completion of this chapter, you should be able to:

- understand the determinants of demand curves
- be able to calculate and use price, income and cross elasticities of demand
- understand the determinants of supply curves
- use price elasticity of supply
- understand how a market equilibrium is determined
- apply demand and supply analysis to particular markets
- appreciate the inter-relationship between markets
- analyse how the market mechanism allocates resources.

Introduction

Getting to grips with how competitive markets work will be key to your developing the skills required for success as a young economist. The theory in this chapter provides the foundations for understanding microeconomics. None of the individual concepts which make up this chapter is particularly hard to understand, and many will appear to be a simple matter of using your 'common sense'. It may take you longer to understand how the different parts of the economic jigsaw fit together, but as long as you spend enough time getting your head round the different sections of this chapter, you will develop a wider and more sophisticated understanding of how competitive economies are meant to work.

This chapter is about demand and supply. These concepts relate directly to the actions of two sets of economic agents:

- consumers – that's us when we demand goods or services

- producers – the firms who supply goods and services.

It is very important to make a rigid distinction between these two sets of actions, which take place independently of each other. Economists model the behaviour of consumers and producers using demand and supply curves. These diagrams can be used to represent the interaction of demand and supply. Once you have understood these two concepts it is possible to use diagrams to show how markets work to set the price of particular goods or services and also to determine how much is actually sold. Individual markets link to each other and chain reactions are set in motion, which theoretically allocate resources to those whose demand is strongest. This is known as the **price mechanism**, which should ensure that consumers determine what is produced and that it is produced at the lowest possible cost. But we start by getting back to basics with an understanding of demand curves.

The determinants of the demand for goods and services

First, it is important to understand what we mean by the term **demand**. Economists make a clear distinction between wanting something and demanding something. There is probably a whole range of things which we want or aspire to having. Most of us fantasise about material goods, exotic lifestyles, fame, fortune and all the rest, but, in the harsh reality of the world we actually live in, many of these wants are unrealistic as we do not necessarily have the means to pay for them. Demand has a very precise meaning in economics – that is, how much of a product or service we are prepared to buy. Wants and aspirations have to be backed up by the ability to pay for the goods or services we desire. If you can't find some way of affording something then you can't, in economic terms, demand it. Economists call this **effective demand** although in practice the 'effective' part of this term often gets dropped.

Demand can be illustrated graphically by making a simple and reasonable set of generalisations or assumptions about customer behaviour:

● The most important influence on the demand for a good or service is its price. Other factors are also important.

● If the price of something you demand rises, and nothing else changes, you are less likely to buy it,

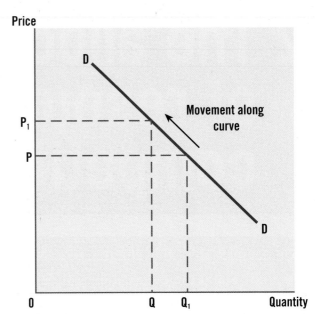

Figure 2.1 Demand curve

whereas lower prices, other things being equal, will lead to higher demand. Again, it is possible to think of exceptions to this generalisation but these do not invalidate this important assumption.

Given these assumptions it is possible to draw a **demand curve** as shown in Figure 2.1.

The quantity demanded of a product or service is measured along the horizontal axis and its price on the vertical. Because of the assumptions we have made about the relationship between the price of a good or service and the quantity demanded, the demand curve D slopes downwards from left to right. If the price is set at OP, the demand will be at OQ_1.

If the price rises to OP_1, there will be a movement along the demand curve showing that the quantity demanded will fall to OQ.

If, on the other hand, the price falls, there will be a movement along the curve showing that the quantity demanded has increased.

learning tip
A movement along the demand curve shows you that the price of a good or service has changed.

Shifts in demand

It would be unrealistic to ignore other factors which may cause the demand for a good or service to change. Changes in other factors are likely to lead to changes in demand. Many other factors can potentially influence the demand for a product or service. Economists group these key variables under the following three headings:

- the price of other goods and services
- incomes
- tastes.

THE PRICE OF OTHER GOODS AND SERVICES

Clearly, the decision to buy or not to buy something is not made simply on the basis of its price. Our choice to buy one product is often made by reference to prices of similar products. Products can be seen as alternatives for each other – for example, a Mercedes might be seen as an alternative to a BMW. Economists call two such goods **substitutes**. If I was thinking about buying a BMW I might change my mind if a similar Mercedes came down in price. If my response was similar to that of other potential customers for BMWs, the quantity demanded at all prices would fall, and this is shown by a shift in demand for BMWs to the left. If on the other hand Mercedes increased their prices, the demand for BMWs might rise and this would be shown by the demand curve for BMWs shifting to the right. These shifts are illustrated in Figure 2.2.

On the other hand, sometimes buying one good or service goes hand in hand with buying another.

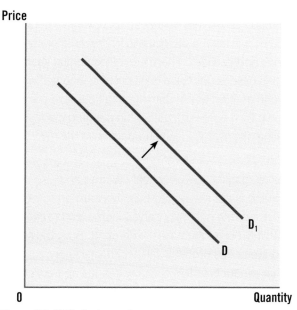

Figure 2.2 Shifts in demand

Products or services that are often bought jointly – for example, cars and petrol – are called **complements**. In this case the relationship between demand and price changes is likely to be different. Rising petrol prices might lead to fall in demand for BMWs and this would be shown by a shift in the demand curve to the left, whereas falling petrol prices might increase the demand for BMWs, leading to a shift in the demand curve to the right.

DEFINITIONS

Substitute: a good or service that consumers might consider as alternatives for another.

Complements: goods or services that are often bought together.

INCOMES

Changes in the level of our income have a powerful effect on our demand for goods and services – the more money we earn, the more we can buy. Because they try to be as accurate as possible, economists focus on 'disposable income' as the amount of money available for spending, after the deduction of income tax and National Insurance contributions. Common sense tells us that an increase in disposable income will lead to an increase in demand for some goods and services. These are called **normal goods**. In this case an increase in disposable incomes will lead to an increase in demand at all possible prices, shown by a rightward shift in the demand curve. Falling disposable incomes would have the reverse effect.

The relationship between real incomes and demand is not always so straightforward. In some cases increases in disposable income lead to even relatively bigger increases in demand. Both BMWs and Mercedes probably fall into this category. Other products in this category include air travel in business class, long-haul holiday destinations and designer label clothes. They are all known as **superior goods** or luxury goods. In this case a given increase in real income leads to a more than proportional increase in demand. The reverse is also true in that falling incomes will lead to a more than proportional fall in demand for these goods or services.

Other products are classified as **inferior goods** in the sense that as consumer income rises, demand for such products falls. We tend to regard smaller cheaper cars, own-label products and fake designer clothes as inferior products. In this case increases in

real disposable incomes leading to falling demand are shown by shifts to the left, but if incomes fall, we would expect demand for inferior goods to actually increase.

TASTES

This term is used by economists to capture a whole range of other influences on demand. At one level, we all like and dislike different things and these personal preferences are likely to affect what we wish to buy. These individual differences are hard for economists to model but it is easier to identify broad trends and changes in **tastes**. Advertisers in particular try to change our tastes in order to increase the demand for particular products or services. Success in fashion retailing often depends on trying to ensure that customers will pay more for styles and products that are considered fashionable.

DEFINITION

Tastes: all those other subjective and personal factors that affect the demand for goods and services.

What if demand changes?

The effect of a change in the price of a good or service on the quantity demanded is shown by a **movement** up or down the demand curve. This was illustrated in Figure 2.1. If any of the other variables change, the demand curve will **shift** either to the right or to the left. Thus if the price of a BMW were to rise and the prices of other similar cars were to stay the

---

DEFINITIONS

Normal goods: those for which demand increases as disposable incomes increase and decreases as disposable income decreases.

Superior goods: goods for which a real increase in income results in a more than proportional increase in demand, and a decrease in a more than proportionate decrease in demand.

Inferior goods: goods for which demand falls as income rises and increases as income falls.

DEFINITIONS

Movement: in demand, indicates that the price of a good or service has changed.

Shift: a shift in demand indicates that a variable other than price that affects demand has changed.

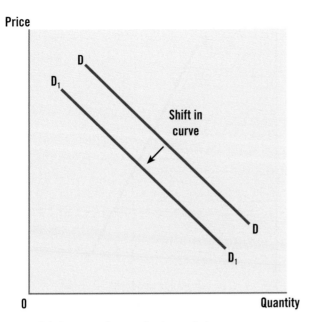

Figure 2.3 Decrease in quantity demanded

same, the demand for Mercedes would rise. This is shown in Figure 2.2 by a shift in demand to the right from *D* to *D₁*.

If changes in the prices of other goods, incomes or tastes were to change in such a way as to decrease the demand for a good or service, then the opposite would happen: the curve should shift to the right. A Ford Fiesta, for example, might be regarded as an inferior good, therefore if incomes were to rise, we might well expect the demand curve to shift inwards to the left from *DD* to *D₁D₁*, showing a fall in demand at all possible prices as shown in figure 2.3.

Changes in tastes can be treated in a similar way. The demand for goods that become more fashionable will shift to the right, whereas a leftward shift would show that something is no longer fashionable.

ACTIVITY ····⟩

Which way will the demand curve for Mars Bars move if:

(a) the price of Twix is reduced

(b) child benefit is raised

(c) eating chocolate is proved to reduce your intelligence

(d) Tesco launches a two-for-the-price-of-one Mars Bar offer?

Price, income and cross elasticities of demand

Elasticity is a measure of responsiveness of one variable to changes in another. Elasticity is a key concept in economics, occurring many times in different contexts. This will probably be the first time you have come across it, so do spend some time making sure your understanding is secure. There are three different measures of the responsiveness of demand to changes in

- price
- incomes
- the prices of other goods.

DEFINITION

Elasticity: a measure of responsiveness between one variable and another.

PRICE ELASTICITY OF DEMAND

As you will remember from the previous section on page 16, economists assume that demand for a good or service will change if its price changes. An increase in price is likely to result in a fall in demand, whereas a cut in price is likely to lead to an increase in demand. **Price elasticity of demand** (often expressed as $^P\varepsilon_d$) is a way of measuring how much demand changes in response to a change in price. Price elasticity of demand can be analysed in three ways:

- by graphs
- in words
- by using a formula.

DEFINITION

Price elasticity of demand ($^P\varepsilon_d$): a measurement of the responsiveness of demand to a change in price.

Graphs

Figures 2.4 and 2.5 show two very different responses in demand to identical reductions in price.

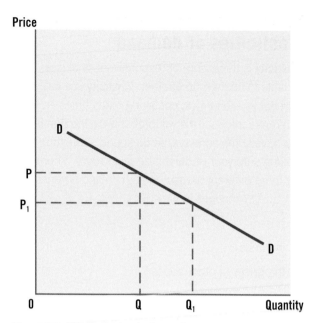

Figure 2.4 Relatively elastic demand curve

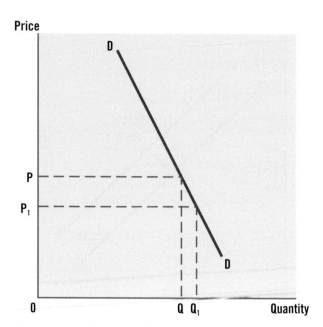

Figure 2.5 Relatively inelastic demand curve

In Figure 2.4, a cut of around 20 per cent in house prices leads to a rise in demand of about 50 per cent. In Figure 2.5, the same price cut causes a much smaller rise in demand – about 10 per cent.

Figure 2.4 shows demand to be very responsive to changes in price. In Figure 2.5, demand is much less responsive. Given the use of the same axis, the slope of the demand curve will indicate the degree of responsiveness to changes in price, that is, the price elasticity of demand.

Understanding how customers might respond to a price change is important to firms. In Figure 2.4, a cut in price would boost revenue spent on a particular product. This can also be shown graphically. Revenue is calculated by multiplying price by sales. The area OP_1 x OQ_1 is larger than OP x OQ. In Figure 2.5, revenue would be boosted if the firm were able to raise its prices. Elasticity of demand has, therefore, massive implications for businesses selecting an appropriate pricing policy.

Words

Using words to describe the differences between Figures 2.4 and 2.5 involves some specialist terminology. If the demand for a good or service is very responsive to changes in price, then the demand is said to be 'relatively elastic'.

If the demand for a good or service is not very responsive to changes in price, then the demand is described as 'relatively **inelastic**'.

DEFINITION

Inelastic: describes a variable that is not very responsive to changes in another.

The formula

This representation of price elasticity of demand is a much more precise and mathematical way of dealing with the relationship between changes in price and changes in demand. Figures 2.4 and 2.5 show different slopes or gradients of a demand curve. The gradient can also be represented by the following equation

$$^P\varepsilon_d = \frac{\% \text{ change in quantity demanded}}{\% \text{ change in price}}$$

If the response to a 10 per cent fall in price were an increase in demand of 30 per cent, these values can be inserted into the equation to give:

$$^P\varepsilon_d = +30/-10$$
$$= -3$$

Alternatively, if the same price cut were accompanied by an increase in demand of just 5 per cent, solving the same equation would give:

$$^P\varepsilon_d = +5/-10$$
$$= -0.5$$

These answers or values are called coefficients and they give an instant insight into the price elasticity of demand. Any value which is greater than 1 shows that demand is relatively elastic, while any value less than 1 represents a relatively inelastic demand.

> **learning tip**
> Note that in most cases the price elasticity of demand will be represented by a negative value. A positive coefficient would indicate that demand rises along with increases in price or falls as price falls. This can happen especially when high prices are associated with greater quality or higher status but such a situation would mean that the gradient of the demand curve would be reversed.

Unitary elasticity

What if the percentage change in price of a good or service were to be matched by the same percentage change in quantity demanded? Those of you who are quick with using your formula will soon have the answer – it is –1. For example if a 20 per cent increase in the price of oil were to lead to a 20 per cent decrease in demand,

$$^P\varepsilon_d = \frac{\% \text{ change in quantity demanded}}{\% \text{ change in price}}$$
$$= -20/+20$$
$$= -1$$

Because the coefficient in these cases is always –1, economists refer to this special case as unity, or **unitary elasticity**.

> **DEFINITION**
>
> **Unitary elasticity:** elasticity in which a change in price leads to a change in demand of the same proportion.

Any value greater than this would indicate relative elasticity and any smaller value relative inelasticity.

Finally, it is important to remember that a curve showing unitary elasticity at all price levels will be a rectangular hyperbola as shown in Figure 2.6.

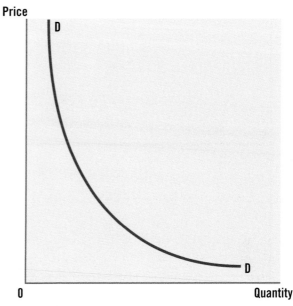

Figure 2.6 $^P\varepsilon_d = 1$

Graphs can also be used to illustrate the two extreme cases. First, what if demand stays constant irrespective of changes in price? This is illustrated in Figure 2.7 and is described as perfectly inelastic.

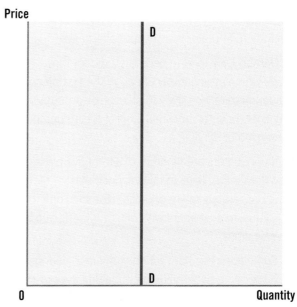

Figure 2.7 Perfectly inelastic demand

The other extreme, or limiting, case is when any amount of a good or service will be demanded at a given price but nothing will be demanded at a higher price. Such a demand curve is perfectly elastic and is illustrated in Figure 2.8.

Price

D   D

0   **Quantity**

Figure 2.8 Perfectly elastic demand

Why do price elasticities differ?

Price elasticities for different goods are likely to differ for four main reasons:

● Demand will be more elastic for those goods which have many *substitutes*, as we would expect consumers to prefer the cheaper alternative.

● Demand will tend to be less elastic for those goods which are relatively cheap in the first place. Consumers are less likely to change their demand if they spend only a very small part of their income on a given good or service.

● If consumers are ignorant of alternative prices, their demand is likely to be less price elastic. Many firms deliberately make price comparisons difficult by confusing customers with different tariffs and specifications.

● Sometimes it is hard for consumers to change their spending patterns quickly, making their price elasticity of demand relatively inelastic in the short run. This can be the case when we contract for

particular services for a given period of time. For example, mobile phone contracts are usually for a year, although providers try to get you to sign up for 18 months.

Do elasticities matter?

Understanding elasticities of demand can be very useful to economists as it enables them to predict the outcomes of a range of changes. Such forecasts are particularly useful to both business and the government.

ELASTICITIES OF DEMAND AND FIRMS

Decision makers in all types of businesses both large and small are almost certainly going to use the concept of elasticity to help them make crucial marketing and production decisions. This will be true whether or not they have studied economics and whether or not they use the term elasticity. Most firms have some scope to set the price that their products and services sell for. When they make these decisions they will, even if it is intuitively, take account of price, income and cross elasticities. Firms that fail to consider the impact of price changes on demand, do not ensure that they are aware of competitor's prices, and are unaware how changes in real incomes are likely to affect the demand for their products are not likely to be successful.

For example, a relatively inelastic demand curve for rail season tickets is shown in Figure 2.9. Suppose the rail company has scope for changing the price up or down from OP_1. If they reduce prices, demand will increase slightly but overall their revenue will fall. The increase in revenue generated by the lower price is not sufficient to compensate for the loss of revenue from all those existing customers who will benefit from cheaper season tickets. On the other hand, what would happen if they increased the price of season tickets to OP_2? In this case, demand would fall slightly but the bulk of passengers would pay the higher fares probably in the absence of any competition. Total revenue would go up from OQ_1xOP_1 to OQ_2yOP_2. Other factors will be involved, but firms facing inelastic demand curves have an incentive to push up prices to increase revenue.

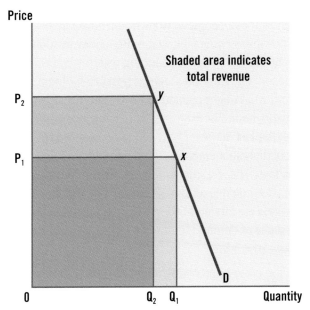

Figure 2.9 **Increase in price leading to increasing revenue**

The situation outlined above would be totally different in a more competitive market. In such a situation firms could increase revenue by cutting prices – again there might be other factors limiting the ability of firms to do this, not least the fear that competitors might do the same. However, as Figure 2.10 shows, firms facing a relatively elastic demand curve can boost revenue by cutting prices.

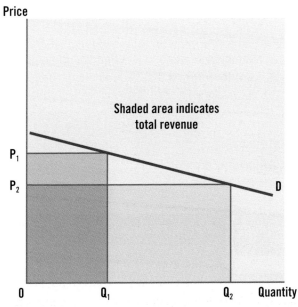

Figure 2.10 **Decrease in price leading to increasing revenue**

ELASTICITIES OF DEMAND AND THE GOVERNMENT

The significance of price elasticity of demand is not lost on governments. It is no accident that goods like alcohol, tobacco and road fuels are relatively highly taxed. The demand for these products tends to be relatively inelastic. Indirect taxes put up prices but the government's tax revenues would increase.

ECONOMICS IN CONTEXT

RAILWAY RIP OFF?

A recent article in the *Daily Telegraph* highlighted a persistent source of confusion to rail travellers. The paper undertook an investigation of rail fares between Blackpool and London and discovered that there were up to 30 different prices for a single route.

Prices varied from £16.50 for the cheapest single to £347 for the most expensive return journey. The cost of the fare depends on what time a passenger travels, what route is chosen, how far the booking is made in advance, whether the return date can be specified, what class a passenger selects and whether the ticket is refundable.

Passenger groups have long campaigned about confusing rail fares. 'Some of the fares on offer are totally baffling,' said Jane Revell, a spokeswoman for Passenger Focus, the independent consumer watchdog.

'There are so many different names for the offers that passengers do not understand what they mean. They are lost when it comes to choosing the cheapest fare. And we know that passengers are constantly frustrated when they find that the person sitting next to them has a cheaper fare that they knew nothing about.'

What makes the situation worse is that the rail companies themselves do not appear to understand the differences between different types of tickets, and studies by *Which* show that potential travellers are often given the wrong information about the cheapest fares.

ACTIVITY ····⋮›

(a) Why do rail companies have so many different fares?

(b) How are rail fares determined in Italy?

(c) Find out the cheapest and most expensive rail fare between where you live and London.

> **learning tip** Don't get the terms mixed up – elastic = stretchy = responsive, inelastic = inflexible = not responsive.

ACTIVITY ····⋮›

BT Broadband recently reduced their monthly charge from £18.99 to £14.99. What would be the price elasticity of demand for their service if demand increased by:

(a) 10 per cent

(b) 20 per cent

(c) 30 per cent?

Income elasticity of demand

Income elasticity of demand measures the responsiveness of the demand for a product to changes in income. It is also represented by a formula, or equation – in this case:

$$^{y}\varepsilon_d = \frac{\% \text{ change in quantity demanded}}{\% \text{ change in income}}$$

> **DEFINITION**
>
> **Income elasticity of demand** ($^{y}\varepsilon_d$): a measure of the responsiveness of demand to changes in income.

> **learning tip** Note: only the bottom of the equation is different from the equation given for price elasticity of demand on page 20.

If the government were to decide to cut income tax, then all those people in work would have higher disposable incomes. Having more money to spend might change people's spending patterns, especially if becoming better off makes it possible for them to afford what might previously have been considered a luxury item. For example, increasing incomes over the last 30 years have led to an even bigger proportionate increase in the demand for foreign holidays. This could mean that a 10 per cent rise in incomes could lead to a 30 per cent increase in the demand for foreign holidays. In other words, income elasticity of demand for foreign holidays would be +30/+10 = +3.

On the other hand, rising incomes have also been associated with a fall in demand for traditional British seaside holidays. So the same increase in income of 10 per cent might be associated with a 40 per cent fall in demand for some British seaside towns.

The income elasticity in this case would be –40/+10 = –4 and, in this case, the coefficient for income elasticity of demand would be negative. Economists call goods such as these *inferior goods*, whereas the more attractive foreign holidays are called *superior goods* (see page 18).

ACTIVITY ····⋮›

Suppose you get the opportunity to work on Sundays rather than Saturdays and you get paid at time and a half. What would be the income elasticity of the following goods and services if your demand changed in the following ways?

(a) spending on public transport fell by 20%

(b) spending on the cinema increased by 50%

(c) spending on petrol rose by 75%.

> **learning tip** By now you should be used to the significance of positive or negative values when interpreting measures of elasticity. Always make sure you include the + or –.

Cross elasticity of demand

In the previous section you will have learned that changes in the price of a given good or service can have an effect on the demand for another good or service. Economists categorise goods as being either substitutes or complements (see page 17). The degree to which demand changes in response to changes in the price of other goods can be measured by using the concept of **cross elasticity of demand**. This is defined as

$$^{x}\varepsilon_{d} = \frac{\text{\% change in quantity demanded of good x}}{\text{\% change in the price of good y}}$$

SUBSTITUTES

If this is applied to the demand for peaches for which a close *substitute* is available, say nectarines, it would be expected that an increase in the price of the substitute (nectarines) would lead to an increase in demand for peaches.

So a 10 per cent increase in the price of nectarines might result in a 40 per cent rise in demand for peaches. The cross elasticity of demand for peaches in respect of changes in the price of nectarines would be +40/+10 = +4.

The value would be much smaller if consumers did not regard these two fruit as close substitutes and vice versa. The size of the coefficient indicates how substitutable the two products are for one another. If there were little **brand loyalty** and a high degree of customer knowledge, the value of the coefficient would be much larger. Moreover if we are considering

two goods which are substitutes, the value of the coefficient will always be positive.

COMPLEMENTS

If two sets of goods are *complements*, the coefficient of the cross elasticity of demand of one good in respect to a change in the price of another will always be negative. For example, a fall in the mortgage rate is likely to lead to an increase in the demand for homes. In this case, a price cut of one good leads to an increase in demand for a complement. So a cut in interest rates which represented a 1 per cent fall in the cost of borrowing may lead to a 10 per cent increase in demand for houses. In this case the cross elasticity of demand for housing in respect to changes in the mortgage rate would be expressed as follows

$$^{x}\varepsilon_{d} \text{ (housing) in respect of the cost of borrowing} = \frac{\text{\% change in quantity of housing demanded}}{\text{\% change in the price of mortgages}}$$

$$^{x}\varepsilon_{d} \text{ (housing) in respect of the cost of borrowing} = +10/-1$$

$$^{x}\varepsilon_{d} \text{ (housing) in respect of the cost of borrowing} = -10$$

This value indicates that the demand for houses is very sensitive to changes in the cost of borrowing, which in turn is closely linked to changes in mortgage interest rates. If two goods are complements, their coefficient for their cross elasticities will always be negative and, as with all the other uses of the concept of elasticity, the smaller the value the less responsive the relationship (and vice versa).

ECONOMICS IN CONTEXT

USA HIT BY PROPERTY PRICE CRASH – SUB-PRIME MISERY

Easy loans have finally taken effect on the US economy. It's funny how the lessons of boom and bust soon get forgotten. Credit has been easy in the USA, but it has been harder and harder to find those who want to take out loans, or rather those who want to take out loans and have the means to repay them.

Until early last 2006 property prices in the USA were ringing. Those with an eye to easy profits and new markets thought that this would take some of the risk out of lending to those on low incomes.

Some financial institutions spent small fortunes on encouraging those on low incomes to take out loans to buy property. They reasoned that rising property prices would provide the lenders with assets to cover the possible defaults on loans. Their greed blinded them to the obvious: that what goes up could come down.

Guess what happened: property prices fell, the US economy looked rocky, and the poor started getting poorer with some falling behind on their repayments. They got evicted. The supply of housing increased. Property prices fell.

The problem was that it did not end there.

Smart people in financial circles had sold on their so-called assets from the 'sub-prime market',

and these had been traded on, but their origins had been disguised so no one knew who held these dodgy assets.

It didn't take long for financial markets throughout the world to get the jitters, and in late 2007 banks started worrying about lending to one another, lest sub-prime securities should be uncovered.

It didn't take long for the shock waves to cross the Atlantic, and they are still reverberating.

ACTIVITY ····

Read the Economics in context case study above and answer the following questions.

(a) Why are house prices falling in the USA?

(b) What effects might this have on the US economy?

(c) What effects might this have on the UK economy?

ACTIVITY ····

Interpret the following elasticity coefficients.

(a) Price elasticity of demand of −0.2

(b) Price elasticity of demand of −3.6

(c) Price elasticity of demand of +2

(d) Income elasticity of demand of −4

(e) Income elasticity of demand of +4

(f) Cross elasticity of demand of −2

(g) Cross elasticity of demand of +2

(h) Cross elasticity of demand of 0.

ACTIVITY ⋯⬩⋮

Work out some cross elasticities for yourself:

(a) Select two clothing brands that you believe are close substitutes.

(b) Devise a suitable questionnaire to collect data to test whether or not you have made a good choice.

(c) Collect your data.

(d) Collate your findings.

(e) Conclude by outlining what you have learned.

ACTIVITY ⋯⬩⋮

Undertake a survey of possible buying intentions in order to determine the likely price elasticity, income elasticity and cross elasticities of demand for a product of your choice. Analyse your findings and report on the main outcomes of your research.

learning tip

Demand elasticities are confusing at first but try to remember three things:

(a) Define by writing out the formula for the elasticity you are using.

(b) Remember that the change in quantity demanded always goes on the top half of the equation.

(c) Small value to elasticity coefficient = relatively weak relationship

Large value = strong relationship

Negative relationship = inverse relationship.

The determinants of the supply of goods and services

We now need to switch to thinking not about consumers as economic agents who demand goods and services, but rather about producers who supply goods and services. Crudely speaking, we argued earlier that consumers will want to buy more if goods are cheaper and vice versa. But what about the behaviour of producers, especially in respect of their willingness to supply goods in relationship to changes in price? At this stage we will make two key assumptions about the behaviour of producers.

● They will wish to produce more goods and services if the price is high than would be the case if the price was relatively low. This assumption is based on the argument that if the price of a good or service rises, **ceteris paribus,** its production will become more profitable. Bigger profits are more desirable than smaller profits; therefore, it is argued that a rise in price will lead to an increase in supply.

● The price of a good or service is the most important variable determining supply.

DEFINITION

Ceteris paribus (Latin: other things being equal): assuming other variables remain unchanged.

Given these assumptions, the relationship between the supply of a good or service and its price can be graphically illustrated by drawing a supply curve as shown below in Figure 2.11.

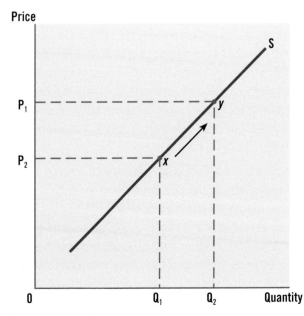

Figure 2.11 Supply curve

Price is measured on the vertical axis and quantity on the horizontal, and the supply curve slopes upwards from left to right. If prices were to rise from *OP* to *OP₁*, producers would want to increase the quantity supplied from *OQ* to *OQ₁* as shown in the movement along the curve from *x* to *y*. The converse (or opposite) of this is true. If prices fall, supply should also fall.

Other factors that determine the supply of goods and services

Although the price of a good or service is considered to be the most important factor affecting supply, changes in other variables are also likely to bring about changes to supply:

- costs of production
- changes in technology
- relative profitability
- business objectives.

COSTS OF PRODUCTION

Costs of production refer to all payments that have to be made in order to produce a good or service. Thus payments to all factors of production need to be taken account of. An increase in wage rates would push up the costs of production and, *ceteris paribus*, this will lead to a fall in profits reducing the incentive to make a particular product or service. This can be shown graphically by shifting the supply curve upwards to the left from *S* to *S₁* as illustrated in Figure 2.12, showing that, at all possible prices, producers will desire to produce less. The reverse argument applies – if costs fall, potential profits rise and supply will rise, shown by a shift in the supply curve to the right, from *S* to *S₂*.

Producers are almost always faced with a range of taxes. Thus, in the UK, corporation tax is paid on the net profits made by businesses. Business rates and national insurance contributions paid by employers are another form of taxation. These taxes paid by firms are treated by economists as another cost of production and an increase in taxes will shift the supply curve upward to the left. Governments

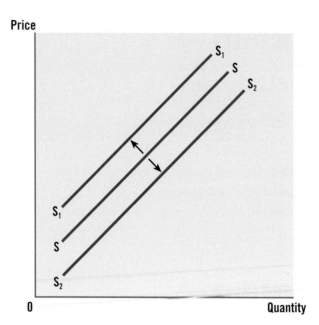

Figure 2.12 Shifts in supply

sometimes give grants and loans as incentives to encourage producers to supply particular goods or services. These subsidies are treated as a reverse tax and if they are increased the supply curve shifts downwards to the right and vice versa (Figure 2.12).

CHANGES IN TECHNOLOGY

Technology refers to the particular way in which factors of production are combined to produce goods and services. Significant economic change is often associated with the adoption of new technologies that cut the costs of production. The introduction of steam power helped create the industrial revolution, the internal combustion engine cut transport costs, and the application of computer-based technologies has more recently enabled producers of many different goods and services to cut the costs of production.

Improvements in technology are often associated with reductions in the cost of production and they can be illustrated in a similar way. The adoption of better and cheaper ways of making something will shift the supply curve downwards to the right. On the other hand, the use of more complex or difficult technologies will shift a supply curve to the left (Figure 2.12).

RELATIVE PROFITABILITY

The importance of profits and the incentive that they offer to producers has previously been considered, but a further issue – especially for those firms who have an easy choice between producing different products and providing different services – is the relative profitability of producing different goods or services. For example, if Tesco can negotiate a better deal with the suppliers of Whiskas cat food rather than Felix, it may be inclined to supply more of the former and less of the latter.

Not all businesses have such easy choices, because changing what is produced or sold may take time. However, the general rule is that if supplying an alternative product becomes more profitable, the supply of the good in question will fall, as shown in Figure 2.12. On the other hand, if the supply of an alternative becomes less profitable, there could be a shift to the right, showing an increase in supply, also illustrated in Figure 2.12.

Business objectives

So far, we have assumed that producers will respond in similar ways to changes in factors affecting their supply of a good or service, and that making bigger profits is likely to be important to all businesses. However, no two businesses are the same when it comes to the prioritisation of different objectives.

● Some businesses are interested in quick profits at all costs.

● Others might place greater emphasis on, for example, ethical considerations.

MAKING MAXIMUM PROFIT

At one extreme there are street and market traders who are probably in competition with others and will want to sell their stocks as quickly as possible, especially if they are dealing with something that is perishable. They are able to alter their prices very easily in response to changes in demand. These changes in prices will not push up costs and a skilled street trader will alter prices to try to ensure that he/she makes as big a profit as possible.

Not all business decision makers respond immediately to small changes in price. Changing prices can be costly in terms of pricing up individual items, maintaining records and arranging for advertising. In this case, rising prices might not lead to increased profits and raised output. Similarly improvements in technology might allow the same level of profit in return for working less hard.

Some businesses pride themselves in terms of their services to the community. They may believe that it is wrong in terms of scarcity to push prices up. They might consider that objectives other than making as much profit as possible are important. Because individual businesses work in different ways it is harder for economists to make simple generalisations about supply.

Market traders need to sell perishable goods fast

Ethical considerations

ECONOMICS IN CONTEXT

FRANCISCO, WILLIAM & JOSÉ

Francisco, José and William are small coffee farmers in Costa Rica. They live in a remote mountain community where people 'start the day working, end the day working.' They love growing coffee. 'I was born in the leaves of a coffee bush,' says Francisco. They also appreciate the freedom of being small producers. 'I'm my own boss. I've got mastery over my own time,' says William. 'I'm an impresario,' jokes José.

So Francisco has this message for Fairtrade shoppers: 'Continue buying coffee grown by small producers. Spread the word among your friends that they can help small producers. Mention our love for our way of life, and our culture and our customs.'

The village of Bajo Caliente has one church, a playing field, two shops and a primary school. It is about 25 km from the nearest town of Miramar, along a rutted dirt road.

There's no source of income in the remote valley other than growing coffee. 'We have no choice,' says José. 'Our plot of land is too small to make money in any other way. Coffee is our only way of getting out of poverty.' However, for the last two years, the price of coffee has been very low – below the cost of production.

Fortunately, Francisco, José and William all belong to a local farmers' cooperative (Coop Monte de Oro), which sells 35–40 per cent of their crop to the Fairtrade

market. 'It's our organisation. They're not exploiting us,' says Francisco. 'When we supplied to a middleman, he paid us when he wanted and we never knew if the payment reflected the market price.' The co-op's sales to the Fairtrade market fetch a price guaranteed to cover the cost of production.

'If it wasn't for Fairtrade, it would be impossible to continue,' says José. 'A lot of people abandon their land and go to the city, which isn't what they're used to. Some only find casual work. Here we have subsistence crops, so we've got something to eat, even if times are hard.'

Source: Fairtrade

ACTIVITY ····

(a) Why might coffee producers be exploited?

(b) How does 'Fairtrade' help coffee producers?

(c) Should we pay more for commodities like coffee?

ACTIVITY ····

Which way will the supply curve for Mars Bars move if:

(a) there is a severe frost in Ghana

(b) producing chocolate truffles becomes more profitable

(c) an ethical chocolate-producing company (for example, Fairtrade) mounts a successful advertising campaign

(d) Mars Bars are shown to improve energy levels?

PRICE ELASTICITY OF SUPPLY

It is very useful for economists to know how responsive the supply of a given good or service is to changes in price. This relationship can be measured by using the concept of **price elasticity of supply**. As with price elasticity of demand this concept can be explained in words, by graphs and by use of formulae.

DEFINITION

Price elasticity of supply: a measure of responsiveness of supply to changes in price.

Words

If it is easy and quick for a producer to change the output of a good or service in response to changes in price then the supply of that good is described as relatively elastic. This means that a given change

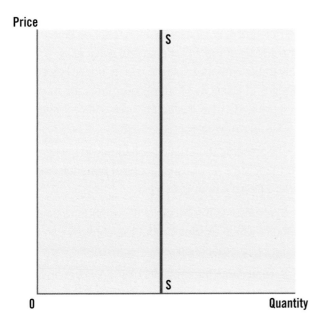

Figure 2.13 Perfectly inelastic supply

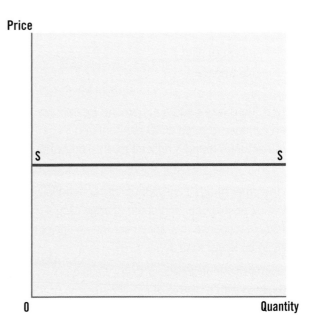

Figure 2.14 Perfectly elastic supply

in price will bring about a more than proportionate change in the supply of that good or service.

Alternatively, if it is difficult and time consuming to change output in response to price changes, then supply is relatively inelastic in that a given change in price will lead to a less than proportionate change in quantity supplied.

Graphs

Graphical analysis can be quickly used to illustrate different elasticities of supply. The diagrams above show the two limiting cases of perfectly inelastic (Figure 2.13) and perfectly elastic (Figure 2.14) **supply curves**.

DEFINITION

Supply curve: this shows the relationship between the price of a good or service and the willingness of a producer to supply that good.

In most cases we would expect elasticity of supply to fall between these two extremes and, unlike unitary demand, unitary elasticity of supply is represented

by a straight line bisecting the origin, showing equi-proportional changes in both price and quantity supplied. This is shown in Figure 2.15 below:

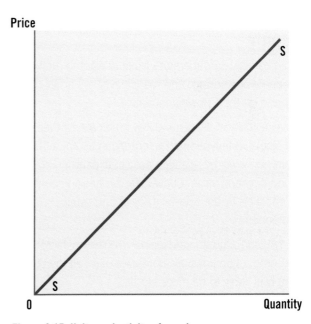

Figure 2.15 Unitary elasticity of supply

The formula

The formula for working out the coefficient is very similar to that relating to price elasticity of demand.

31

It is:

$$\text{price elasticity of supply} = \frac{\% \text{ change in quantity supplied}}{\% \text{ change in price}}$$

Thus if there was a surge in demand for cars leading to an increase in price of 10 per cent and if car manufacturers found it difficult to raise output by more than 2 per cent, the coefficient would be +0.2.

On the other hand, if car manufacturers had large stocks of unsold cars and could change output quickly in response to a price rise, the coefficient is likely to be larger than 1.

The opposite analysis also applies. Falling prices are associated with a decrease in willingness to produce and supply. Some producers are able to adjust quickly to falling prices, while others will find it harder to do.

It is very unlikely for a negative coefficient to occur, as this would mean that producers expand production in response to a fall in price or cut output in response to a rise in price.

Factors affecting the elasticity of supply

If prices rise, producers are likely to want to respond by increasing supply, and responsiveness is likely to depend on the following factors.

● Availability of stocks and raw materials. (If there are stocks of finished goods, components and other materials, it will be relatively easy to expand production and sales. Conversely, expansion could be checked by the unavailability of one small component.)

● Unused productive capacity. (If existing factories and production lines are not being used all the time, supply is likely to be more elastic.)

● Availability of imports. (Many industries are global and companies can switch supplies from contracting markets to those that are growing.)

● Availability of suitably trained labour. (The difficulty and extra costs of attracting skilled workers may limit the responsiveness of producers in meeting increases in demand.)

The significance of these factors can be viewed in a different way by using the concept of 'time' – the supply of most products and services is likely to become more elastic over a longer timescale. Changes in elasticity of supply over time are shown in Figure 2.16. This illustrates three different time periods shown where:

● S represents the elasticity of supply in a very short timescale as unused stocks of materials and under-utilised labour is used

● S_1 represents the elasticity of supply for a longer period in which existing productive capacity can be brought into production

● S_2 represents the elasticity of supply over an even longer period to allow for the acquisition of a new plant and machinery along with the training of new workers.

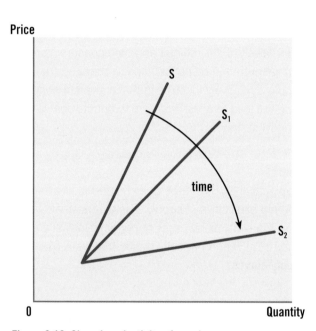

Figure 2.16 **Changing elasticity of supply**

The significance of technological change

Technological change refers to changes in the way in which goods and services are actually produced. Over the last two decades tremendous advances have been made in communications technology. We all know about the importance of IT in our lives, but there have been similar, if less spectacular, advances in air and sea transport. These developments have been paralleled by the growth of transnational corporations – many of which have more economic power than most nations. Nissan and Shell are examples of such transnational corporations.

The cumulative effect of these changes is often referred to as globalisation. It is now possible for production and sales to be organised on a global scale, which means that the supply of many products and services has become more and more elastic.

ACTIVITY ⋯⋮

Suppose there is an increase in demand for cereal bars leading to a 10 per cent increase in price, what would be the price elasticity of supply if output rose by:

(a) 0 per cent

(b) 2 per cent

(c) 8 per cent?

ACTIVITY ⋯⋮

1 What factors are likely to affect the elasticity of supply in the following markets?

   (a) wheat production

   (b) electrical generation

   (c) T-shirt manufacture.

2 Which supply is likely to be most responsive to changes in:

   (a) demand

   (b) price?

ACTIVITY ⋯⋮

How might you interpret the following coefficients for the elasticity of supply?

(a) 0

(b) +0.1

(c) +1

(d) +4

(e) −2

ACTIVITY ⋯⋮

Devise a series of questions to be used when interviewing local producers about how quickly they change output to meet changes in demand. It probably won't help much to use the concept of elasticity of supply, but that is what you need to try to find out. If you are doing this on your own, try to interview three producers of different products. You might get some more comprehensive results if you undertake this as a class activity. Write up your results in the form of a report.

The determination of market equilibrium prices

So far we have considered consumers and producers, those who demand and those who supply independently of each other. It is important for you to clearly distinguish between the actions of these two sets of economic agents but even more important to understand how their two potentially conflicting sets of objectives might be reconciled. Markets provide the theoretical meeting place for those who demand goods or services and those who supply them. Don't be rigid in your thinking of what a market place might look like. Many different kinds of markets exist. The earliest markets moved around the country. They were often celebrated as fairs and special events at which all kinds of resources were traded. Some were devoted to selling surplus production at harvest time. Others involved selling labour to the highest bidders.

Cattle markets retain some of the features of these earlier trading events but for most of us city centres and shopping malls are the new markets. However, there are many other forms of market, including:

- classified advertisements
- the stock market
- wholesale markets
- futures markets
- auctions
- flea markets
- grey markets
- the Internet.

This list could easily be extended, but regardless of the form and frequency of such markets they all involve two sets of economic agents: buyers and sellers together with the means to make a deal.

Market equilibrium

As demand curves and supply curves are drawn against the same axes, it is possible to superimpose one on top of another – as shown in Figure 2.17, which is based on the housing market.

The demand for new houses slopes downwards to the right. It is likely to be relatively inelastic, as there are not many close substitutes. This factor is likely to outweigh the significance of housing taking up a very large portion of most customers' budgets.

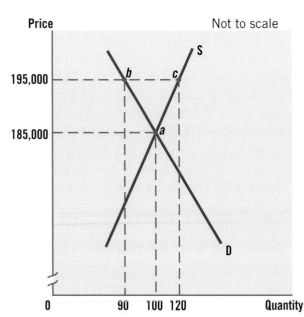

Figure 2.17 Market equilibrium

Supply slopes upwards to the right. As far as new houses are concerned, stocks are likely to be limited, and the acquisition of sites and acquiring planning permission are likely to take time, making the supply relatively elastic.

The point *a*, where the supply and demand curves cross, shows the price at which demand and supply are equal. In the example given in the diagram, the average price of a new house coming onto the market will be £185,000. In a given area, 100 houses would be sold each month. This is called the **equilibrium price**, and in a free market this will be established automatically.

If, for some reason, the price were to be £195,000, demand would equal 90, whereas supply would be 120. The producers of new houses would be attempting to sell more than could be sold. This **excess supply** of 30 homes would mean that some houses were being built, but not sold. Stocks of unwanted houses would build up and sellers would be tempted to cut prices.

Falling prices would make new houses more attractive to some consumers – for example, those on lower incomes, who might now be able to borrow enough money. However, some builders may find house building less attractive and seek alternative building contracts. Demand would rise as supply would fall.

According to price theory, this process will stop when the equilibrium price is reached. This pincer movement towards equilibrium is shown by movements *b* and *c* along the demand and supply curves. The process by which markets are brought into equilibrium is called **market clearing.**

The same logical analysis can be applied to a situation in which new houses are being sold for less than £185,000. **Excess demand** would apply and some prospective house buyers would be forced to go without. New houses coming onto the market would be snapped up quickly, and enterprising estate agents might well attempt to take advantage of the shortage of new houses by raising their prices.

This process would set a similar pincer movement in operation to that described earlier. Rising prices would put off some potential house buyers but would also make house production more attractive. Demand would fall and supply would rise until equilibrium is reached.

learning tip

The key point to remember is that as long as demand curves slope downwards to the right and supply curves slope upwards to the right, and as long as they both cross, there can only be one equilibrium – and that is the price where demand is equal to supply. In other words, both buyers and sellers can make a deal.

Markets and changes in demand

As noted earlier, demand curves shift if any of the following change:

● the prices of substitutes

● the prices of complements

● consumers' incomes

● consumers' tastes.

DECREASE IN THE PRICE OF A SUBSTITUTE

Consider the market for seats at the Centre Court for the Wimbledon All-England Open Tennis Championship. This particular market is illustrated in Figure 2.18. In this case the Centre Court capacity is fixed at 15,000 and this would appear as a vertical line as shown by *SS*. Demand is relatively inelastic, represented by *DD*, giving an equilibrium price of *P* and ticket sales of *OQ*.

DEFINITIONS

Market clearing: the process by which changes in the price of a good or service bring about equilibrium between demand and supply.

Excess demand: occurs when the demand for a good or service is greater than the supply.

ACTIVITY ····⫶

Stella McCartney's one-off collection for H&M went on sale at 9 a.m. on 10 November 2005. A queue had been forming outside since 7 a.m. By 9.05 a.m. the collection had sold out.

Draw a demand and supply diagram to explain the situation outlined above.

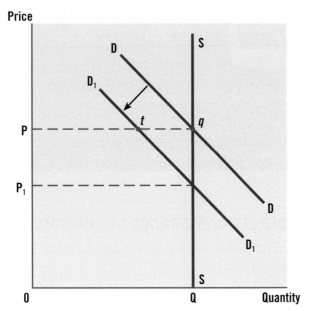

Figure 2.18 Falling demand

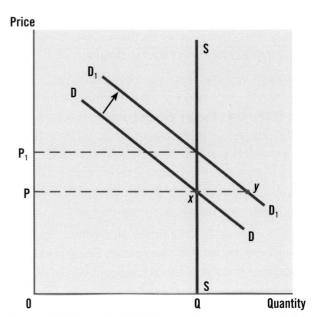

Figure 2.19 Increasing demand

Those thinking of buying a ticket will consider not only the price of the ticket, but also the price of alternatives. This would include prices of tickets for other courts or a whole range of other leisure products. If, for example, a Test cricket match were being staged in London at the same time and seat prices for that were reduced, some people might be attracted to cricket rather than tennis and this would cause the demand for Wimbledon tickets to fall – as shown by the shift from DD to $D_1 D_1$. If the price were to remain at P there would be disequilibrium between demand and supply. Supply would exceed demand by tq. Excess supply would exist – that is, some tickets would be unsold. The managers of Wimbledon might consider cutting prices to OP_1 in order to make sure all seats were sold. This change in price would be described by economists as being the outcome of 'market forces' at work.

DECREASE IN THE PRICE OF A COMPLEMENT

A number of other products or services are likely to be jointly consumed by visitors to Wimbledon. Travel to the courts, the famous strawberries and cream, and perhaps having something new to wear, could be considered to be complements. So, reduced public transport prices to Wimbledon could result in an increase in demand for Wimbledon tickets, as shown in Figure 2.19. In this case, demand increases, as

indicated by the shift to the right from D to D_1. If the price remained at P, excess demand of xy would occur. This would give Wimbledon's managers the opportunity to raise seat prices and a new equilibrium could be established with a higher price at P_1. If they didn't raise the prices, opportunities would arise for ticket touts outside to exploit the situation by selling tickets at inflated prices.

CHANGES IN INCOMES

If the country as a whole becomes better off, potential ticket sales at Wimbledon are likely to rise. Studies show that the income elasticity of demand for 'products' such as this is highly positive. If incomes in general rise, it is likely that the increase in demand for tickets will be proportionately greater and the effects of this would be similar to those illustrated in Figure 2.19.

If the product or service under consideration were an inferior good, then an increase in income would be associated with a fall in demand; the demand curve shifts to the left, leading to a fall in prices and sales.

CHANGES IN TASTES

The effects of changes in tastes can be modelled in the same way. If a good or service becomes more fashionable, demand shifts to the right resulting in higher prices and sales. On the other hand, going out of fashion would be represented by a shift in demand to the left, leading to falling prices and sales.

ACTIVITY ····⟶

Use demand and supply diagrams to predict what will happen to the price and sales of tennis rackets if:

(a) there is a rise in membership fees for tennis clubs

(b) footballers get even higher incomes

(c) there is a reduction in income tax

(d) cat gut (once used for stringing tennis rackets) is shown to be carcinogenic.

Markets and changes in supply

Changes in supply are considered in this section in the context of agricultural production and the focus will be on a growing agricultural market, that for organically grown carrots. In this case, the supply

curve will shift if any of the following changes occur:

- changes in costs of production
- technological changes
- changes in the objectives of producers.

THE MARKET FOR ORGANIC CARROTS

The market for organic carrots can be analysed like any other market by focusing on demand and supply. As noted earlier, the demand for organic produce is growing. In 2006 sales of organic food and drink in the UK increased by 22 per cent. Moreover, the demand for organic carrots is, arguably, relatively inelastic if we assume that buyers do not consider non-organic produce a close substitute.

When it comes to supply, it is reasonable to assume that the supply curve slopes upwards to the right as shown in Figure 2.20. It is harder to generalise about the elasticity of supply. It takes UK farmers at least three years to switch from conventional to organic production, making their supply relatively inelastic. However, organic carrots are traded globally,

ECONOMICS IN CONTEXT

UK ORGANIC SALES HIT £2BN – UP 22 PER CENT – AVERAGING £7 MILLION GROWTH PER WEEK.

Organic food and drink sales in the UK nudged the £2 billion mark for the first time in 2006, with a sustained market growth rate of 22 per cent throughout the year.

Launched to coincide with the start of Soil Association Organic Fortnight 2007, the Soil Association's definitive annual Organic Market Report shows continued strong growth and dynamic public support for organic food, drink, textiles and health and beauty products.

Retail sales of organic products through organic box and mail order schemes and other direct routes increased from £95 million

in 2005 to £146 million in 2006 – a staggering 53 per cent growth, more than double that experienced by the major supermarkets.

Organic textiles and the booming organic health and beauty sector are experiencing particularly strong growth. 2006 saw a 30 per cent increase in the number of health and beauty products licensed with the Soil Association. At current growth rates, the UK market for organic cotton products is estimated to be worth £107 million by 2008.

Despite the steady growth in demand for organic food over the past decade, some key sectors

are still failing to meet demand. Organic livestock sectors are dependent on supplies of organic feed, but UK self-sufficiency in organic cereals fell below 50 per cent, during 2006, increasing our reliance on imported organic grains. The cost of livestock feed, whether for organic or non-organic farmers, is rising as a result of recent poor global harvests, increasing diversion of cereals into biofuel production and rapidly rising demand particularly from China and India.

Source: Soil Association Organic Market Report 2007

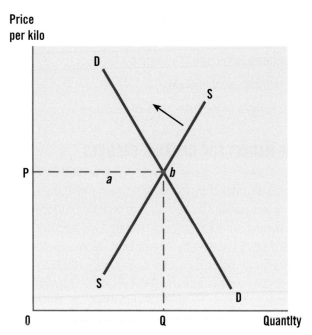

Figure 2.20 Market for organic carrots

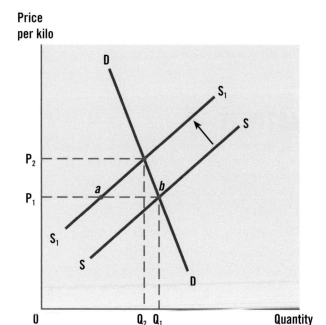

Figure 2.21 Increasing production costs

which means that suppliers in the UK can be more responsive to changes in demand, especially if UK consumers are prepared to pay more than customers in other countries.

> **learning tip**
>
> Notice the use of phrases like 'it could be argued' and 'it is harder to generalise', indicating that this analysis is a bit more speculative and the writer does not want to give the impression that answers or assumptions are easily made.

This analysis indicates that the equilibrium price will be at *OP* and sales will be at *OQ*. However, this will change if other variables change.

INCREASING COSTS OF PRODUCTION

Organic producers face additional costs in order to assure buyers that their produce is really organic. So the Soil Association, which promotes organic production methods, operates a certification scheme to guarantee the organic origins of products. If it

were to increase its registration fees, organic carrot producers would face an increase in costs. This is shown in Figure 2.21 by the leftward and upward shift in supply to S_1.

If the price were to remain at OP_1 per kilo, demand would now exceed supply by *ab*. Excess demand means that some potential buyers might have to go without. Enterprising greengrocers might raise their prices. The price would be likely to rise until a new equilibrium is reached. In this case, demand would be equal to the reduced supply with a price of OP_2 per kilo, and sales would fall to OQ_1.

IMPROVEMENTS IN TECHNOLOGY

Alternatively, an improvement could be made in the production process that reduced costs of production. Potential profits would be higher, production would be more attractive and the supply curve would shift downwards to the right. If the old price were maintained, disequilibrium would arise: supply would be greater than demand. Prices would fall until a new equilibrium had been established, showing both a lower price and higher sales. This is illustrated in Figure 2.22 where increasing supply from *S* to S_1 leads to a fall in price from *OP* to OP_1 and increase in supply from *OQ* to OQ_1.

Price
per kilo

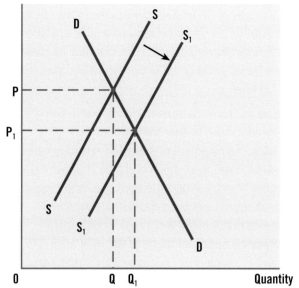

Figure 2.22 Highly elastic demand

OBJECTIVES OF PRODUCERS

An increasing number of farmers are turning away from inorganic fertilisers, herbicides and pesticides, and may prefer to adopt organic techniques for ethical reasons. This trend is likely to lead to an increase in the supply of organic products (as shown in Figure 2.22). The long-term effect of these trends is that the supply and sales of organic carrots (and other products) should increase and prices should fall.

ECONOMICS IN CONTEXT

UNDER THE WEATHER

Rainfall in many parts of the UK in 2007 was greater than has been officially recorded since records began, and although it is not possible to be precise about the effects of this abnormal weather, agricultural production in the UK has been hit. Organic crops have been flooded and consequently the supply has shifted upwards to the left, leading to higher prices and lower sales for domestically produced produce. The particular features of the markets for many agricultural products are explored in greater detail on page 90. Some economists and farmers have argued that governments should regard agricultural markets differently from others which are less likely to be affected by events which cannot reasonably be anticipated.

ACTIVITY

How might the price and sales of hot chocolate in the UK be affected by:

(a) easier access for African producers to European markets

(b) a new outbreak of foot and mouth disease in the UK

(c) hurricanes in the West Indies

(d) lower tea prices?

The application of demand and supply analysis to particular markets

It should be clear that if any of the key variables that determine the demand or supply for any product or service change, then the equilibrium will change, leading to a change in price and sales.

The stages outlined in the Learning tip can be used to analyse aspects of the following markets:

● crude oil

● health care

● footballers.

learning tip

Get into a routine with market analysis.

1 Know the basics: demand normally slopes downwards from left to right and supply slopes upwards.

2 Label your axes.

3 Think about the relative size of demand and its possible elasticity.

4 Do the same for supply.

5 Draw a graph.

6 Find the initial equilibrium.

7 Change a variable.

8 Predict the outcome.

9 Ask yourself – is this realistic?

10 Is there anything special about this market?

CRUDE OIL MARKET

Crude oil is one of the most important resources used directly and indirectly to produce a wide range of goods and to provide an important energy source. In the short run, demand is likely to be inelastic but in the longer run it is possible to find alternatives.

The supply of crude oil is ultimately finite as it is a non-renewable resource. However, prospectors are still finding new supplies of crude oil, and actual deposits can vary in quality and ease of extraction. There is little doubt that the current demand for oil is increasing at a faster pace than the discovery of new reserves. Some experts believe that world supplies of crude oil will peak next year. However, it is very difficult to get accurate and reliable data on oil reserves. The major suppliers such as BP, Exxon and Shell are reluctant to reveal commercially sensitive data. Moreover governments own 90 per cent of reserves and their statistics cannot be relied on.

The extraction of crude oil usually requires extensive and expensive investment and this is likely to make its supply relatively inelastic in the short run. Crude oil is not very useful in the form in which it spurts from beneath the Earth's crust. It has to be transformed to enable it to be used to power vehicles, make chemicals, produce plastics and make foodstuffs. Limits in refining capacity can also make the supply inelastic. For these reasons, the demand and supply of diesel fuel to motorists in the UK in September 2007 can be represented as in Figure 2.23. This shows that world demand has increased from D to D_1, taking the UK price per litre over the £1.00 level.

Figure 2.23 can be used to model peace being restored to Iraq, or the, some would say highly unlikely, development of improved relations between the USA, European Union and Iran. The two Middle Eastern countries have the third and forth biggest proven reserves of oil in the world. Peace and understanding might well boost world supplies, shifting the supply of diesel to the right from S to S_1 and bringing down prices to 75p/litre as well as boosting sales.

ACTIVITY ⋯⦂

The following article probably represents a more realistic scenario for the crude oil market. Use demand and supply analysis to model the effects of:

(a) a cut in world production of 2 million barrels a day

(b) successful exploitation of Canada's oil sands.

> Six of the largest oil suppliers to the USA are poised to cut their global exports by nearly 2 million barrels a day by 2012, ramping up pressure on supply and price, and intensifying the focus on one of the last great deposits open to private investment: Canada's oil sands.
>
> The projected cut, amounting to seven percent by Mexico, Saudi Arabia, Venezuela, Nigeria, Algeria and Russia, reflects the growing struggle in these countries to grow production and manage their own soaring rates of oil consumption, says Jeff Rubin, chief market strategist and chief economist at CIBC World Markets.

HEALTH CARE MARKET

The market for health care in the UK is more difficult to model as for most people health care is free, provided by the National Health Service and funded

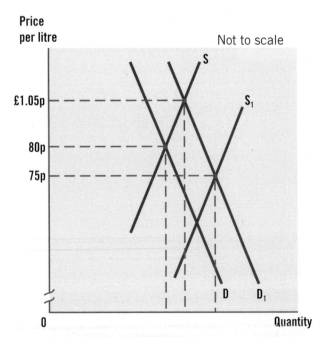

Figure 2.23 Rising fuel prices

by the government through taxes that we all pay. The medical care market is arguably the largest individual 'market' in the UK, and is the largest single employer in Europe. Although the NHS is not directly part of the market economy, demand and supply analysis can be used to highlight some of the issues that make health care in the UK such a controversial and politically sensitive issue.

First, we have to consider a hypothetical demand for NHS health care. The population of the UK is aging, and our expectations about receiving health care are rising. It is possible to argue that private health care is a substitute for some NHS users, but the demand for health care is likely to be relatively inelastic – as will be the supply: doctors and nurses take years to train. Building hospitals and new provision cannot be achieved quickly. Supply problems are made worse as the NHS is government funded: there will always be competing demands for government spending. Moreover, governments don't like raising taxes and would probably prefer to reduce taxes.

This means that we don't have a conventional equilibrium between the demand and supply of health care. The demand at a given time outstrips the supply. If health care were part of the market system, the price of health care would rise until demand equalled supply. We are left with excess demand, which in turn gets translated into waiting lists.

World-class footballers such as Wayne Rooney are in demand and can earn huge salaries

£676,000 a year or £13,000 a week. An elite group tops the £1 million-a-year mark. Can this be justified in economic terms? Can demand and supply analysis help understand why they earn in a year what will take most of us 25 years?

We have to make some adjustments to the graphs used earlier: instead of price on the vertical axis we measure footballers pay, and on the horizontal axis quantity becomes numbers of footballers employed in the Premiership.

Footballers are a different kind of commodity compared to houses or organic carrots. They are demanded to help build teams to win major competitions, the League, the Cup and the Champion's League. Successful teams such as Manchester United, Chelsea and Arsenal are international brands earning millions from television rights, merchandising and ticket sales. Given these incentives, these clubs are prepared to pay to get the best players. The demand for premiership footballers is represented in Figure 2.24 – it is high and relatively inelastic.

ACTIVITY ⋯⋮

1) Try drawing demand and supply curves based on the analysis of the health care market outlined above.

2) Use demand and supply diagrams to explore the implications of making UK residents pay for medical care.

SPORT AND LEISURE MARKET

One of the major controversies in many sports is whether or not famous sports people should earn so much. This is clearly a *normative* statement, but economic analysis can provide a possible explanation of the high earnings. Recent data indicates that the average UK premier league footballer earns

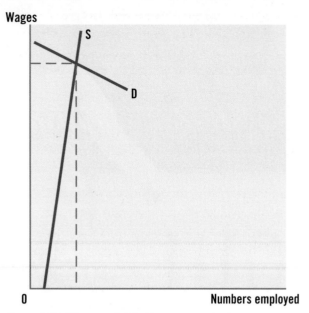

Figure 2.24 Why some footballers earn so much

When it comes to the supply – it's almost the reverse. There are very few world class players. Although teams try, they cannot be manufactured quickly. Their supply is highly limited and very inelastic. The combination of demand and supply leads to the high rate of pay.

The inter-relationship between markets

Knowing how individual markets work is a key step to understanding how the whole market economy works. No individual market works in isolation. Changes in one will lead to changes in others, which will have further effects. These chain reactions have a big impact on our lives (for example, they can cause us to become richer or poorer). They can also have an impact upon the environment.

The inter-relationships between markets can also be explored by investigating what happens when new products and suppliers enter a market. This is illustrated by the impact of David Lloyd Gyms on a growing section of the leisure industry relating to personal fitness. The former tennis player, David Lloyd, spotted a gap in a growing market and in 1982 opened the first David Lloyd fitness centre. There are now 59 clubs in the UK, with some 300,000 members. They tend to be sited where access by car

is easy, and they tend to be much larger than other gyms. This development will have led to changes in related markets:

● The demand for *complements* such as sports equipment will have risen.

● The demand for *substitute* services such as those provided by local authorities may have fallen.

● The **derived demand** for fitness instructors will have risen.

● The demand for suitable sites may have diverted demand for development sites away from alternative uses such as retailing. This is an example of **composite demand** when a resource such as development land can be used for different purposes. The success of David Lloyd Gyms may have pushed on the value of development land to the detriment of alternative retail uses.

● One of the factors which has helped make David Lloyd succeed is that developers have increased the supply of suitable land. More shopping centres have been built and this has increased the supply, and potentially reduced the cost, of sites for new gyms. This relationship between markets is called **joint supply.**

DEFINITIONS

Derived demand: a situation in which the demand for a good or service is determined by the demand for another good or service; usually relating to the demand for labour being determined by the demand for a final product or service.

Composite demand: occurs when a resource can be demanded for different purposes.

Joint supply: occurs when a resource can be used for a number of different purposes.

The next section develops how markets might be inter-related by examining what happened in the housing market in London and south-east England in 2004/6 to show how markets for a series of products or services are interlinked.

Local market inter-relationships

The housing boom of 2004/6 was caused by a major imbalance between the supply and demand for housing. Greater London is home to many different businesses, corporate headquarters, government departments and so on. Although people do exist on low incomes in London, the city contains a disproportionate number of people earning high incomes. House buying has a high positive income elasticity of demand, and the demand for houses in London and the south-east has always been stronger than in other parts of the country.

DEMAND

The demand for workers with building skills was subsequently high, boosting the earnings of bricklayers and other skilled trades. Estate agents found both sales and high profits easy to achieve. The demand for all kinds of building materials rose. Earnings of workers and the profits of the owners of such businesses also climbed. Rising house prices in London forced some potential buyers to look further afield, increasing the demand for housing in areas around London and causing a similar chain reaction as increases in demand in one market rippled over into closely related markets.

SUPPLY

The supply of houses in the short run is relatively inelastic, resulting in relatively high house prices. At the end of 2006, the cheapest starter home in London was about £210,000. People moving away from London could make large profits selling in London and buying relatively cheaper property elsewhere. Land prices continued to rise in the early part of 2006.

EFFECTS ON THE WIDER LOCAL MARKET

All of the above only describes part of the picture. There are great pressures to turn farmland into new estates, road congestion is getting worse and so on. It is easy to see how such ripples and waves would set off further reactions. It is also possible to anticipate how the rise in property prices in the south-east might reach out and affect the whole local economy.

Any local economy consists of thousands of interconnected markets, each with its own demand and supply curves, shifting and adjusting to change after change. The key links between these individual markets are price changes.

Thus, the rise in the price of houses is a signal to those who supply associated products, like paint, nails, furnishings and washing machines, that they should consider increasing their supplies and raising their prices. These products are all complements and they are likely to be in **joint demand** and any increase in the demand for housing is likely to also lead to an increase in demand for this category of products.

Rising house prices may deter some potential house buyers and they may look for alternative provision. Renting a house is an obvious *substitute*, and it is likely that rising demand for new houses will lead to rise in the demand for rented accommodation accompanied by an increase in rents. This kind of relationship between two goods is called **competitive demand.**

Increased demand for housing will increase the demand for bricklayers and plasterers. This relationship is referred to as a *derived demand* as the demand for builders is based on or derived from the demand for new housing. Rising incomes in the building trade are a signal that attracts more workers to move to the region and more young people to undertake training.

Rising profits lead to increases in the share prices of leading building firms. The demand for water, electricity and other utilities also rises.

DEFINITIONS

Competitive demand: occurs when a buyer can choose between similar products or services.

Joint demand: a situation in which products or services are bought together.

National inter-relationships

The impact of the property boom was not confined to the south-east. Brickmakers in Bedford, timber suppliers in Scotland and screwmakers in Birmingham, for example, are all likely to have experienced growing order books. Demand for their products would have risen, as would the demand for labour and other resources. A whole series of demand curves shifted to the right, and prices and outputs rose.

Ever-growing congestion and rising land prices in the south-east might encourage some employers to relocate to other parts of the country. Spreading business activity from London also affects motorways and rail links.

Global effects

The effects of the property boom spread beyond the UK. Foreign suppliers of building materials, furnishings and white goods (refrigerators, washing machines and the like) enjoyed increased demand for their products. Workers from other parts of Europe have been attracted to the UK because of labour shortages – especially in the hotel and catering industries. The property boom has spread to northern France and Ireland, as those with increasing incomes look for holiday and weekend homes.

Factor markets

The market system includes a whole series of markets for land, labour, capital and enterprise. Collectively, these are called factor markets. They play a crucial role in ensuring that customers get the goods and services they wish to purchase. Although economists consider that there are special features of these markets, demand and supply analysis is used to model the behaviour of those working in factor markets.

DEMAND FOR FACTORS

In many ways, *factors of production* are like any other product that is traded in the marketplace. They have a price. For example, the price of labour is the wage or salary that has to paid. Rent is the return

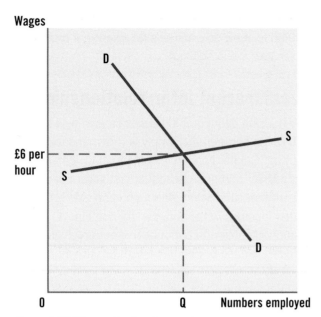

Figure 2.25 Wage rates for shop workers

earned by the owners of land. Profit is a reward for enterprise. Interest or dividends can be seen as the price paid to the owners of money or capital. If a factor of production is expensive, then – other things being equal – demand is likely to be low. If, on the other hand, it is cheap, demand will be high. Thus, the demand for building land will be lower as it becomes more expensive. In other words, the demand for factors is likely to slope downwards from left to right, as shown in Figure 2.25.

Similar analysis can be applied to the supply of factors. If you assume that the owners of factors of production want a good financial return, then the supply of land, labour, capital or enterprise can be treated in a similar way to that of any other commodity. The supply of workers to higher-paying jobs is likely to be greater than that to similar jobs paying lower wages. Alternatively, if wages are low, then the supply is likely to be low. This means that a supply curve for any factor will slope upwards to the right as shown in the diagram above.

FACTOR MARKET EQUILIBRIUM

Factor market equilibrium is illustrated in Figure 2.25. Although this looks like other demand and supply diagrams, the axes measure different variables. Thus, the market for shop workers in Cheltenham can be modelled using demand and supply analysis. Wages are represented on the vertical axis and numbers employed on the horizontal. The equilibrium wage rate is given as £6 per hour, at which the demand for shop workers is matched by the supply. Any change in demand and supply will lead to the establishment of a new equilibrium.

DERIVED DEMAND

Final goods like cars or houses are demanded for what they are. Factors are demanded because they are required to produce something else. In the example used earlier, footballers are employed because it is hoped that they will contribute to the success of their club. The nature of demand for that final product will have a direct impact on demand for the factors required to produce that product. For example, the demand for pesticide-free land will increase as a result of the increase in demand for organic foodstuffs. On the other hand, the demand for meat-processing equipment will fall if the demand for meat products falls.

Thus, although the demand curve for a factor of production looks like any other demand curve, its gradient and position will be heavily influenced by the demand for the final product. If the demand for that final product is highly price elastic, it is likely that demand for factors to make that product will also tend to be relatively elastic. Similarly, if the demand for the final product is relatively inelastic, factor use is likely to be more stable.

ACTIVITY ····⁝

How far can the concepts of demand and supply be used to explain the differences in earning between successful pop bands and those struggling to make ends meet?

How markets and prices allocate resources

This section further develops the preceding explanations of how individual markets work and interact with each other, and focuses on how the market mechanism works to allocate resources and co-ordinate the decisions of buyers and sellers.

Much of the following is based on the work of Adam Smith (1723–90), one of the most famous economists to have lived. In his book *The Wealth of Nations* (published in 1776), Smith argued that there was an 'invisible hand' which linked producers to consumers and society as a whole. Smith's choice of the term invisible hand was meant to convey to his readers that the market mechanism would work automatically to link buyers and sellers to resolve the economic problem of what to produce, how to produce it, and whom to produce it for. He also argued that freely operating markets would also work to everyone's advantage

THE MARKET MECHANISM

There are three sets of economic agents whose independent actions are linked by the market mechanism:

● consumers – whose motive is to consume as many products and services as possible for the minimum outlay

● producers of goods and services – who will seek to make as much profit as possible

● owners of factors of production – who will sell land, labour, capital and enterprise to the highest bidder.

Smith argued that if each of these sets of agents acted selfishly to pursue their own objectives, the market system would ensure that resources would be used to produce those goods and services which were most in demand. The starting point for this mechanism to work is the consumer. If markets are competitive and if they are allowed to operate freely, Smith argued, consumer wishes would be paramount. Economists call this principle 'consumer sovereignty'. In other words, the consumer is king. The market mechanism should work in the way shown in the flow diagram illustrated in Figure 2.26. This shows how the market mechanism works to co-ordinate thousands and thousands of independent decision makers and ensure that resources are allocated effectively. Prices have a crucial function

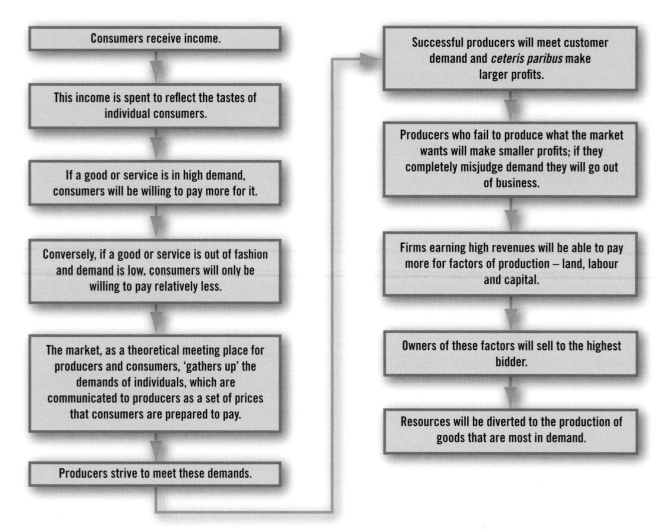

Figure 2.26 Consumer sovereignty

in ensuring that the market mechanism works in this way. They:

- ration scarce resources
- provide incentives to producers
- signal to producers, consumers and owners of factors.

RATIONING

Consumers have unlimited wants yet resources are scarce. If a resource is relatively scarce and demand is high, the price will be high, and supply will be rationed out to those consumers prepared to pay the high price. On the other hand if a resource is relatively plentiful, and demand is low, the price of that resource will also be low, ensuring that more of that relatively plentiful resource is actually used.

INCENTIVES

High demand leading to high prices is an incentive for firms to produce more as, other things being equal, profits will be higher. Low demand is associated with low prices on the other hand, which are likely to be associated with lower profits which would act as a disincentive for the production of goods and services.

SIGNALS

Rising prices indicate to producers and consumers that a good or service is in short supply and/or that the demand is rising. This provides a signal which can help the decision making of both producers and consumers. Falling prices may indicate that a good or service is in greater supply and/or the demand is falling.

Assessing the effectiveness of markets

At this stage it is important to understand the main assumptions that have been made in developing this model of the market mechanism. First, it has been assumed that markets are competitive, and firms are forced by competition to do their very best to produce those goods and services which are most in demand. If they don't, their profits will be reduced and ultimately they could go out of business. If a producer has little or no competition, there will be less of an incentive to produce what the consumer wants. Ultimately, if there is only one producer of a particular good or service, consumers might be forced to buy whatever was produced and also to pay more, as they would not have any substitutes to turn to.

Second, the market mechanism may allocate goods effectively but it makes no allowances for inequalities in income and wealth. Goods and services are allocated to those prepared to pay the highest price. If there is a high level of income inequality, goods and services will be produced to satisfy the demands of the rich and wealthy. In extreme circumstances this might mean that the better off consume the bulk of available resources and the poor go without. This is a *normative* question but one that is very relevant in assessing the effectiveness of markets.

The third assumption that will be challenged in considerable detail in Chapter 4 is that markets actually work in the way that has been described. Markets might for a number of reasons fail, and if this happens the market mechanism may not work or may produce outcomes which lead to a misallocation of resources.

ACTIVITY ⋯⋮

(a) How do consumers decide (in a free market economy) which resources get used to produce which goods and services?

(b) Why is competition so important in a free market economy?

(c) What happens to ineffective firms?

ACTIVITY ⋯⋮

Use the Internet to find out what is happening to the price of wheat.

(a) Use demand and supply analysis to explain these trends.

(b) What is likely to be the impact on consumer behaviour?

(c) How will producers be affected?

(d) Identify other markets that will be affected by the changing price of wheat.

3 Production and efficiency

On completion of this chapter, you should be able to:

● understand the benefits of specialisation, the division of labour, trade and the role of money

● analyse production, productivity and productive efficiency

● use and give examples of economies and diseconomies of scale.

Specialisation, division of labour, exchange and the role of money

The way by which goods and services are produced in our economy has developed over the last 3,000 years as we have moved from a subsistence existence to being part of a global economy. Three sets of factors have contributed to these changes:

● specialisation and the division of labour

● the development of trade

● the role of money.

SPECIALISATION AND THE DIVISION OF LABOUR

Specialisation and the division of labour are two very closely related concepts. The **division of labour**, whereby different individuals, groups, regions or even countries undertake to produce particular goods or services, has been recognised as an important concept since Greek times. Plato envisaged that every state would 'need a farmer, a builder, and a weaver, and also, I think, a shoemaker and one or two others to provide for our bodily needs.'

Adam Smith and others developed the notion, and argued that the division of labour enables **specialisation,** which would lead to even further increases in production. He used the example of pin manufacture and explained that production would become more efficient if labour was divided up into the different operations required to produce a box of pins. Moreover, dividing up labour in this way would enable individual workers to become even more skilled and productive at their appointed tasks.

DEFINITIONS

Division of labour: when different individuals, or wider groups, undertake different roles within the productive process.

Specialisation: the concentration on a particular part of the production process, or on the production of a particular good or service that is likely to lead to an increase in productivity.

These philosophical discussions about improving production were paralleled by changes in society that led to the application of the division of labour and the benefits of specialisation. In an earlier stage of our economic development – best described as **subsistence** – tribes or other groups of people within societies attempted, through their own labour, to produce enough food and basic products to survive. In its most primitive form, this would involve hunting and gathering plants and fruits. Some people in the

Hunter-gathering is still a way of life in Papua New Guinea

world still live in this way but, by our standards, living in this way is both difficult and dangerous. Poor harvests could result in too little food to go round, and natural disasters such as floods or earthquakes could wipe out shelter and possessions.

DEFINITION

Subsistence: situation when a society is at best only able to produce enough food and basic products to survive.

Around 3,000 to 5,000 years ago in the UK, some tribes became more settled and farmed the land to produce enough to live on. Subsistence economies that became more successful were able to produce more food and other goods than needed for immediate survival. They were able to store unused produce to provide insurance against unforeseen disasters. These surpluses could also be traded with other groups producing surpluses. Local trade such as this developed in the British Isles around 3,000 years ago and would have involved barter, whereby one commodity was swapped for another. Thus, a

division of labour between different tribes and social groups developed – for example, some who may have specialised in producing simple iron weapons would trade these with others who specialised in the production of grains and foodstuffs. This trade enabled greater prosperity and higher standards of living.

The division of labour and specialisation has continually developed over time.

The growth in size and importance of cities and towns encouraged a further division of labour between urban and rural areas. In the industrial revolution in the UK in the 18th–19th centuries, manufacture of cotton, woollen goods, ships, trains and other engineering products largely took place in cities, leaving the production of primary products including food to the countryside. Within factories, workers specialised in different tasks leading to mass production as typified in the early 20th century by the manufacture of the Model T Ford.

Division of labour and specialisation have been taken further as the *globalisation* (see page 33) of production and consumption has intensified. Throughout the 20th century, trade between economies grew and grew and we are all now producers and consumers in a global market. Improvements in communications, better and quicker transport links, the relatively free movement of capital, and political changes associated with the collapse of the Soviet Union in the early 1990s, have all contributed to the process of globalisation.

ACTIVITY ┄┅

The UK once had thriving clothing and footwear industries of which little remain today. Recent estimates indicate that 90 per cent of clothing and footwear sold in the UK is imported, the bulk coming from China and the Far East.

1 Is this good or bad?
2 How might economists answer this question?

THE DEVELOPMENT OF TRADE

The development of effective ways of **exchange** of surplus goods and services – more commonly referred to as trade – is a prerequisite if societies are going to benefit from greater specialisation and the division of labour. If two or more groups of countries are producing more than they can consume of particular goods and services, trade is a means by which both groups can benefit from specialisation and the division of labour. Successful trading requires:

- markets to enable buyers and sellers to 'meet'

- stability and the development of institutions to resolve any differences that might arise

- effective communications between buyers and sellers

- efficient and relatively cheap transport.

These four key variables have become even more important as economic activity has grown and now takes place on a global scale involving different peoples, different cultures, and different economic systems.

DEFINITION

Exchange: the trade in and exchange of goods and services.

If we look at economic development over time, developments in trade have had dramatic effects in raising the standard of living of many people. In recent years information and communication technology (ICT) developments have revolutionised communications and provided for the development of electronic markets, while at the same time air and sea transport has become quicker and relatively cheaper. Although this can all be disrupted by war and conflict, the development of international institutions such as the World Bank and World Trade Organisation (WTO) represents attempts to encourage greater trade.

THE ROLE OF MONEY

The third key element in economic development has been the importance that is attached to the role of **money** as a medium of exchange. Primitive societies had to rely on barter, which was not a very effective means of exchange. In the jargon of economists, barter requires 'a double coincidence of wants'. In other words, if I have specialised in the production of cider and someone else in the production of pork, the other person has to want cider and I have to want pork for barter to work.

DEFINITION

Money: a means and medium of exchange.

Money simplifies this process and early societies found that shells and other small precious items provided a more convenient means of exchange. It was a relatively short step to using coins made of valuable metals. This occurred around 3,000 years ago. The next stage – which has gradually developed over the last 700 years – involved using coins of little intrinsic value, and to using paper, and more recently electronic methods to enable exchange to take place. As long as whatever is used as a medium of exchange is trusted, it should work.

In ancient societies shells were used as an early form of money

Production

As you will have seen on page 4, production is about the transformation of factors of production into goods and services. You need to know more about three aspects of production:

- productivity
- productive efficiency
- costs of production.

PRODUCTIVITY

This refers to the output of a factor of production measured over time. The input–output diagram (Figure 3.1) can be used to help to understand the importance of **productivity** within an economy.

Figure 3.1 Input/output model

> **DEFINITION**
>
> **Productivity:** output for a given factor of production over a period of time.

The output of a good or service can be increased by increasing the amount of factors of production that are used in its production, but output can also be improved by increasing the productivity of any of the factors of production – in other words, by using land, labour, capital and enterprise more efficiently. Economists and politicians pay considerable attention to increasing productivity of labour and this can be achieved in a number of ways:

- financial incentives – bonuses and commissions paid to those who produce or sell more
- organisational changes to improve efficiency and/ or promote better working practices
- technological improvements to increase the output of workers by investments in more productive machinery

- training – to increase skill levels of workers.

Labour productivity is usually measured in terms of output per worker for a given time period.

> **DEFINITION**
>
> **Labour productivity:** output per worker over a given period of time – usually per hour.

> **learning tip**
>
> A common source or error is for students to confuse production with productivity. Production refers to how, and how much of, something might be produced. Productivity usually refers to the output per worker per hour.

PRODUCTIVE EFFICIENCY

Economists are concerned with the concept of **productive efficiency** of the whole economy. An economy is said to be productively efficient if it is not possible to increase the output of one good or service without reducing the output of other goods and services. This is illustrated on the production possibility curve in Figure 3.2.

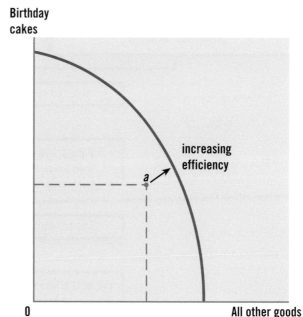

Figure 3.2 Production possibility curve

In the example, the output of birthday cakes is represented on the vertical axis and that of all other goods on the horizontal. At any point on the production possibility curve, the output of cakes can only be increased by reducing the output of other goods, by switching factors of production from the production of other goods to the production of cakes. On the other hand, if this economy is producing a combination of cakes and other products represented by any point to the left of the production possibility curve, it cannot be described as being productively efficient. Thus, if the economy is at *a*, not all

resources are being used efficiently and it would be possible to increase the production of both cakes and other goods by moving to the right until the production possibility curve is reached.

In Chapter 2 Adam Smith's 'invisible hand' was used to discuss how a free market economy might work. Smith argued that if markets are truly competitive, individual producers would have no choice other than to be productively efficient. They would be forced by market pressures to produce outputs whose costs of production were minimised. This concept relates to the basic question 'How are goods and services produced?' It is argued that that if markets are truly competitive, costs of production for an individual firm will be squeezed to a minimum, and the whole economy would be productively efficient. Freely operating markets should enable the price mechanism to work as described in the flow chart (Figure 3.3), which traces the impact on the whole

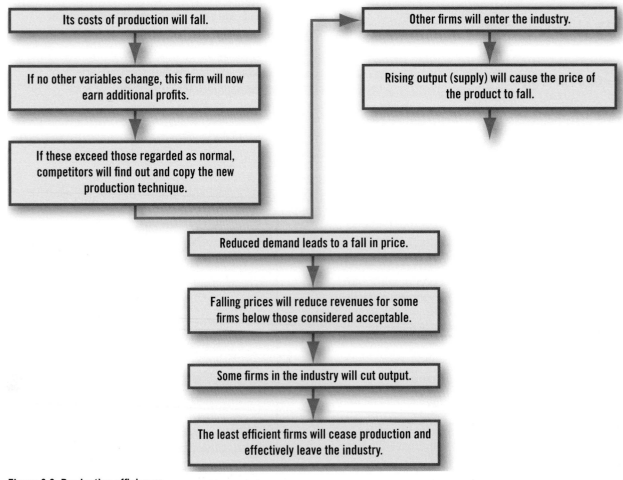

Figure 3.3 Productive efficiency

economy if one firm operating in one industry discovers a new, more efficient way of making what it produces.

Assume your company discovers a new process which speeds up the time that it takes to make birthday cakes. As long as firms compete with each other market forces will ensure that:

● any tendency by one firm to be more efficient and cut costs will be copied by competitors

● if any one firm is less efficient than its competitors, it will go out of business to the benefit of more efficient firms.

This is a continuing process that should result in ever-growing efficiencies in those markets that are truly competitive.

ACTIVITY ⋯⋗

Use a production possibility curve diagram to illustrate a decline in productive efficiency within an economy.

ACTIVITY ⋯⋗

Use average cost curves to illustrate what might happen if an individual business finds a better and cheaper way of producing a good or service.

COSTS OF PRODUCTION

As the production side of the market economy is the sum or aggregation of all the decisions made by individual producers, it is useful to examine the behaviour of individual firms.

At this stage, it is assumed that individual firms operate within competitive markets. This means that individual firms will be concerned about losing customers to the producers of substitute goods. At the same time, individual firms will probably try to do better than competitors producing alternatives. Therefore, competition should ensure that individual firms try to produce the same good or service more cheaply than competitors. This means, as Adam Smith

pointed out, that firms in a competitive economy have an incentive to produce at the lowest possible cost.

Cost of production can be divided into two categories according to the time taken to change inputs of the factors of production in order to change output:

● short-run average costs

● long-run average costs.

DEFINITIONS

Short run: the period of time during which it is only possible to change the input of one factor of production.

Long run: the time taken to change inputs of all factors of production.

learning tip
The difference between the short and the long run can vary tremendously between different industries – from weeks in the clothing industry to years when it comes to the supply of airports in the UK.

Short-run average costs

In the **short run,** it is assumed that the firm can only change the use of one factor of production – usually

Too many workers in a cake factory will increase the factory's costs

labour, while in the long run, *all* factor inputs can be changed. Suppose a firm producing birthday cakes was faced with an increase in demand. If this firm wished to increase profits, it would be expected to increase the output of birthday cakes. If the birthday cake factory was not working to capacity, one of the most obvious ways of increasing output would be to ask existing workers to work overtime. If demand had increased significantly, the business might consider introducing a shift system to enable birthday cakes to be produced 24 hours a day, 7 days a week. In this example, the company would be increasing its use of one factor of production – labour. A point would be reached when the physical limitations of the size of the factory, numbers of mixing machines, available ovens and so forth would prevent any further expansion of output. Taking on more and more workers would actually become counter-productive.

If we consider this process and relate it to the cost of producing each cake – the **average cost** – we would find out that the cost of producing each cake would get less and less until an optimum point was reached, after which increasing output by taking on more workers would start to push up the price of each cake. This relationship between output and costs of production in the short run is illustrated in Figure 3.4.

Costs are measured on the vertical axis and output on the horizontal. If we focus on employing more labour to increase output, the average cost of producing each cake will fall. For example, if more workers were employed, increasing output from *OX* to *OY*, the actual cost of producing each birthday cake would fall from £2.00 to £1.50. The recruitment of more workers would lead to further decreases in average cost, but once this falls to £1.25, average costs starts to increase. This means that *OZ* is the point of maximum efficiency – or lowest possible average cost in the short run. Beyond this level of output, employing more workers will push up the average costs of production. Workers will get in each other's way, making the factory less efficient, and this would be reflected in increasing average costs.

Long-run average costs

In the **long run** it is possible for firms to change levels of output by changing inputs of all factors of production and the relationship between average costs and output is very different to that which applies in the short run.

To continue with the example of the cake-making firm, in the long run they might consider buying in more machinery – more mixing machines, bigger ovens and more vans to distribute their cakes. In terms of the factors of production, the firm would be increasing its inputs of capital. If the owners decided that they needed bigger premises, the movement to a new site would represent a change in the factor input of land. Common sense tells us that changes like this will generally take longer than changing labour inputs. In the long run, average costs could fall, stay the same or even rise. It will all depend upon the existence or otherwise of economies and diseconomies of scale which are explained in the following sections.

Short-run average cost

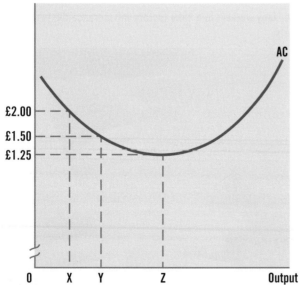

Figure 3.4 Short-run average cost curve

Economies and diseconomies of scale

The preceding analysis focused on the short run, and it was shown that short-run average cost curves are U-shaped. This does not apply in the long run, when it is possible to change all factor inputs. This opportunity to vary all factor inputs can have a big effect on costs in the long run. Long-run average costs of production could:

● fall because of **economies of scale**

● rise because of **diseconomies of scale**

● remain the same because of **constant returns to scale.**

DEFINITIONS

Economies of scale: decreases in *long-run average costs* attributable to the growing size of a firm.

Diseconomies of scale: increases in long-run average costs associated with the growth of firms.

Constant returns to scale: these occur when long-run average costs do not change as firms grow larger.

These three situations can be illustrated in Figures 3.5-7, relating long-run average costs to output.

Economies of scale

These can be further subdivided into:

● **internal economies of scale**

● **external economies of scale**.

Long-run
average cost

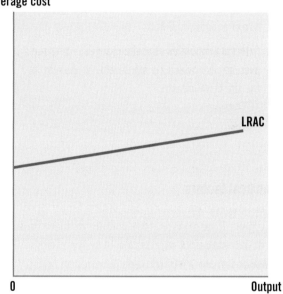

Figure 3.6 Diseconomies of scale

Long-run
average cost

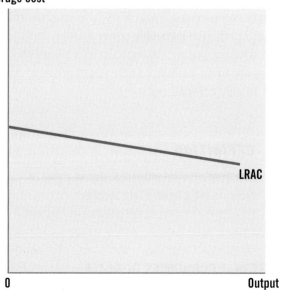

Figure 3.5 Economies of scale

Long-run
average cost

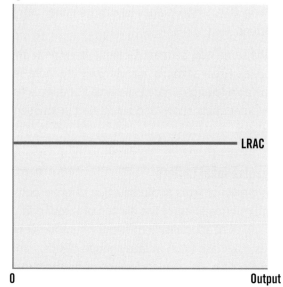

Figure 3.7 Constant returns to scale

INTERNAL ECONOMIES OF SCALE

Internal economies of scale relate to a growth in the size of the individual firm and include technical factors, organisational factors and market power.

Technical factors

As firms grow, producing and selling larger outputs can make it 'economic' to automate or mechanise particular stages of production in order to drive down costs. Henry Ford used production line techniques to mass produce cars that were much cheaper than those produced more traditionally. Similarly, wide-bodied planes such as the Airbus 300 series have lower running costs per passenger mile compared to a smaller aircraft such as the Boeing 707. Larger planes tend to be more fuel-efficient.

In the same way, as manufacturing firms grow and produce larger saleable outputs, they are more likely to be able to afford more expensive but more efficient computer applications and automated production methods.

Organisational factors

The growth of firms and production of larger outputs enables firms to apply the division of labour and principles of specialisation. Those who work for small firms may have to undertake a range of jobs, and will find it hard to develop cost-saving skills and expertise in particular fields. As firms grow, they can afford to employ specialists in finance and marketing and

so on, and this can result in cost savings, leading to falling long-run average costs.

Growth and higher revenue can allow firms to invest more heavily in research and development. This is especially important in those industries in which the rate of change is rapid – for example, electronics and pharmaceuticals. These sectors of the global economy tend to be dominated by giant firms such as Sony and GlaxoSmithKline. Their growth leads to greater research efforts, which lead to the development of new products and the establishment of new sources of competitive advantage.

Market power

Firms that grow larger can exercise more power in the various marketplaces in which they operate. Expanding output can allow companies to negotiate larger discounts from suppliers. In the UK, the major supermarkets are said to be able to compel prospective suppliers of foodstuffs to accept ever-lower prices while maintaining ever-higher standards.

Larger, wealthier companies can afford to devote larger amounts of their resources to advertising, which is particularly important in branding and the development of global markets. Transnational companies have the power to influence governments and are in a stronger position than smaller companies to use bribery or take advantage of corrupt business practices.

Larger companies are also likely to have larger market shares and such **monopoly** power enables them to use different pricing strategies to limit competition. They are more likely to be able to cut prices to drive out smaller competitors.

EXTERNAL ECONOMIES OF SCALE

These can be very beneficial to some firms, as they can bring the benefit of long-run cost reductions without additional expenditure by individual firms. External economies of scale relate to changes in long-run costs that are associated with the expansion of a particular industry rather than an individual firm.

External economies of scale are often associated with the growth and concentration of particular industries in defined geographical areas. This can attract related businesses, reducing transport costs and making collaboration more possible. Local schools and colleges are more likely to provide relevant vocational training, which will also benefit local businesses, helping them to reduce long-run average costs. These factors help to explain why biotech businesses are attracted to the Cambridge area and software manufacturers to Silicon Valley in California.

Diseconomies of scale

However, there are factors that can lead to the increasing size of firms being associated with *rising* long-term costs. Such diseconomies of scale can also be both internal and external to the firm in question.

INTERNAL DISECONOMIES OF SCALE

These can be classified in the same way as economies of scale. Technical diseconomies of scale often relate to technological constraints. For example, ships that are built beyond a certain size require different methods of construction, which can result in increasing average costs. Their size might be such that ports and particular routes are no longer usable.

Organisational diseconomies are probably relatively more significant as the growth in size of businesses is often associated with increases in red tape and bureaucracy. Companies employing tens of thousands of workers are more difficult to manage, communications can be slower and less effective, and both workers and managers might be less motivated. All these factors might contribute to rising long-run costs.

Growing size does not automatically bring greater market power. Large, dominant companies might be slower in responding to market trends. They are likely to be more distant and less responsive to the demands of their customers. There are many examples of companies that have expanded and

lost touch with their customers. Xerox was once the world leader in the photocopier market but it is now struggling to survive. In the UK, businesses such as Marconi and ICI have been forced to de-merge and downsize in order to try to survive.

EXTERNAL DISECONOMIES OF SCALE

In the same way that particular geographical areas can be associated with the complementary growth and development of related businesses, the decline of particular firms and industries can drag down the fortunes of others. Some of the worst social and economic problems in the UK are associated with the failings of particular industries – shipbuilding on the Mersey and Clyde and coalmining in South Wales, Yorkshire and Nottinghamshire are two obvious examples where many small businesses have not survived because of external changes.

The significance of economies and diseconomies of scale

In traditional economic theory, there is no automatic formula that can be applied to the average costs of firms as they grow in size in the long term. In some industries – for example, motorcar manufacture – potential economies of scale that benefit firms able to produce in large scale for a global market are enormous. This can mean that some businesses have a great incentive to grow larger and that some industries are dominated by a handful of large companies. In extreme cases this can lead to the development of monopolies. By definition, a monopolistic market is one in which there is no direct competition and whether or not this is in the public interest is a major issue for economists and politicians. This is explored in much more detail in the A2 section of your course.

The existence of diseconomies can also affect the structure of particular industries. Over the last 20 years many formerly large businesses have been broken up. It is argued that the bureaucratic costs of running large businesses may discourage the growth of firms. In other businesses, especially where more traditional methods of production are used, diseconomies of scale may be more significant.

When it comes to your exam, you will be expected to draw an average cost curve and to know about economies and diseconomies of scale. However, it can be helpful to know what these other cost concepts mean and about the distinction that economists make between the short and the long term. You will definitely be expected to know all this and more when it comes to the A2 part of your course.

ACTIVITY ⋯⋯∗

How competitive is the UK economy?

Undertake research into two different industries and produce case studies of one that you consider to be competitive and one that is uncompetitive. Identify the main features of each and assess what changes would make the less competitive industry more competitive.

ACTIVITY ⋯⋯∗

Find out how large firms in your area have responded to the challenges of the single European market.

ECONOMICS IN CONTEXT

SINGLE EUROPEAN MARKET

One of the key features of the EU is the creation of a single European market within which there are no barriers to trade. This has involved the removal of duties and tariffs which previously existed and also involves the free movement of workers between EU countries. For many countries in the EU but not the UK, the creation of a single European market has been accompanied by the adoption of a single European currency also designed to facilitate trade between EU members.

These developments provide both threats and opportunities to UK-based firms. They have access to a much wider market, and if they succeed in selling into this bigger market they can enjoy economies of scale – companies like Vodaphone have been able to do this. It also means that companies can specialise, again enjoying economies of scale as they can concentrate production on a few large production plants. For example, Unilever produces Cornetto ice creams in three main locations across Europe including their plant at Gloucester. Those UK companies that succeed in the single European market have the opportunities to boost their sales and cut long-term costs. But those that find it difficult to compete with more efficient firms based on mainland Europe are likely to be faced with bleaker futures.

4 Market failure

On completion of this chapter, you should be able to:

- understand what economists mean when they use the term market failure
- identify 'public goods'
- analyse positive and negative externalities
- distinguish between merit and demerit goods
- assess the extent to which monopoly constitutes market failure
- assess the extent to which factor immobility can lead to market failure
- assess the extent to which inequalities in the distribution of wealth and income might contribute to market failure.

The meaning of market failure

Market failure is a major concept that you are expected to understand for your AS examination. It is a blanket term used by economists who recognise that if markets are left to themselves, they may produce socially unacceptable outcomes. Freely operating markets might produce too little of socially desirable goods, or too much that is socially undesirable. The question of what is socially desirable or undesirable can partly be a value judgement but economists have developed a set of concepts which help us clarify how a freely operating market economy might not necessarily allocate resources effectively.

DEFINITION

Market failure: occurs when the market system produces socially unacceptable outcomes.

ACTIVITY ····⁑

Identify other markets which may work well, work partially or even be missing. Explain and justify your answer.

THE HOUSING MARKET

Distinctions in economics are not always black and white. Markets do not necessarily completely fail – partial market failure can occur in which markets work for some economic agents but not others. For these, markets may be missing entirely. Housing is a good example of this. The majority of the population in the UK live in homes which they own, and, although it can be a long drawn-out process, it is relatively easy to sell one house and buy another, leaving buyers and sellers satisfied and having no adverse effects on others. If, however, your income is relatively low and you want to live in a area of high property prices, you may find that you are excluded from the housing market – there are degrees of exclusion – and it might be that you qualify for government help which gives you access to this market. However, for those sleeping rough or in homeless accommodation it could be argued that the housing market does not exist. Economists call this a **missing market**.

> **DEFINITION**
>
> **Missing market:** a situation in which there is no mechanism by which the needs of potential buyers and sellers can be reconciled.

Public goods

The market system works on the principle that the individual who purchases a particular product or service will consume and 'enjoy' that product. If I choose to go to the cinema, the purchase of my ticket enables me and no one else to sit in a given seat and watch a movie of my choice. I make the judgement as to how much I am prepared to pay to see the film and this reveals something of my tastes and preferences. Cinema seats for particular movies are something that the free market will try to supply in response to demand. In a free market, those who derive the greatest satisfaction from the consumption of a good or service are thought likely to be prepared to pay the most. In this way, resources are rationed to those who believe they will benefit most. Most goods and services provided in the UK economy fall into this category and collectively they are called **private goods.**

> **DEFINITION**
>
> **Private goods:** goods whose consumption by one person means that they cannot be consumed by another.

There are, however, goods or services for which it is difficult to identify who benefits most and who should pay for their provision. The principle that those enjoying a good or service should pay for it works well enough with consumer goods, but it is harder to apply to a range of services such as the police, roads, flood prevention and defence. It is impossible to predict who needs the police and when, and it would be hard to work out a means by which consumers of police services would actually pay for the resources they may have used. These are called **public goods**.

> **DEFINITION**
>
> **Public goods:** goods to which the principals of non-rivalry and non-excludability apply.

Economists argue that public goods have two important features that differentiate them from other goods:

● **non-rivalry,** which means that if one person consumes a good or service, others are not prevented from doing the same. For example, I benefit from improvements to the pavements near my house, but my benefit does not stop other pedestrians from enjoying similar benefits.

● **non-excludability**: this has a similar meaning in that once a public good is provided to one person, it is not possible to stop others from enjoying it. Thus I may choose to pay for improvements in street lighting at the entrance to my drive, but I can't exclude others from benefiting from this provision. This is called the **free rider** problem.

> **DEFINITIONS**
>
> **Non-rivalry:** situation in which consumption by one person does not reduce the amount available for consumption by others.
>
> **Non-excludability:** where once something is provided it is not possible to exclude others from benefiting.
>
> **Free riders:** those who receive but don't pay for the benefits of a good or service.

This means that some goods and services, like 'law and order' and public health, may not be supplied by the free market. This provides a reason for government intervention, in that the state might provide, or subsidise private firms to provide, them.

Turning public goods into private goods

Over the last 25 years, countries around the world have looked to providing more goods and services using market systems rather than by government intervention. Both left- and right-wing governments have favoured this approach, but it is particularly difficult to turn public goods into private goods. Thus, it is possible to get businesses to pay private sector firms to give added levels of security, but privatising the police or the army or the courts system is probably not feasible. Thus, the use of 'private defence contractors' in Iraq has been the subject of recent debate, especially in light of their immunity from prosecution.

One area of possible success has been in road pricing systems. New ICT-based technologies mean that it is possible to calculate what use individual drivers make of which roads at what times, and to charge for road use. Experiments in Singapore have been copied with some success in other parts of the world, and the UK government has said that it might be interested in moving towards a national form of road pricing.

ECONOMICS IN CONTEXT

'PAY-AS-YOU-GO' ROAD CHARGE PLAN

The UK government is considering charging road users up to £1.34 a mile in 'pay-as-you go' road charges.

They have been considering the scheme for over two years but are concerned about the political impact of their proposals.

It has been argued that the charges would cut congestion and would replace road tax and petrol duty. Ministers have argued that the change was needed if the UK was to avoid the possibility of 'LA-style' gridlock within 20 years.

Every vehicle would have a black box to allow a satellite system to track their journey, with prices starting from as little as 2p per mile in rural areas, and going up to £1.34 for peak use in urban areas.

ACTIVITY ····⦂

What are the economic arguments for and against the proposals in the Economics in context case study?

Positive and negative externalities in consumption and production

Another source of market failure occurs when the market system fails to account for all costs and benefits associated with the production of a given good or service. In the market system it is assumed that you pay for what you get. However, economic transactions can be more complicated because of the third-party effects of any transaction between a consumer and a firm. Figure 4.1 illustrates what may happen in a transaction in which firms supply goods to consumers in return for payment. There may be unintended third-party effects whereby others are positively or negatively affected by the transaction. These are called *externalities*.

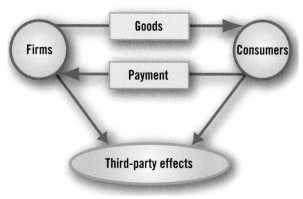

Figure 4.1 Third-party effects

It can be argued that, if markets are left to themselves,

- too many goods and services will be produced that have harmful third-party effects, and

- too few goods and services will be produced that have beneficial third-party effects.

NEGATIVE EXTERNALITIES

A whole range of industrial and commercial activities can give rise to **negative externalities**. Pollution of various kinds is an obvious example. Some businesses may pay little regard to the effects of their activities on others. Pure water might be used to cool, clean and wash, only to be returned to rivers and water courses as pollution. Forests are exploited for their timber, giving rise to erosion, floods, infertile soil and even global warming. Anti-social behaviour by consumers of alcohol and tobacco can affect the well-being and health of 'innocent' third parties.

DEFINITION

Negative externalities: these occur when the production and/or consumption of a good or service imposes additional costs on a third party.

NEGATIVE EXTERNALITIES AND MARKET FAILURE

Negative externalities are significant to economists because their existence places additional costs on other members of society. This provokes controversy about the strengths and weaknesses of the market system. For example, we all know there are links between smoking tobacco and a range of serious diseases. Treatment of patients with smoking-related diseases means that the National Health Service (NHS) and private health insurance companies are faced with additional expenditure.

Smoking can have harmful third-party effects

If markets operate freely and effectively, the price that a customer pays for a product or service should represent the actual costs involved in the production of that product or service. If this production generates additional costs that are incurred by other members of society, the market system can be said to have failed.

In Figure 4.2 below, S_1 represents the costs of production faced by the producer of a good. These are known as the marginal private costs. *MSC* includes

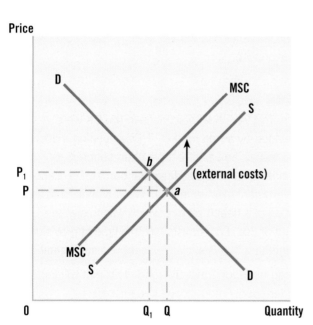

Figure 4.2 Negative externalities

the additional external costs that the production of this product creates. This is known as the marginal social cost curve and is made up of two parts: the **private costs** and the **external costs**. These added together represent the **social costs**, that is, the full cost to society of making the product or providing the service. If there were no government or other intervention, the market equilibrium would be reached at *a*, where *OP* would be the price charged for the product and *OQ* would represent the quantity sold.

However, if it were possible to calculate the external costs, these could be added to the private costs. If consumers were required to pay the full social cost of production, a different equilibrium would prevail at *b*, giving a higher price of OP_1 and reduced sales of OQ_1.

In other words, a freely operating market would lead to lower prices and higher outputs of goods having harmful environmental and/or social consequences.

ACTIVITY ⋯⋮

Make a list of those economic activities that generate negative externalities. Choose three that you consider to be most harmful to society and, if you have the opportunity, compare your choices with those of others in your class.

POSITIVE EXTERNALITIES

Unintended external effects do not necessarily lead to greater costs for society as a whole. Some economic transactions generate more beneficial third-party effects. Thus, the provision of clean piped water will directly benefit those who are supplied but it may also contribute to better standards of health, less illness and disease, and greater productivity. Similarly, improvements to education and training may benefit society as a whole, as well as those individuals who are directly concerned with the improvements.

The existence of **positive externalities** is illustrated in the diagram in Figure 4.3. In this diagram, *D* represents the demand from individuals – that is, the marginal private benefit gained from purchasing a particular good or service – and *S* represents the costs of providing that good or service. The market

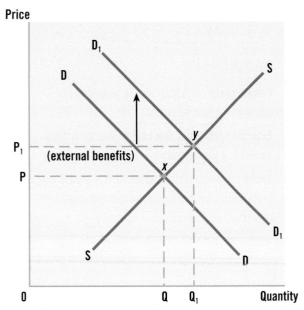

Figure 4.3 Positive externalities

equilibrium is given at *x*, with a price of *OP* and sales of *OQ*.

If, however, it were possible to quantify the positive externalities associated with the provision of this good or service, they could be represented by *D1*, showing the full social benefits that would benefit society as a whole. If these additional benefits were to be taken into account, output would be increased to *OQ1*.

In this example of market failure, freely operating markets would be said to be failing because fewer socially useful goods would be produced.

> **DEFINITION**
>
> **Positive externalities:** these occur when the consumption of a good or service provides additional benefits to a third party.

> **ACTIVITY ····⫶**
>
> Make a list of those economic activities that generate positive externalities. Choose three that you consider to be most beneficial to society and if, you have the opportunity, compare your choices with those of others in your class.

> **ACTIVITY ····⫶**
>
> Use demand and supply diagrams to illustrate the externalities associated with the purchase of:
>
> **(a)** a packet of cigarettes
>
> **(b)** energy created by nuclear power
>
> **(c)** membership of a gym.

Merit and demerit goods

There are two further categories of goods and services which the market system may under- and over-provide.

MERIT GOODS

Prior to 1947, health services in the UK were provided by a free market. Those needing a doctor had to pay, and poor people often suffered ill-health because of this financial barrier. The Labour government elected in 1945 was committed to the notion of a health service which was free at the point of use. Economists call this type of provision of something that is socially desirable a **merit good**.

It can be argued that the market system will tend to under-supply merit goods because of:

● imperfect information

● positive externalities.

Thus, governments may feel that if consumers were left to themselves they might make poor economic decisions, especially in relation to health and old age. Individuals have no way of knowing if they are likely to need health care in the future and because their information is imperfect they may make inadequate

> **DEFINITION**
>
> **Merit good:** something considered to be socially desirable but which is likely to be under supplied by the market system.

provision. This argument can be extended to justify government spending on measures to promote healthier lifestyles such as subsidies made to sports.

The encouragement of a healthier, fitter workforce also has third-party effects in terms of increasing productivity and decreasing the demands on health services. The existence of positive externalities provides governments with another reason for the provision of merit goods.

Other merit goods include the provision of library services, job centres, state education, and health and recreational services. In each case, there may be significant positive externalities that could be used to justify tax-funded government provision to ensure that full social benefits are enjoyed.

DEMERIT GOODS

A free market system might also produce goods and services that society believes to be socially harmful and to involve negative externalities. Left to themselves, consumers may demand and consume commodities known to be harmful to themselves and to impose costs on the rest of society. For this reason the government intervenes and introduces various measures to reduce the consumption of commodities such as alcohol and tobacco. The provision of other goods and services such as cannabis, prostitution and offensive weapons is banned. Arguably, value judgements affect what the government decides to ban and what to control.

Goods that are judged to be harmful to society are called **demerit goods**. Governments may judge that, if left to their own devices in a free market, people would over-consume products or services which may be damaging to both individuals and society as a whole. It might be that the production of demerit goods involves the generation of significant negative

DEFINITION

Demerit good: something that is considered to be socially undesirable but is likely to be over supplied by the market system.

externalities, and this could be used to justify intervention to limit production and therefore protect society.

learning tip
Students who have a weak understanding of economics get public goods and merit goods muddled up. Make sure you can define both and avoid making that mistake.

ACTIVITY ····⫶

Suppose you were Prime Minister with power to ban the production of a good or service on the grounds that it was a demerit good – what would you choose? What economic reasons would you give for your choice?

Monopoly and the allocation of resources

One of the key assumptions underpinning the merits of market-based economic systems is that competition between suppliers will provide an incentive to keep costs down and meet consumer needs. Competition is likely to be much reduced if the output of a particular good or service is in the hands of a small number of suppliers. The most extreme example occurs when there is a *monopoly* which is theoretically defined as occurring when one organisation is the sole producer or provider of a good or service. Pure monopoly of this type is not common as it is usually possible to find an alternative good or service which could be regarded as a substitute. Nonetheless, in the real world individual firms strive to make their products or services different from those of their competitors. Moreover, many industries are dominated by a small number of larger firms that are able to exercise monopoly power, and the UK government defines a monopoly as a market in which a firm has a 25 per cent or more market share.

THE COST OF MONOPOLIES

Monopoly power distorts free markets because such firms:

- can charge higher prices than would be the case if there were more competition

- can be less efficient than firms operating in a competitive market

- distort the allocation of resources by reducing output and limiting customer choice to a smaller range of products than would be the case if there were more competition.

HIGHER PRICES

If a company has monopoly power, it will have much greater freedom to set its own prices – for example:

- A petrol station that has no local competitors is likely to charge more for its petrol.

- We are likely to pay more for branded goods than we do for non-branded goods.

But if there is a lot of competition, individual companies will be strongly influenced by the prices charged by other businesses. If they increase their prices, they will fear the loss of sales to competitors. Economists describe companies that have market power as **price makers**. If they know that demand for their product is relatively inelastic, they can boost revenue by putting up prices. In other words, a monopolist provides goods or services for which there are few close substitutes. This is shown diagrammatically in Figure 4.4. The diagram shows a relatively inelastic demand curve for a product produced by a monopolist. In this case the firm could cut production from OQ_1 to OQ and this would increase sales revenue from OQ_1aP_1 to $OQbP$. If they were faced with more competition the demand curve would be relatively more elastic and a cut in production could result in a relatively more significant loss of sales leading to a fall in sales revenue.

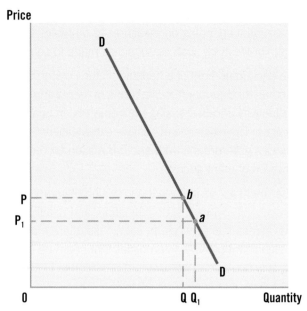

Figure 4.4 Increasing revenue

> **learning tip**
> Remember your work on elasticity. If there are few substitutes for a good or service, the demand is likely to be relatively inelastic. If the price elasticity is less than –1, any reduction in output will lead to an increase in revenue. If you consider a competitive market where the price elasticity of demand will be greater than –1, any reduction in output will lead to a fall in revenue.

This analysis has other implications. For example, a monopolist in this situation will have less incentive to keep costs low because if it is a price maker, it can pass on additional costs to its customers.

Another aspect of market power is that a monopolist can also charge different sets of customers different prices for the same product. For example, a Mazda 323 car is nearly £5,000 more expensive in the UK than in the rest of Europe. This particular form of monopoly power is called price discrimination. Companies have used this technique to boost profits by charging higher prices to those with more inelastic demands and lower prices to those whose demand is relatively more elastic. This is becoming an increasingly common practice.

DEFINITION

Price maker: firm that has elements of monopoly power that enables it to set the price that consumers pay for its goods or services.

RESTRICTED CHOICE

Monopolies can exploit the dependence of their customers on their products by restricting choice. Henry Ford was famous for saying that customers could buy a Model T Ford in any colour, as long as it was black. More modern forms of this kind of behaviour include limiting the number of retailers allowed to sell particular products. Some electrical goods manufacturers do this, arguing that particular expertise is required to sell their products. Such practice makes it easier for manufacturers to ensure that retailers do not cut prices.

ACTIVITY ····⁖

Survey prices of television sets in local stores. What evidence does this reveal of competition in this particular market?

SOURCES OF MONOPOLY POWER

Monopoly power can exist for a number of reasons:

● **Barriers to entry** – economists use this technical term to describe how there may be barriers stopping new firms from entering or leaving an industry.

These include high capital costs, patents and policies followed by monopolists. Barriers to entry are probably the single most important source of monopoly power, especially as many industries require ever larger amounts of capital to fund technological changes.

DEFINITION

Barriers to entry: factors that prevent firms entering or leaving an industry.

● Natural monopolies exist when it is clearly cheaper and more efficient to have a single supplier, for example, the National Grid. There would be wasteful duplication of resources if there were a number of competing national grids.

● Competitive advantage associated with size. It is very hard for other retailers to compete with Tesco because they dominate so many different markets.

● Product differentiation – this occurs when customers perceive similar products to be different.

ECONOMICS IN CONTEXT

SUPERMARKETS OFF THE HOOK?

In November 2007, the Competition Commission concluded that Britain's consumers were getting a relatively fair deal from their supermarkets but that suppliers were not.

They looked at the behaviour of 24 supermarkets and concluded that the industry was broadly competitive. However, two pricing policies were not judged to be so. They were:

● selling loss leaders
● charging higher prices in some areas.

The commission felt that dealing with these examples of uncompetitive behaviour would cause more problems than they would solve. But the commission did find that 30 practices of supermarkets in relation to suppliers were not competitive. These included late payment, changing contracts and expecting suppliers to contribute to retailers' costs.

Companies also create market power, and what might be described as illusionary choice, by marketing very similar products under a range of brand names. The two major soap powder manufacturers Unilever and Proctor & Gamble are experts at this strategy.

ARE MONOPOLIES AN EXAMPLE OF MARKET FAILURE?

The answer to this question based on the analysis so far is clearly a yes. Monopolies can force up the price of goods they produce beyond that point at which the price paid represents the actual costs in terms of resources used, that is, productivity inefficiency. Moreover, they can limit the supply of products. In short, they can result in a misallocation of resources. However, that is not the whole story.

Benefits of monopolies

Like most controversial topics in economics, there are also strong arguments in favour of monopolies, as well as against. These include the benefits of:

● economies of scale

● innovation

● greater choice.

ECONOMIES OF SCALE

As noted in the previous chapter, monopolies will tend to be large companies. If they produce high volumes of particular products, they may be able to cut costs of production because they enjoy economies of scale. The largest supermarkets have been able to invest millions in using IT to record sales, make orders, change stocks and control expenses that could not be afforded by smaller competitors. Larger businesses can also force down the prices of their suppliers and use specialisation to reduce costs.

Economic research indicates that for many industries long-run average costs are as illustrated in the diagram in Figure 4.5. This is based on the diagrams on page 55 showing the three theoretical situations in which there might be economies of scale, diseconomies of scale and constant returns to scale.

In this example, increasing output from *OX* to *OY* results in significant economies of scale, especially as automation and the computerisation of activities takes effect. This is followed by a phase of relatively constant returns to scale, but there is also a point, say *OZ*, beyond which a business becomes large and excessively bureaucratic, leading to diseconomies of scale and rising long-run costs.

The strongest argument in favour of monopolies is that if output in an industry is spread between a large number of small firms, then none of them ever reach the size required to enjoy significant economies of

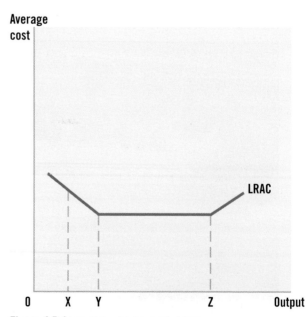

Figure 4.5 Long-run average cost curve

scale. The controversy associated with supermarkets in the UK is an example of this – Sainsbury, Asda, Morrisons and Tesco are all big enough to enjoy economies of scale and reductions in long-run average costs that can never be attained by smaller grocery retailers.

INNOVATION

Large companies with monopoly power might be more able to afford research and development that lead to the creation of newer and better products. Major drug companies like GlaxoSmithKline use this argument to justify their monopoly position in the provision of some drugs.

GREATER CHOICE

It has been argued that competition can actually produce very limited or illusory choice for consumers. Thus, one small car or brand of soap powder is much like another. Monopolies can offer clear choices. For example, the different radio or television channels provided by the BBC are said to offer a greater range of choice than their commercial rivals.

> **learning tip**
> Economic arguments can be developed to both support and defend monopolies. The important point is that monopoly power can be used to distort free markets and lead to a possible misallocation of resources. However, economies of scale can lead to the more effective use of resources. Whether or not this happens in practice is a job for economists to investigate.

ACTIVITY ···

Undertake an assessment of the behaviour of the following instances of monopoly power. Are the monopolies acting in the public interest?
(a) Microsoft
(b) BA flights between London and New York
(c) your nearest post office.

Immobility of factors of production

Free markets require factor mobility. Land, labour, capital and enterprise are all meant to be attracted by the prospect of better returns and repelled by the threat of worse returns. There are many reasons why this might not be so.

LAND

Economists define land as including not just farms, factory sites and building lots but also those resources contained within the Earth's crust. Whereas natural resources such as timber, minerals and energy can be relatively easily transported and switched from use to use, particular sites with particular qualities are more likely to be locked in time and space.

LABOUR

Free market theory assumes that workers work primarily for money and that changes in wage and salary levels not only signal to workers that they should consider changing employment but that they should also be geographically mobile. In spite of higher wages elsewhere, some workers are reluctant to leave areas of high unemployment such as Cornwall, Merseyside and Teesside. Family and community links are hard to break. It is not clear what primarily motivates workers. Some workers indicate that 'job satisfaction' is more important than financial return. Others value 'status'. Given the complexity of human behaviour, economists have to be very careful when making assumptions about motivations.

CAPITAL

Finance capital has become a much more mobile factor of production compared to land and labour. Governments have historically tried to control international flows of finance capital but such intervention has become increasingly difficult and ineffective, especially as global capital markets have developed. If investments in a particular sector or country become more attractive relative to those in others, finance capital is likely to flow to that new use, away from uses where the returns are less.

ENTERPRISE

By definition, enterprise should be the most mobile of all factors. If enterprise is about taking risks and identifying where greatest profits can be made, it follows that entrepreneurs will be mobile in pursuit of profit. However, as with labour, human factors are likely to influence decisions of entrepreneurs. Thus, owners of small businesses may be reluctant to sack workers when orders fall. Alternatively, there is evidence to suggest that some owners forgo greater sales and profits associated with growth because such expansion may threaten lifestyles and informal relationships with employees.

ACTIVITY ····⋗

LABOUR MOBILITY

Of all the factors of production, the degree to which labour is mobile or immobile is of most interest as it actually involves not just the weighing up of economic factors, but also social, cultural and interpersonal relationships. Imagine that you are unemployed, single and in your 20s in the following situations:

(a) living in the West of Ireland in the 1840s

(b) living in Torbay in 2008

(c) living in Krakow, Poland, in 2008.

Would you move to London in search of work? What factors would influence your decision?

Imperfect knowledge

If the price mechanism is to work effectively to allocate resources, both buyers and sellers need to be well informed about the market in which they are operating. Economists use the following concepts to analyse why some markets work better than others.

● Symmetric information – indicates that both buyers and sellers are reasonably well informed about the products or services in a particular market. In this case both parties can make rational decisions as to whether or not they should buy or supply the product in question.

● Asymmetric information – this describes a situation in which either the buyer or the seller knows more about the product or service than the other party to the transaction.

If consumers are to make informed and effective choices about the products and services they may wish to purchase, they need knowledge and understanding of the prices and qualities of potential purchases. In theory, they need perfect knowledge, which is the term used by economists to describe a total and all-encompassing knowledge. However, numerous studies indicate that consumer knowledge is far from perfect:

● Customers perceive differences between products when there are none.

● Keeping track of the prices of competing products is too demanding for all but the most expert buyers.

● It is sometimes assumed that customers base purchases on rational decisions, that they are consistent and not swayed by irrational considerations. But customer choices are often unpredictable. Fashions and tastes change, as do perceptions as to what is good quality.

Imperfections in customer knowledge imply that markets may not respond quickly to changes in demand or supply conditions.

Inequalities in the distribution of income and wealth

A freely working market will create both losers and winners. For example, many British and other European farmers are currently losers because they are finding it increasingly difficult to compete with cheaper imported foods and cope with changes in customer tastes away from products such as meat. Similarly, the coal industry in the UK has almost disappeared because of the greater use of alternative energy sources and the availability of cheap imports.

Other members of our economy can also be described as losers. These include:

● some older people whose skills are no longer in demand

● young people who lack both skills and qualifications, and

- owners of businesses that have become uncompetitive.

On the other hand, the price mechanism rewards those owners of resources who are able to produce goods and services in anticipation of changes in demand. Free markets result in inequalities, one outcome of which might be the existence of poverty for losers and material benefits for the winners. This might not be socially acceptable.

The distribution of rewards

Not only do free markets create inequalities in income, but also they allocate resources to those members of society who are prepared to pay the most. As noted earlier, some economists have likened the price mechanism to a system of votes:

- Each pound of income is the equivalent of one vote.

- Those with the most votes will determine not just what is produced for society but who consumes such production.

- If there is a shortage of a good or service, competition between buyers will force up prices until equilibrium between buyers and sellers is reached.

- Those who cannot afford the market price of the good or service will go without.

Those members of society who have larger incomes will be able to consume more resources than those with relatively smaller incomes. Some people would regard such inequalities as unfair.

ARE INEQUALITIES AN EXAMPLE OF MARKET FAILURE?

This is hard to answer. Some economists argue that inequalities are an example of market failure but there is nothing in the analysis of the working of free markets that indicates that markets are able to make such moral judgements. Other economists would argue that it is up to politicians and governments to make judgements about fairness.

ACTIVITY ····⋗

Suppose that government is considering making the private sector the only provider of education in the UK. Produce a report:

- outlining no more than three economic arguments in favour of the proposal

- outlining no more than three economic arguments against the proposal

- explaining, using economic reasoning, whether or not the government should proceed with this proposal.

ECONOMICS IN CONTEXT

INCOME INEQUALITIES

According to the Disability Unit in the Department for Work and Pensions, disabled people have income which is, on average, less than half of that of people who are not disabled.

Those from ethnic minority groups have lower average earnings than the white population. However, there are differences between minority ethnic groups,

with Indian men having slightly higher average earnings than white men. Pakistani men have significantly lower earnings. There is a slightly different pattern for women, with Black Caribbean, Black African, Chinese and Indian women earning more than white women.

21 per cent of those aged over 65 were classed as living in poverty

in 1998. The EU average for that year was 17 per cent. Ireland had the most over-65s in poverty (35 per cent) and the Netherlands the fewest (7 per cent).

What economic reasons can you offer to explain these inequalities? Do these provide a sufficient explanation? Justify your answer.

Source: Economic and Social Research Council

5 Government intervention in the market

On completion of this, you should be able to:

● understand why governments may intervene in markets

● use economic models to evaluate methods which governments may use to correct distortions in individual markets

● understand how and why government intervention might result in government failure and misallocation of resources

● use economic models to evaluate the effectiveness of government intervention in health, housing, agriculture, transport and the environment.

The rationale for government intervention

You are getting close to the finishing line for Unit 1 – your introduction to microeconomics, and by now you should be able to use demand and supply analysis to understand how markets determine the prices and outputs, and also model the effect of changes in key variables. You will have also learned that competitive markets can in theory ensure that economic welfare is maximised, that goods and services are produced as cheaply as possible, and that resources will be used to produce those goods and services for which there is an effective demand.

However, the last chapter on market failure should have made you look at market-driven outcomes more critically. In reality, markets don't necessarily work in the way that microeconomic theory, going back to Adam Smith, predicts. There are many reasons why markets might not allocate resources effectively. These include:

● monopoly power

● externalities

● imperfect information

● factor immobility

● possible political and social objections.

The existence of any of these factors provides governments with a rationale for government intervention, and in this chapter you will critically examine the effects that government policies might have. However, governments, like markets, can fail in the sense that their intervention may have unintended outcomes. Four markets will be examined in greater detail.

learning tip Don't forget that different economists and different political parties advocate very different policies to remedy market failure.

learning tip

Watch out for the political pitfalls that young economists sometimes fall into. Always try to be objective, always try to explore different viewpoints and arguments. This does not mean you have to sit on the fence but examiners get put off by students who get into political rants on controversial issues like the health service.

Methods of government intervention to correct distortions in individual markets

There are a number of methods that governments have developed to correct or minimise the adverse consequences of market failures. These include:

- indirect taxation
- subsidies
- price controls
- buffer stocks
- pollution permits
- state provision
- regulation
- persuasion.

INDIRECT TAXATION

One of the most significant examples of market failure occurs when the price paid for a good or service fails to reflect the real cost in terms of resources. This means that some goods and services are under-priced in terms of the actual resources used in their production and leads to a misallocation of resources in the sense that over-supply will occur.

© Mark Stivers 2008

Arguably, pollution that is not paid for by the consumer of the polluting product or service presents economists and governments with a major problem, especially pollution that contributes to global warming as this presents us with a significant threat to the continuation of life as we know it.

What can the USA and other countries do to limit carbon emissions? In theory the government could use the powers that it has to raise **indirect taxes** to ensure that the price that we pay for goods and services takes into account – *internalises* – the

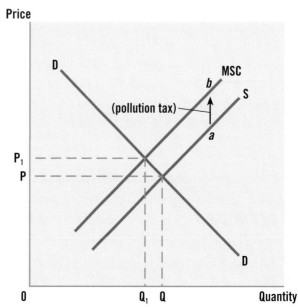

Figure 5.1 Internalising negative externalities

ECONOMICS IN CONTEXT

HOW CAN GLOBAL WARMING AFFECT OUR LIVES?

Global warming is sometimes referred to as the most dangerous experiment ever conceived. We do not know what the full effect of radical climate change will be on our environment, but we do know that even a modest rise of 2°–3°F (1.1°–1.7°C) could have dramatic effects.

In the last 10,000 years, the Earth's average temperature hasn't varied by more than 1.8°F (1°C). Temperatures only 5°–9°F cooler than those of today prevailed at the end of the last Ice Age, in which the north-east USA was covered by more than 3,000 feet of ice. Leading scientists assert that a rise of three degrees would cause famine and drought and threaten millions of lives. It would also cause a worldwide drop in crop harvests of between 20 and 400 million tonnes, threatening 400 million more people with famine, and put up to 3 billion people at risk of flooding and lack of access to fresh water supplies.

Few ecosystems could adapt to such a dramatic temperature change, with the result that half the world's nature reserves and a fifth of coastal wetlands would be destroyed. Global sea levels could rise by more than 20 feet if the ice shelves in Greenland and Antarctica collapsed, which is a distinct possibility if temperatures continue to climb. Droughts and wildfires will occur more often. More than a million species worldwide could be driven to extinction by 2050.

The biggest contributor to global warming is CO_2 emissions. The USA produces far more carbon dioxide than any other country in the world. According to the latest figures from the Department of Energy, the USA produces 22 per cent of all CO_2 emitted into the atmosphere – 5,912.21 million metric tonnes in 2004. That is more than China and India together (17% and 4.1% respectively), more than Russia (6%), Japan (4.7%), Australia (1.4%) and more than the whole of Europe put together 17.2%).

In the USA, the major sources of CO_2 emissions stem from burning fossil fuel such as coal, natural gas and oil. We burn coal and natural gas to produce electricity and energy for our homes, businesses and factories, while most of the oil is burned to power transportation – planes, buses and especially cars. However, all of the technology that produces this energy is outdated and inefficient. We can continue to live our lives by putting more efficient technology to use, and by getting more energy from clean sources, like wind and solar.

negative externalities or 'carbon footprint' associated with the production of a given good or service. This approach is illustrated in Figure 5.1. The MSC (marginal social cost) curve indicates the true cost of producing and if a government is able to calculate accurately the external costs attributed to a polluting company, it could introduce a tax equal to the vertical distance *ab*. This would force consumers of this product to pay a price that represented the full cost to society of its production. Output would be reduced to OQ_1 and the government would actually use the price mechanism to cure market failure.

This approach is one which some governments plan to use in order to limit carbon emissions. For example, Germany and Portugal have announced plans to link levels of car taxation to emission of CO_2 from a given model of car. In the UK, tax on company cars and annual excise duty are linked to CO_2 emissions.

DEFINITION

Indirect taxes: taxes levied on goods and services which only have to be paid by consumers purchasing such products.

Does this mean that we have – with a diagram and a paragraph – solved the problem of global warming? – Sadly not. There is little doubt that making sure consumers pay the actual or real cost of what they purchase would go a long way to rationing our scarce resources more effectively, but governments are faced with three major problems:

● calculating the amount of externality

● dealing with the political unpopularity of imposing significant taxes on goods and services which may not previously have been taxed

● pollution and climate change being global problems requiring co-operation between different countries.

These problems will be considered in greater detail on pages 79–93 which deal with government failure.

SUBSIDIES

A subsidy can be represented to be a reverse tax that can be used to encourage greater provision of goods and services for which there are positive externalities. This method is illustrated in Figure 5.2, which shows that the government is using the price mechanism to try to ensure that the price paid by consumers internalises positive externalities. The government could estimate the value of the positive externality and pay a **subsidy** to producers equal to

this amount – shown by the vertical distance ab. The outcome would be production rising to OQ_1 and price falling to OP_1. If the government were able accurately to estimate the positive externality, it could boost production of a product or service that a free market would over-price and under-produce. However, as with taxes, this simple theoretical solution is not necessarily so simple to achieve in practice.

> **DEFINITION**
>
> **Subsidy:** payment to a producer to encourage greater production of a good or service.

PRICE CONTROLS

Price controls may be used to deal with inequalities generated by free markets, and with merit and demerit goods. Governments can intervene by using price controls. These can be maximum prices, which limit what can be charged for a good or service. They may be used to encourage the consumption of merit goods or to compensate for inequalities caused by free markets. A number of governments in developing countries impose maximum prices for basic foodstuffs in order to ensure that poor people avoid going without. For example, the prices of flour, oil and sugar in Egypt are regulated by the government. This will usually involve fixing a price below the market equilibrium, as illustrated in Figure 5.3. This shows that this form of price control will create excess demand. This is illustrated by the horizontal line at OP, below the market-clearing price of OP_1.

The effect of this form of government intervention will be to create excess demand of ab, and the government would then be faced with problem of dealing with shortages. For this reason, price controls of this type are often associated with some form of

> **DEFINITION**
>
> **Price control:** the imposition of a maximum and/or minimum price by a government; that could be above or below *market equilibrium*.

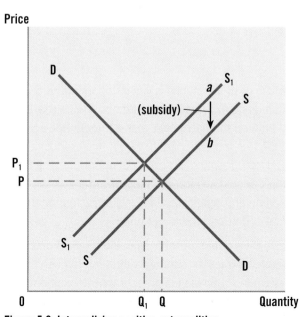

Figure 5.2 Internalising positive externalities

Price

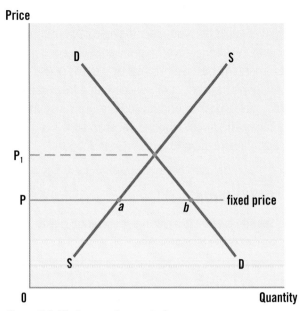

Figure 5.3 Maximum price control

rationing in order to ensure 'fair shares'. In this case, market-based methods have to be backed up by the use of direct controls.

Governments might also introduce minimum prices, especially if they wish to encourage production. If these are set above the equilibrium that would apply without government intervention, producers would be encouraged to produce more than consumers would be willing to buy. This excess supply is shown in Figure 5.4 where a fixed price at OP_1 would lead to overproduction of *xy*.

Price

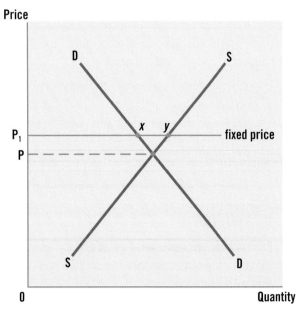

Figure 5.4 Minimum price control

As will be examined in greater detail later in this chapter (see page 89), the European Union's Common Agricultural Policy (CAP) has involved setting minimum prices for a range of agricultural products. It does this to increase agricultural output and to protect farmers' incomes, but in some cases the result has been the accumulation of vast surpluses of unsold agricultural products.

BUFFER STOCKS

Buffer stocks can be used to reduce the undesirable effects of widespread fluctuations in prices that will occur if demand and/or supply changes frequently. It could be argued, for example, that unpredictable changes in the weather are likely to affect harvests, leading to fluctuations in the prices of agricultural products. Although this is not technically an example of market failure, it might be argued that fluctuating prices cause farmers problems, as their incomes are likely to fluctuate widely. Moreover, consumers and other users of agricultural products may find decision making more difficult in periods of uncertainty.

DEFINITION

Buffer stocks: stocks held by a government or government agency that can be used in an attempt to stabilise prices.

The use of buffer stocks is illustrated in Figure 5.5. In this diagram price is measured on the vertical axis and time on the horizontal; *tp* is a target price and *mp* the free market price. In 2005, overproduction would have resulted in additional supply, forcing the market price down to *OP*. The government could intervene and purchase surplus supply, forcing the actual price up to the target price.

These government purchases could be stockpiled; if in the following year shortages threaten to push the price up to P_1, release of government stocks from the previous year will bring down prices to the target level. In this way, prices would be stabilised, not

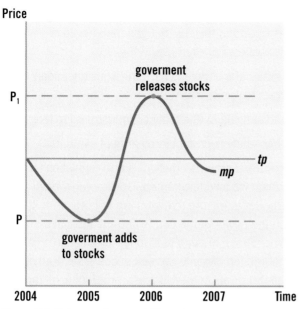

Figure 5.5 Using stocks to stabilise prices

only protecting farmers' incomes but also benefiting consumers.

It is easy to see how this apparently simple policy could go wrong. It involves forecasting future possible harvests, and setting a price that will in the long run balance demand with supply. Overestimates will result in the accumulation of unsold stocks and underestimates to shortages.

POLLUTION PERMITS

Another market-based means of limiting some negative externalities is for the government to use **pollution permits.** The government decides to restrict pollution by a given amount and then gives or sells permits to polluters to emit a certain amount of waste. These permits can then be bought and sold. A company successful in cutting its pollution could sell its permit to one that was less successful in doing so. The company producing the lower emissions would gain and the heavier polluter would be forced to pay. By setting an overall limit to how much pollution

DEFINITION

Pollution permits: permits sold or given to potential polluters in an attempt to limit pollution.

ECONOMICS IN CONTEXT

The *European Union Emission Trading Scheme* (EU ETS) is the largest multi-national, greenhouse gas emissions trading scheme in the world and is a main pillar of EU climate policy.

Under the EU ETS, large emitters of carbon dioxide within the EU must monitor and annually report their CO_2 emissions, and they are obliged every year to surrender (give back) an amount of emission allowances to the government that is equivalent to their CO_2 emissions in that year. The installations may get the allowances for free from the government, or may purchase them from others (installations, traders and the government). If an installation has received more free allowances than it needs, it may sell them to anybody.

In order to make sure that real trading emerges (and that CO_2 emissions are reduced), EU governments must make sure that the total amount of allowances issued to installations is less than the amount that would have been emitted under a business-as-usual scenario. The total quantity to be allocated by each EU member state is defined in the Member State National Allocation Plan (NAP).

The EU ETS is divided into two phases – the first phase (2005–07), applies to 12,000 installations, representing approximately 40 per cent of EU CO_2 emissions, including the production and processing of ferrous metals, mineral industry (cement, clinker, glass and ceramic bricks) and pulp, paper and board activities.

The second phase, due to run from 2008 to 2012, is much more ambitious as it includes:

- all greenhouse gases, and not only CO_2
- aviation emissions
- non-EU members – Norway, Iceland, Liechtenstein and Switzerland – joining the scheme.

The jury is still out on the effectiveness of phase 1 – critics have suggested that the initial allowances were too generous, not resulting in significant cuts in CO_2 emissions. Others have said that it is too soon to judge.

The success or failure of this policy will be largely determined by the outcomes of phase 2, especially in respect of aviation emissions.

ACTIVITY ····⋮

Use the Internet to monitor the effectiveness of the EU ETS.

would be allowed, governments could reduce this negative externality. However, it would be left to market forces to determine where emissions would be reduced.

This method of tacking negative externalities has become more popular with some governments in recent years.

STATE PROVISION

Governments may make the judgement that the arguments in favour of particular merit goods are so convincing or the positive externalities so overwhelming that the market system should be completely by-passed by the state. In the 19th century the market system did little to ensure that water suppliers were safe and that wastes were properly disposed of, so local government stepped in to fill the gap. Since then other services have been provided by the UK government. Most children are educated in state-provided and tax-funded schools. Similarly, the government pays for the armed services, police, courts and road building and all governments in the world intervene to provide some of these kinds of services.

Increasingly, many governments have tried to move away from state provision in the belief that market-based provision is more efficient, or because of the potential political popularity of lower taxes. It is argued that state-owned or -run provision is more inefficient because, unlike market-based provision, there are less likely to be financial incentives to reward success or to punish failure.

REGULATION

We take for granted the many company and civil laws that provide a framework to protect consumers, producers and factor suppliers from being exploited. This legal framework helps ensure that markets work and are trusted. Such confidence is vital, especially in matters relating to banking and company finance.

Governments often go further than just providing the legislative framework to support markets. They also use direct controls to limit the negative effects of market failure. Governments have the power to pass laws and use the existing legislative framework

in an attempt to control and constrain the behaviour of firms and industries that generate negative externalities. For example, in the UK:

- emissions of potentially dangerous chemicals are subject to regulations
- advertising by the tobacco industry is limited
- car safety is promoted by annual car tests.

There are countless other rules and regulations, most of which we take for granted. Governments have the power to ensure that laws are not broken but even the power of the courts and the judicial system are not strong enough to stop the production and consumption of some demerit goods – the market for illegal drugs in the UK exists and functions much like any other free market and there seems little that successive governments can actually do to cut the consumption of cannabis, ecstasy, and heroin. Recent efforts by the government to promote healthy eating in schools also appear to have had limited success.

PERSUASION

Finally, if all else fails, governments fall back on education and persuasion.

Some people consider that changing customer and producer behaviour to ensure greater account is taken of externalities is so complicated that it is more effective in the long term to change the attitudes of those who demand and supply products and services that create negative externalities. It could be argued that much of any government's work is concerned with persuasion in the form of advertising, political campaigning and so on. Changing attitudes to education, healthy living, sustainability, preventive medicine and so on can all be seen as attempts to change free market outcomes. For example, the UK government part-funds the Health Education Council, whose role includes encouraging people to eat healthier diets. If these approaches are successful, the effects will be fed through the market system. It can be argued that demand for organic produce is a result of greater awareness of healthy eating.

Producers usually favour voluntary codes aimed at educating consumers into changing their tastes and consumption patterns away from demerit goods, or those for which there are negative externalities.

Government failure

Government failure is the term that economists use to describe how government intervention in the market may lead to a loss rather than a gain in economic welfare. In other words, government actions might actually lead to a worse allocation of resources than that achieved by markets. In the previous section, possible sources of government failure were mentioned, and these are dealt with more fully below. Policies might fail because of:

● inadequate information

● conflicting objectives

● administrative costs

● unintended effects

● short-termism.

INADEQUATE INFORMATION

The success of many of the policy options outlined in the previous section rely on the government having excellent data and information on the markets in which they wish to intervene. For example, if a government is using some form of tax to correct a negative externality, it has to be able to estimate

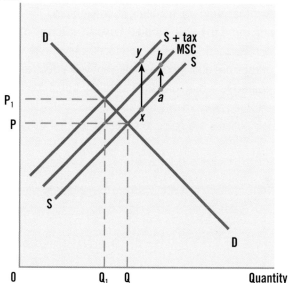

Figure 5.6 Potential government failure

accurately the external costs. If its estimates are too high, then the market will be further distorted. This theoretical example is illustrated in Figure 5.6, where the government overestimates the external costs involved in the production of a given good or service.

In the diagram above, the additional tax is set at *xy* rather than *ab*, resulting in consumers paying more than the product is worth in terms of resources used. This does not necessarily mean that resources are allocated less efficiently or effectively compared to a market-based solution, but it does mean that governments need really accurate data if their policies are going to succeed. Even if this

requirement is satisfied, this type of policy relies also on forecasted or projected data which by its nature is likely to be less reliable than historical data.

Making the wrong decisions about data can also affect the effectiveness of policies designed to even out price and output fluctuations. This is illustrated in the two diagrams above in which the 'wrong' target price is set.

In Figure 5.7 the target price is set too high, resulting in the accumulation of ever bigger stocks. Figure 5.8 shows the effects of setting too low a target price and in this case buffer stocks would soon run out.

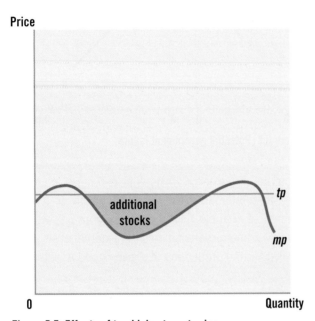

Figure 5.7 Effects of too high a target price

CONFLICTING OBJECTIVES

Politics can be seen as a means of reconciling conflicts, and this often involves making compromises between different objectives. Conflicts can occur for many reasons. Politicians are themselves economic agents, as are the civil servants who are meant to put policies into practice. Politicians are faced with many different influences, from the media, pressure groups, employer organisations, trade unions, not to forget the electors who determine whether or not they hold power. It is not surprising that what might start out as a clear economic objective can end up as a messy compromise.

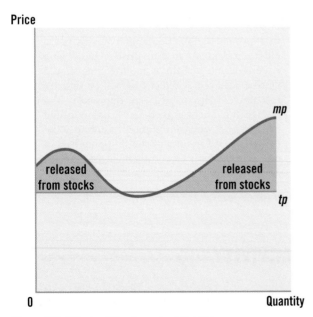

Figure 5.8 Effects of too low a target price

ECONOMICS IN CONTEXT

WHEN POLITICS AND ECONOMICS MEET

In the 1960s, when the steel industry in the UK was still nationalised, it was argued that the government should build a new integrated steel-making plant that would take full advantage of the economies of scale involved and enable British Steel to compete internationally. The Labour Party was in power at the time and its MPs from both Scotland and South Wales were very influential. A compromise was made with one half of the steel works built in Scotland and the other half in Wales – so much for integration and economics of scale.

Transport policies are another political battleground. The road-building lobby is strong and powerful, ecological groups can grab the headlines. It is almost possible to feel sorry for politicians, who have to try to reconcile political popularity with economic good sense.

Reconciling political differences is even harder in an international or global context. This is particularly significant in dealing with negative externalities. Pollution and pollutants do not recognise national boundaries. Countries need to agree common approaches. The failure of the US government to cut greenhouse gas emissions is considered by some to be one of the biggest threats facing global society.

ACTIVITY ···:>

Research and analyse an example of what might happen when economics and politics meet.

ADMINISTRATIVE COSTS

Governments and civil servants make mistakes, and these errors can add to costs. The UK government has attempted to improve the management and efficiency of the NHS by computerising medical records. Interventions such as these – as with research and development into new weapons – are notorious for going over budget. Moreover, the imposition of any control or regulation necessitates sanctions for non-compliance. Well-meaning legislation can result in spiralling administrative costs.

ECONOMICS IN CONTEXT

GOVERNMENT FAILS WITH SCHOOL DINNERS

Prime Minister Tony Blair, in a response to campaigning by Jamie Oliver, developed a £500m package to transform school dinners. However, a recent Ofsted report said that the number of pupils opting for school lunches had dropped by up to 25 per cent in some areas. It found that a rise in the cost of the healthier meals was putting some pupils off, as was the removal from some menus of such favorites as chips and crisps.

ACTIVITY ···:>

Use demand and supply diagrams to assess the effectiveness of your school/college in promoting healthier eating.

Changing the behaviour of people involves affecting complex and deep-rooted attitudes. Government spending on public relations campaigns is not always successful, as illustrated by the government's recent efforts to promote healthy eating in schools.

UNINTENDED EFFECTS

The growth of **parallel markets** is a good example of unintended effects, especially if the result of government policies is to create shortages of goods that are in demand. Parallel markets arise when maximum prices are set so that shortages of products or services are created. Some customers

DEFINITION

Parallel markets: illegal markets that often arise when governments try to suppress markets in particular goods.

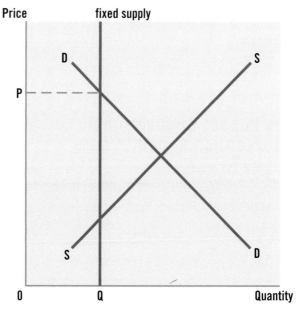

Figure 5.9 Potential for illegal market

are prepared to pay more than the set price, and this creates a new or unofficial market for such products. If governments introduce maximum prices in times of war, they usually outlaw illegal parallel markets. As they are illegal, lawlessness is encouraged, and this may have further repercussions. Much of modern gangsterism in the United States is said to have developed in the 1920s–30s when many states banned the consumption of alcohol.

The incentive for parallel markets to develop is shown in Figure 5.9 above, which shows the supply of a good is fixed at *OQ*. Some customers are prepared to pay up to *OP* for these limited supplies. This could provide an incentive to engage in illegal activity.

SHORT-TERMISM

Democratic governments are always likely to have an eye on the electoral consequences of any decisions. This can lead to favouring those decisions which are likely to have a quicker effect, especially if that is likely to be popular with the electorate. The example on page 81 of government responses to a series of television programmes about healthy eating in schools might be described as **short-termism**.

DEFINITION

Short-termism: choosing options for their likely short-term effect while neglecting their possible long-term effects.

The impact of government intervention in health care

The provision of adequate health care can be seen as a merit good, which, if left to market forces, would be under-supplied. Positive externalities would be lost and inequalities increased. It has been argued that increased government spending on the National Health Service has not resulted in the expected improvements in the quality of provision. The NHS is the biggest single employer in Europe and perceptions as to its effectiveness or otherwise

are likely to have a major effect in determining which political party is elected at the next election. Therefore, closer examination of the economics of health care may provide you with some good insights into how economists might analyse the merits or otherwise of both state and private sector provision.

Market provision of health care

If health care were provided by market forces, it is easy to answer the what, how and for whom questions because health care would be just like any other commodity. The price of individual treatments would be determined by the forces of demand and supply. It is reasonable to assume that the demand for health care with respect to changes in price would slope downwards from left to right, showing that more care would be demanded if prices were low and vice versa. This is illustrated in Figure 5.10 which is about hip replacements.

If the supply of health care was in the hands of privately owned firms seeking to make a profit, it is reasonable to assume that they would be willing to supply more hip replacements at higher prices and vice versa. The equality between demand and supply would determine the equilibrium price. Any increase in demand as shown by the shift from D_1 to D_2 would lead to an increase in price and this would result in a new equilibrium being established with price at

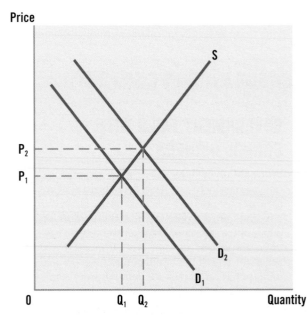

Figure 5.10 Privatising health care

OP_2 and the number of operations performed at OQ_2. This increase in price would signal an increase in potential profits and would encourage other suppliers to expand provision and might attract new businesses to enter this market. Further signals would lead to an increase in the supply of hip joints, expansion of operating facilities, and supply of suitably trained staff. Thus resources will shift from less profitable and rewarding provision. The price mechanism would take care of individual tastes, so those wanting a quick new hip would pay more to be operated on more quickly. Those who could not afford the market price might elect to go abroad for the operation if that was cheaper, while those without the means to purchase replacement hips would have to put up with what they have got. The price mechanism or market system would ration available resources and waiting lists would disappear.

Firms introducing more efficient hip replacements would be rewarded by high profits and the inefficient would go out of business. In short, the market system should ensure an effective allocation of resources.

If only the world were so simple. It could be argued that this market system:

- would not work because of inadequate information
- would fail to take account of positive externalities
- leads to increased administrative costs
- would be unfair.

INADEQUATE INFORMATION
It is one thing to buy a washing machine or tumble dryer. It is possible for potential consumers to get a good idea of the strengths and weaknesses of different brands, to understand about after-sales service and energy use. Similarly, manufacturers, through market research, can have a pretty good idea of their potential markets. Both buyer and seller can be relatively well informed about their potential choices. It is not so easy with health care. We might have some idea of our care needs now but what about in the future? Disease and illness are not necessarily predictable. Health insurance is possible but, again, it is hard to predict what level of cover you might require. These issues are compounded because we are living longer, medical science is advancing and our expectations about having healthy lives are increasing.

POSITIVE EXTERNALITIES
Economies with low life expectancy, in which disease and illness are commonplace, face enormous difficulties, as evidenced by the plight of those African countries worst hit by HIV/AIDS. On the other hand, it can be argued that everyone benefits if the working population is fitter and healthier and more productive. Simple measures like immunisation have a profound effect on whole societies. However, if it was left to the market system, some people would pay for protection against measles, mumps, TB and the like but others wouldn't. From a society-wide perspective, leaving immunisation to market forces would not work if some chose not to pay for immunisation.

INCREASED ADMINISTRATIVE COSTS
The USA relies on a market system to provide health care insurance for those who can afford it and uses state provision for those who cannot. The market system is particularly complicated and its administrative costs are very high. This is partly because the system gives doctors and hospitals incentives to provide expensive services and all kinds of checks and balances are needed to prevent people taking advantage of insurance. Researchers from the Harvard Medical School estimate that the administrative costs of the US health system are more than $1,000 per person per year, which is three times the amount spent in Canada, which has an NHS-style medical system.

FAIRNESS
Economists are not meant to stray into areas of value judgement but it is hard to remain neutral when it comes to health care. Should the poor die because they cannot afford health care? Should the rich use health resources for cosmetic treatment? Perhaps a market system would give better incentives for people to take better care of their health. However, there is ample evidence that UK electors prefer a health

Is cosmetic surgery the best use of health resources?

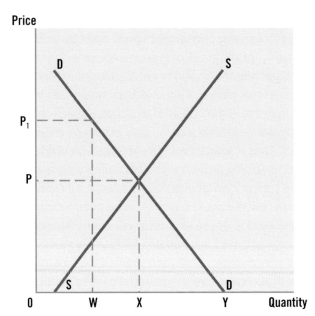

Figure 5.11 **Rationing in health care**

system that is free at the point of use and provided by the government, not by the market.

Does the NHS work?

The market failings of private medical provision outlined above provide a rationale for the direct provision by the government. However, the NHS, as we all know, is not without its problems. Three main issues dominate discussion as to the future of the NHS:

● rationing

● funding

● decision making.

RATIONING

The market system uses prices to ration scarce resources. The problems facing the UK health service can be illustrated by a demand and supply diagram concerning the repair of a broken leg. Figure 5.11 shows that, if left to market forces, a typical leg repair would cost OP and OX numbers would be treated. However, this service is provided at zero cost to the patient, leading to excess demand XY – incidentally this shows that OW people would be prepared to

'go private' to pay up to OP_1 for this treatment. This market model shows that supply and demand are not equal, and some means has to be found to ration out the available resources. Traditionally, queuing has been used to do this. Patients have to wait for all but emergency treatments.

FUNDING

The previous analysis points to a major funding issue – the cost to the government of funding all medical services at zero cost puts pressure on other demands for government expenditure and/or raising taxes. This presents a political dilemma as electors demand better health care, and do not appear to be prepared to vote for a party that says that improvements in the NHS will be funded by higher levels of taxation. The government's response to this has been to try to raise productivity in the health service.

DECISION MAKING

Making decisions within the health service has been undertaken historically by consultants – many of whom also work privately. They are economic agents with their own agendas. In theory, clinical needs should determine how resources get allocated. The government has tried to reduce the power and influence of consultants and has intervened to appoint managers who have to work to achieve targets. On the surface, this makes decision making more transparent but targets are often crudely framed. Hospital managers are under pressure to treat as many patients as possible and it has been argued that this has been pursued at the expense of cleanliness and hygiene – UK hospitals have one of the highest rates of MRSA in Europe.

The impact of government intervention on market outcomes in housing

The housing market is usually broken down into three interconnected markets:

● owner-occupation

● private renting

● social housing.

The first two of these are market based, while social housing involves particular forms of government intervention.

OWNER-OCCUPATION

This is the most common form of housing ownership in the UK. In 2006, 72 per cent of households in the UK were owner-occupied. For most people, buying a house represents the largest individual purchase they are likely to make in their lifetime. The overwhelming majority of house purchases are financed by mortgages, which are a form of long-term lending. Repayment of mortgages is usually monthly, and the main influence on the size of repayments is the interest rate. If the mortgage holder fails to keep up his or her payments, the bank or building society that lent the money can repossess the property, sell it and use the proceeds to repay the outstanding loan.

It should be obvious from the above that many factors affect the demand for owner-occupied houses – not

least the interest rate and consumer confidence. It is possible to argue that, *ceteris paribus*, the demand for houses will be greater if prices are low and vice versa. Hence, the demand curve for owner-occupied houses will slope downwards from left to right.

When it comes to the supply of homes for owner-occupation, there are two interconnected markets:

● newly built houses

● second-hand properties.

The production of new houses for owner-occupation is dominated by nationally known companies such as Bovis, Wimpy and Westbury, which are in business to make profits. However, the majority of properties coming onto the national housing market are second-hand. They are almost exclusively owned by their current occupiers, whose motivations in deciding whether or not to offer their property for sale are very complicated. Anticipated sale price is a key factor, and recent trends indicate that rising house prices are associated with greater preparedness to sell. If home owners believe that prices are not going to rise they are less likely to put their homes on the market.

The suppliers of both new and second-hand houses are likely to be more willing to supply houses if prices are relatively high and less willing if prices are low. Hence the supply of housing slopes upwards from left to right.

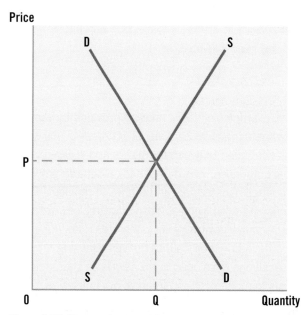

Figure 5.12 House prices

Although this is a complex market, the price of owner-occupied houses will be determined by interaction of demand and supply, as shown in figure 5.12 above.

THE PRIVATE RENTED SECTOR

In the UK, about 10 per cent of households are part of this sector (which is significantly less than in most other European countries). This sector tends to be one of extremes, consisting at one end of luxurious accommodation and at the other of some of the worst housing in the UK. The demand for the latter comes from those excluded from other housing sectors. For the whole market, the price (rent) will be determined by demand and supply.

SOCIAL HOUSING

'**Social housing**' is the name now given to both local authority-owned and housing association-owned housing. Both sub-sectors are, or have been, government funded and exist to compensate for the failure of the other two markets (owner-occupation and private renting) to ensure an adequate supply of affordable housing.

DEFINITION

'**Social housing**': housing subsidised by the government, mostly provided by local authorities and housing associations.

Early examples of social housing provided by various charitable trusts go back about 100 years. This work was continued between the 1920s and 1980s by local authorities, which undertook extensive provision of council houses, flats and estates to replace slums and raise living standards for the less well off. Conservative governments in the 1980s encouraged tenants to buy their council houses. Housing associations developed in the 1960s as charitable trusts to modernise and improve old houses as another means of providing decent housing to those in need. In many places in the UK, housing associations have taken over from local authorities as the main providers of social housing.

Social housing is not a market in the way that other markets have been described in this book. In most cases, the needs of potential tenants are assessed and points are given according to various criteria – for example, the number of children in a family and the state of existing accommodation. Available housing is then (theoretically) allocated to those in greatest need. Normal demand and supply analysis is not appropriate.

ACTIVITY ····⋗

What will happen to the price of owner-occupied housing if:

(a) income tax is cut

(b) interest rates are raised

(c) the supply of privately rented properties is cut

(d) land prices increase?

DOES THE HOUSING MARKET WORK?

For many people, the housing market works reasonably well. Rented and bought properties are rationed by price but these markets can take a long time to clear. In England and Wales this is partly because of institutional factors in actually reaching a point at which contracts can be agreed, and partly because buying and selling a house involves many other potential changes in people's lives. The basic problem with the housing market in the UK is that long-term demand is growing more quickly than long-term supply. Some might argue that this is actually an example of market failure. This imbalance between demand and supply occurs because there are more households in the UK than there are, in the jargon, housing units. This is becoming an increasing problem as more marriages end in divorce, creating an even greater demand for housing. It has been estimated that 350,000 new housing units are required each year if supply is to keep up with growing demand, but in 2006 the housing stock grew by just 200,000. There are many reasons for the relative inelasticity of supply of new housing:

- slowness of the planning system which regulates house building

- resistance of existing home owners to the building of new houses near by – often known as Nimbyism (not-in-my-back-yard-*ism*)

- preservation of the countryside

- fear of flooding.

ACTIVITY ⋯⫶

Find out where there are plans significantly to increase the housing stock in your area. Describe and assess the strength of opposition to these plans. Is the opposition based on normative or positive economic argument?

It could be argued that the housing market fails because of:

- both positive and negative externalities
- income inequalities.

EXTERNALITIES

The existence of what we now call 'positive externalities' associated with good housing and 'negative externalities' associated with poor housing was first identified in the mid-19th century. Employers such as the Cadbury family, who cared greatly about the well-being of their workers, provided decent housing for them because they recognised that well-housed workers were more productive. In this way, housing could be seen to be a merit good.

On the other hand, bad housing was, and is, associated with crime, illness and disease. It imposes negative externalities and additional costs on the rest of society.

For these reasons, the provision of housing by the private sector has been seen to be a source of market failure, giving a rationale for the intervention of local and national governments and the voluntary sector.

INEQUALITY

The existence of significant externalities coupled with an imbalance between demand and supply

of housing have created significant inequalities within housing markets. In the UK, there has been a long-term under-supply of housing in those areas in which needs are greatest. This contributes to the use of bed-and-breakfast accommodation as emergency housing and to the considerable problem of homelessness.

On the other hand, the well off can afford to live in large, under-utilised and luxurious accommodation. Some would argue that the existence of such inequalities is not morally justifiable.

In an effort to deal with these aspects of market failure, the UK government has used:

- subsidies

- rent controls.

SUBSIDIES

Poor people on low incomes tend to have the greatest problems in buying or renting decent quality accommodation. UK governments have used a variety of approaches to make housing more affordable. Currently, two are used to increase the supply of affordable housing:

- housing benefits

- low-cost government loans.

Housing benefits

These are an additional welfare payment that can be paid to tenants on low incomes in both social housing and housing provided by private landlords. The effect of these is to boost low incomes to enable poor people to afford rents, which are market determined. This is analysed in Figure 5.13, which shows the impact of giving subsidies to the less well off.

The effect is to shift the demand for rented accommodation up to the right. If the supply of this kind of housing is relatively inelastic, the outcome will be a relatively large increase in rents and a relatively small increase in the supply of rented accommodation. In some ways this could be argued to represent government failure, as the unintended outcome of this intervention is to boost the incomes of landlords.

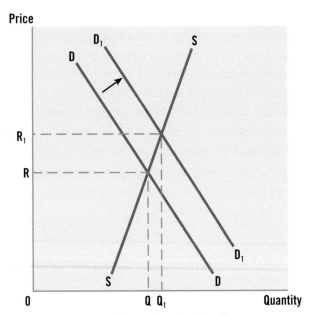

Figure 5.13 Possible effects of housing benefits

Low-cost government loans

The government provides loans to housing associations, which use them to build houses or renovate houses to an acceptable standard. The theoretical effect is to increase the supply of housing and push down rents, as shown in Figure 5.14. The theoretical effect in this case would be to reduce rents and increase the supply of housing and this is arguably a better outcome than that achieved by paying housing benefits.

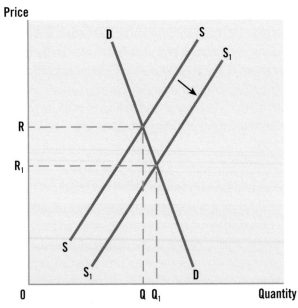

Figure 5.14 Possible effects of housing subsidies

RENT CONTROLS

The rents of social housing provided by both local councils and housing associations are not directly set by market forces. If this were the case, rents would rise until demand equalled supply and those on low incomes would be left homeless.

Rents are set at what is called an 'economic level'. This means that the total revenue earned is meant to be equal to the total costs of providing such housing. As indicated earlier, some tenants are given additional income to help them pay such rents, and housing associations may be able to borrow funds at discounted rates.

GOVERNMENT FAILURE

To some extent, government intervention can lead to government failure in which the outcomes of intervention have not been as planned and in some cases have made things worse.

This is vividly illustrated in the outcomes of the major slum clearance schemes undertaken in the 1950s and 1960s. Local councils were given subsidies to demolish large areas of sub-standard housing in inner cities and replace them with new housing estates, including tower blocks. Some estates were built without facilities such as shops, while others were not adequately maintained. Resettling people into the new estates involved great social change, and family and friendship patterns were disrupted. These changes resulted in effects that were never anticipated – for example, vandalism, social isolation and crime. Some of these estates are now being demolished and planners are reverting to more traditional housing designs meant to promote a greater sense of community.

Finally, until the 1980s, governments tried to limit the rents payable to private landlords. The effect of this in some areas, especially where housing was in short supply, was to create an unofficial market. One form of this was 'key money': in order to rent a flat or even a room, prospective tenants had to pay the landlord or agent large sums of money. Those who refused or fell into rent arrears were often forced out of their homes.

More recently, the pressure to build more homes has meant that planning permission has been given for developments in areas liable to flooding. In the summer of 2007, insurance claims resulting from flooded housing have been estimated to stand at £3 billion, which is leading to higher premiums for all – arguably a negative externality resulting from government intervention.

The impact of government intervention on market outcomes in agriculture

Economics throws up paradoxes and contradictions. In some ways the UK agricultural industry is more competitive than any other. For any given agricultural product there are many suppliers, producing very similar commodities. Individual suppliers have relatively little influence over the price they receive for their outputs, and customers have a very wide choice of produce grown not just in this country but globally. Given the earlier analysis about competitive markets, it would be reasonable to expect that the UK agriculture industry is relatively efficient. There is some evidence to support this in that fewer than 2 per cent of the UK population are employed in the industry and, in addition to exports, they produce 60 per cent of domestic food needs. Manufacturing of food products is also a highly developed, efficient industry. The market system is responsive to the changing demands of buyers and although it is possible to identify both negative and positive externalities, mainly associated with the value that we place on the countryside, there are no obvious examples of market failure to justify government intervention. However, agriculture is one of the most regulated and subsidised market sectors in the UK. There are three main reasons for this:

● strategic considerations

● concern about the incomes of farmers

● the political influence of farming lobby groups across Europe.

STRATEGIC CONSIDERATIONS

For hundreds of years, UK governments have had concerns about the ability of the agricultural industry to supply sufficient foodstuffs in times of conflict or war. This approach was justified in two world wars in the 20th century, when the Germans attempted to blockade the country to prevent imports of food, raw materials and armaments. For this reason farming was heavily regulated and in times of war farmers were directed as to which crops they should grow. Though this form of direction ended over 40 years ago, successive governments have continued to take a keen interest in farming and agriculture ministries have been very powerful.

Similar considerations have affected policies developed by other European countries, especially those such as France and Spain in which the farming lobby is more influential. In 1958 the founder members of the Common Market, as the EU was then known, created a **Common Agricultural Policy (CAP)** designed to promote European self-sufficiency in food production. This involved the creation of tariff barriers and quotas to limit imports of food into the EU from the rest of the world.

These policies were applied to the UK when it joined the European community in 1973 and their effect is shown in Figure 5.15. Restricting imports of foods into the EU has the effect of increasing prices paid by consumers. *SW* represents the world supply of sugar and *SE* the European supply. If there were no intervention, customers in the UK would pay the world market price at OP_1 but because of tariffs and quotas they are forced to pay OP_2.

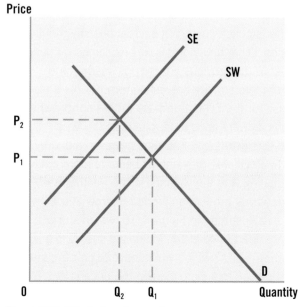

Figure 5.15 Effect of customs union

DEFINITION

Common Agricultural Policy (CAP): European Union policies to protect farmers' incomes and encourage agricultural production within the EU.

FARMERS' INCOMES

Although many farmers have resented what they might see as political and bureaucratic interference, they have also benefited from subsidies and incentives. Maintaining farmers' incomes and protecting rural ways of life were also important aspects of the CAP. The main way in which farmers' incomes were protected was by guaranteeing them a minimum price for their produce.

POLITICAL INFLUENCE OF FARMERS

As noted earlier, farmers across Europe are politically powerful. Large landowners are often very wealthy and smaller landowners can be very defensive of their traditional lifestyles. Many farmers tend to be conservative and resistant to change.

THE CAP IN CRISIS

The Common Agricultural Policy of the EU is seen by many economists as an example of government failure. One of the intentions was to maintain buffer stocks to even out fluctuations in agricultural prices. (The theory of this was explained on pages 76–7 in the previous chapter.) If weather and other factors made harvests unpredictable it made sense for the EU to purchase excess supply when harvests were good, and to release this when harvests were poor. Farmers, however, aided by technological improvements became more adept at dealing with the vagaries of the weather and agricultural production tended to grow and grow. This is illustrated in Figure 5.16, which shows a guaranteed price at OP, increased supply to S_2 and a surplus of XY which would have to be purchased and placed into store to keep the price at OP. The outcome of this example of government failure was that the EU built up stocks of 'unwanted' food

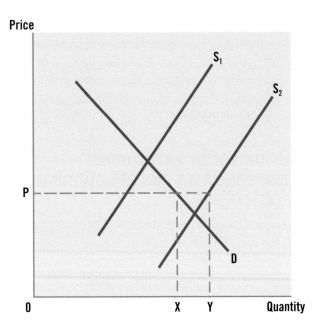

Figure 5.16 Possible effects of guaranteed prices

products such as beef, olive oil and wine. Not only did holding these stocks push up the costs of the CAP, the EU was also left with the dilemma of what to do with them. Some of the excess stocks were sold to the Soviet Union, which then re-exported them back to Europe. Subsidies were given to sell unwanted stocks into African countries, which in turn threatened the livelihoods of local producers, and some stocks were destroyed. The EU has attempted to reform the CAP and move away from guaranteed minimum prices and has subsidised farmers not to use up to 10 per cent of their land for the production of cereal crops.

One of the incentives to change CAP has come from its costs. By 2000, 50 per cent of the EU's budget was spent on agriculture. The enlargement of the EU to include countries, such as Poland, with relatively large agricultural sectors has forced further changes. Current budget plans involve a progressive reduction in the proportion of the EU budget devoted to CAP – in 2007 it stood at 40 per cent.

Another criticism of CAP is that the main beneficiaries are wealthy landowners rather than low-income farmers in greater need. For example, the Queen receives some £400,000 in annual subsidies from the EU for her Sandringham estate in Norfolk.

Single payments scheme

As part of the reform of CAP, the EU has introduced a new scheme to provide farmers with additional income according to the number of hectares under cultivation rather than subsidies for producing particular crops. A set amount is allocated to each member state and then this is divided between the total number of applicants. No payments can be made until all claims have been verified. First payments under this scheme were due to be paid in January 2006 but by the end of that year this had not been completely achieved. The new system of support is said to be more complicated than the one that it replaced, and in 2007 farmers were still complaining that they had not received payments to which they thought they were entitled.

The impact of government intervention on market outcomes in transport and the environment

The final section of this chapter involves a brief outline of the market for transport and focuses on its relationship with the environment.

TRANSPORT TRENDS IN THE UK

In recent decades there have been three major trends:

- an overall increase in demand
- a shift from public to private transport
- an increase in air travel.

INCREASE IN DEMAND

The overall increase in demand for transport reflects a variety of factors, including the increased importance of international trade, people living further away from their place of work and relatives, people undertaking more holidays and holidays further afield, hypermarkets and places of entertainment being built outside of city centres, and increases in output.

These changes increase the need and frequency of transport of both goods and people. At the same time the relative cost of international transport has fallen, which again contributes to increased use.

CHANGE FROM PUBLIC TO PRIVATE TRANSPORT

The change from public to private transport is illustrated in Figure 5.17. A noticeable feature is

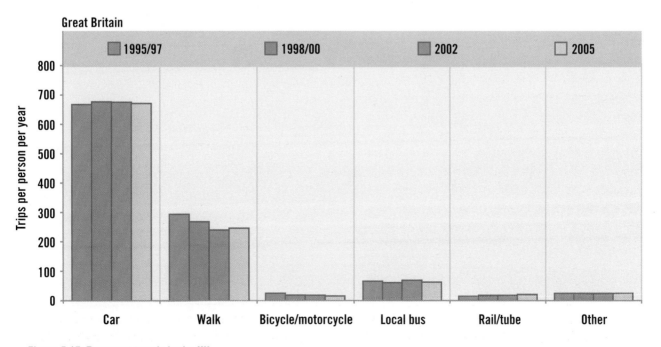

Figure 5.17 Transport trends in the UK

the significant rise in travel by car and fall in travel by bus. The diagram shows the rapid growth in car transport and the fall in bus and coach transport (as a percentage of total passenger transport). This is also reflected in the switching of the transport of goods domestically and in Europe to privately owned road hauliers, away from railway use.

In terms of demand, transport by private car can be seen to be a superior good in that expenditure tends to increase more than proportionately to income. However, some forms of transport, such as local buses, cycles and motor bicycles, appear to be characterised by a negative income elasticity of demand.

INCREASE IN AIR TRAVEL

There have been significant increases in the use of air transport for both goods and services. It was estimated that over half of UK households would travel by air in year 2007, primarily to European short-haul destinations. This expansion in air travel is partly related to the impact of low-cost

Budget airlines have helped to increase air travel

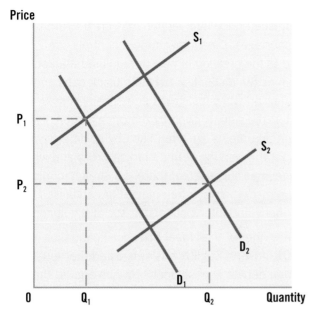

Figure 5.18 Impact of budget airlines

airlines such as the Irish-based Ryanair, which is now the third largest airline in the world. It also indicates that air travel is a superior good characterised by a relatively high positive income elasticity of demand. The impact of these two factors is shown in Figure 5.18.

The shift from D_1 to D_2 represents an increase in demand because short-haul air travel might be a superior good, while the move from S_1 to S_2 shows a reduction in costs of travel introduced by the budget airlines. The outcome is that prices fall from P_1 to P_2 and sales of seats increase from Q_1 to Q_2.

NEGATIVE EXTERNALITIES

The growth in road traffic provides a good example of negative externalities, especially as the demand for road transport has risen more quickly than the supply of suitable roads. Since 1980, the length of the UK's road system has increased by 10 per cent while at the same time total traffic use by passengers and freight has risen by 73 per cent. This has resulted in reduced average speeds and longer journey times. Congestion tends to be concentrated on particular motorways, the M1 and

M6 and the M5 in summer, and in the larger urban areas, especially London.

Congestion is also a problem when there are accidents and roadworks. It has become increasingly difficult to maintain and repair the major road arteries without causing massive disruption to traffic flows.

Economists differ in their predictions as to the future demands for road transport. Some models predict that journey times will get slower and slower and that particular combinations of events could result in gridlock, in which traffic becomes frozen. Department for Transport data indicate a projected increase of 48 per cent in demand for roads by 2026. Other forecasts from the Commission for Integrated Transport suggest that by 2010 congestion is likely to rise by 65 per cent overall and on motorways by 286 per cent. These projections make future planning for the growth of road traffic particularly difficult, especially as some future policy decisions might be very politically unpopular.

In Figure 5.19, the marginal social cost (MSC) curve represents a negative externality, congestion being an obvious example in transport economics.

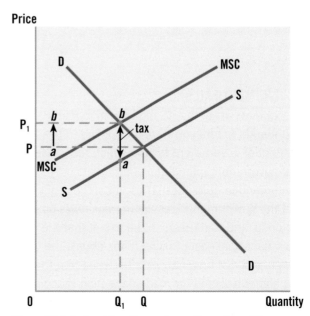

Figure 5.19 Indirect taxation and negative externalities

The graphical analysis can be used to show that if the government could calculate the additional costs on society of road congestion and were to introduce a tax equivalent to the vertical distance *ab* it would be able to ensure an optimum allocation of resources. At OP_1 and OQ_1 an equilibrium is reached at which customers are paying the total cost to society for the road space that they are using.

You will have learned to identify the effects of positive externalities and the possible use of government subsidy to achieve an optimal allocation of resources (see page 87). Thus again, it is possible to argue that having an efficient means of bringing workers quickly to work in London or any other major city might have significant positive externalities, more leisure/work time, happier less stressed workers, and less pollution. Again, in theory, if the government could put a monetary value on these benefits, it might be possible to use subsidies to achieve a socially more desirable allocation of resources.

ACTIVITY ····⋮

Does the price paid for air travel reflect its full social costs? What problems might an economist have in calculating the negative externalities associated with air travel?

GOVERNMENT FAILURE

In the final part of the AS module on markets and market failure you were introduced to the concept of government failure, which recognises that government intervention in markets may lead to unintended outcomes. Thus, it can be argued that the government does not impose taxes on motorists and road users to the extent that the marginal social cost of using roads equals the marginal social benefits, with the result that there is a higher demand for road space than is socially desirable. Even worse, there are no taxes on the supply of aircraft fuel – one of the major sources of pollutants which are thought to damage the

ozone layer and contribute to global warming. Misplaced price intervention may create surpluses or shortages. Direct government controls can lead to the creation of new unregulated markets such as the distinction between black cabs and mini or private cabs. Taxes and subsidies may distort the signals given by the price mechanism. Such arguments are often used by politicians who favour the working of free market forces and who sometimes suggest that there is a straight choice to be made between free market or capitalist solutions and interventionist or socialist solutions.

The winner of the Nobel Prize for Economics in 2001, Joseph Stiglitz, has suggested that much of this debate is misplaced. He has argued that free market ideology is fundamentally flawed, as 'whenever information is imperfect and markets incomplete, which is to say always, then the invisible hand works most imperfectly'. He goes on to argue that government interventions 'can improve upon the efficiency of the market' and that one of the roles of government is to try to remove imperfections in information flows. He suggests that it is more useful to discuss the appropriate balance between governments and markets.

> **learning tip**
>
> Transport markets are likely to fail because of the existence of significant externalities, both positive and negative. Governments often intervene in transport markets to improve the efficiency and effectiveness of resource use and this may improve or exacerbate the efficient allocation of transport resources.

SUMMARY

Traditional economic analysis tends to regard commodities such as air, water and even the land itself as free goods. As our understanding has developed, we now recognise that nothing is free. The world is full of examples that show the limits of such short-term thinking – rivers, lakes and seas that can no longer sustain life because they have been used to cool, wash and clean without thought for the consequences. One of the challenges to economists when dealing with environmental issues is to devise ways of fully accounting for the impact of economic activity on the environment. Does the price paid by air travellers accurately reflect the possible long-term costs that may arise from possible climate change? Similarly, does the price paid by motorists include the long-term costs of their contribution to global warming?

ACTIVITY ····⟩

Conduct your own research into the extent to which one of the following markets might be said to fail, and assess the relative methods of different forms of intervention to improve the allocation of resources:

- market provision of dental health care
- private housing in rural areas
- chicken and eggs for household consumption
- rickshaws in London.

Exam Café
Relax, refresh, result!

Relax and prepare

How do you revise?

Abi

The first thing I did was to find a revision corner which I can call my own. I'm so lucky, I have a bedroom of my own. But friends with larger families have taken over the kitchen table (with permission from their parents, of course) or set up a desk and chair in the garage. I also know friends who have found a table in the local library which they think of as their own. If none of these is possible, have a word with a trusted teacher, in confidence, to see if the school can help you to find a revision space. The important thing is that you should have some peace and quiet for revision, without interruption. Some people find that they can revise better in company, so that, for example, a pair of friends or a 'trio' can meet in each other's houses for a 'swot' session. From time to time during these sessions they'll question and 'test' each other.

I know lots of people who say that they can only revise with loud music on their headphones. I'm not at all sure about this, I suppose it's a matter of taste.

Finlay

Our psychology teacher said that classical music, especially Mozart, playing quietly in the background, can actually help you think! I wonder if that's true? It's worth a try. But anyway, what I think is very important is to make a revision timetable. What works for me is to revise little and often. I say: don't leave it all to the last minute. Start now, and while you are learning, keep reviewing your work, constantly.

How many days are there to the next series of exams? Divide this by the number of subjects: that's the average number of days you have for each subject. Every day, when I've finished my normal homework, I revise a subject for a short amount of time. So revision doesn't come in one huge chunk at the end of the course, you learn the subject as you go. I keep a chart, showing which subjects I've revised every day. It's difficult to start the routine at first, but once you get into the habit, it makes exam preparation so much easier, it saves time in the long run, and you actually enjoy your work much more because it improves your confidence if you are keeping up with the subject and understanding it properly.

Seren

Something I did almost at the start was to collect past papers from the exam board for each of my subjects. Some teachers provided them, but when I asked one of the teachers for past papers, he didn't want me to have them, and said it was 'too soon', I don't know why. So I bought them from the exam board. It's incredible, but some of my friends don't even know which exam board's papers they are preparing for! Either they can't be bothered to find out, or their teacher hasn't mentioned it yet. AQA has a good website with specimen papers and mark schemes, and their past papers can be bought at reasonable cost. As an economist, think of this as an 'investment'!

When you have a good set of past papers, use 'cut and paste' (or scissors and glue) to group the questions together by topic, then put them in a ring binder. That way, you can see how often certain topics come up, and you can see the 'style' of the questions. With the mark-schemes you can also see the answers! This way, you should find that there are no nasty surprises in the actual exam. With any luck, it'll all look familiar.

Refresh your memory

Revision checklist

Can you ...?	Turn to page ...
Define economics and describe what economists do.	2
Explain the different factors of production and, given a particular economic resource (for example, oil), classify it (state which factor it 'belongs' to)	4
List the economic objectives of individuals, firms and governments	7
Define opportunity cost	9
Use a production possibility diagram to illustrate the use of resources	10
Given a statement or question, say whether it is positive or normative	12
Use movements along a demand curve to describe how price affects quantity demanded	16
Use shifts of a demand curve to show how market changes other than price can affect demand	17
Use movements along a supply curve to describe how price affects quantity supplied	27
Use shifts of a supply curve to show how market changes other than price affect supply	28
Define elasticity and explain price, cross and income elasticity of demand and price elasticity of supply	19, 32
Explain how price elasticity of demand affects total revenue	22
Use supply and demand diagrams to show how changes in market conditions can change price and quantity	42
Explain the rationing, incentive and signalling functions of price	46
Define specialisation and explain its importance	48
Define productive efficiency and illustrate it on a production possibility diagram	51
List examples of economies and diseconomies of scale	55
Define 'market failure'	59
Distinguish between public and private goods	60
Distinguish between merit and demerit goods	64
Describe the 'barriers to entry' that may lead to monopoly power	67
Outline the possible disadvantages and advantages of monopoly	68
Discuss how different types of market failure can affect the allocation of resources	72
Explain how and why governments might use indirect taxation, subsidies, price controls, buffer stocks, pollution permits and state provision of goods and services	73
Give examples of government success and government failure when intervening in health care provision, housing, agriculture, transport and the environment	82–95

Key word quiz

Define:
1. Market
2. Demand
3. Equilibrium
4. Productive efficiency
5. Public good
6. Merit good

Student answers

These are answers to part (d) of the following data-response question:

'If there is a "national housing shortage", how should the government deal with it?' (25 marks)

Javed's answer

Examiner comments:
Javed starts well, by clearly stating three options. What is more, he realises that not intervening in the market is one of the options.

Examiner comments:
Two sides of an argument are attempted here.

A government has three basic options when it comes to the housing market: it can build houses itself, encourage the private sector to build or play no role at all.

If the government was to build houses itself, it would carry a very high cost to the government. Building houses isn't cheap but it does mean that any financial reward that comes about helps to pay off the debt of building houses. It would also be very easy to push its own developments quickly through planning, bringing a new supply to the market place sooner.

By encouraging the private sector to build houses, the government will incur a lower financial cost. It could do this by providing grants to house builders (see diagram) or by relaxing planning and making houses easier and quicker to build. By giving a grant to house builders, the government will increase supply, a shift to S2. This will increase the quantity from OQ to OQ2 and reduce the price to OP2. The problem for the government with this option is that their plans may not work and the market will remain unchanged. One reason why the plans may not work is because the private sector might not be interested in building different types of houses in different areas of the country. They might only want to build four-bedroom executive-style houses in the south-east of England, because this is where the profits are. But the country might need single-bedroom flats in the north-west. So the subsidies to get them to change their minds might have to be very large indeed, making it cheaper for the government to do the job itself, through council house building or by paying housing associations to build 'affordable' housing.

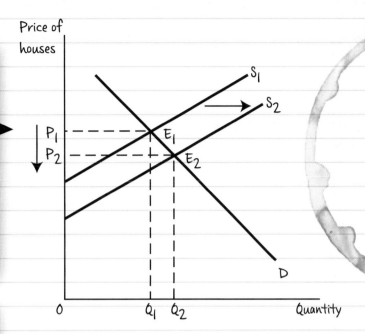

Of course the diagram refers to new houses only. It should be remembered that the majority of houses are already built, so it can take a long time for changes in the price of new houses to affect the general housing market. The flow of new houses is small compared to the existing stock.

The final option is to play no part at all in the housing market. This option would have no financial cost and therefore no reward. Unfortunately, this is a very poor option: it could easily lead to market failure, as the market would not provide to all those who required housing. In the end, there would be an opportunity cost. The government might have to intervene in the market eventually, and a fix might be expensive.

Therefore, overall I believe that the best option is to encourage the private sector. The cost that this would incur would be much lower than building houses itself and although there is a risk that it would have no effect on the market, I believe that this risk is almost non-existent.

Examiner comments:
The use of relevant diagrams is good practice in economics. Javed's diagram is accurately drawn, and he discusses it in a sensible way. He uses it to predict the effects of an increase in housing supply. There is a lost opportunity here because Javed could have discussed the meaning of the phrase 'affordable housing'.

Examiner comments:
An excellent point worth making and well expressed here.

Examiner comments:
More missed opportunities here, where the concepts 'market failure' and 'opportunity cost' could have been elaborated a little. Other ideas which could have been introduced here include 'externalities' and the idea of good housing as a 'merit good'.
Overall: There is some attempt to use economic terminology, some of which is used well. Good use of a diagram. The answer is logically structured, and there is some attempt at evaluation. QWC (quality of written communication) is not perfect but is acceptable. Manages to achieve entry to Level 4 ('good analysis but limited evaluation'). 17 marks.

Examiner comments:
There is potentially a valid economic point here, but it is not developed.

Examiner comments:
A very woolly statement.

Examiner comments:
Imprecise terminology indicating that the idea of 'public good' is not clearly understood.
Clumsy phraseology, meaning not clearly conveyed.

Examiner comments:
Again, a relevant idea (subsidies) is introduced, but is not developed.

Examiner comments:
Why would this affect inflation? Is a balance of payments deficit being confused with a budget deficit here?
Overall: An insubstantial answer with very little hard economics. QWC is not good. The 'evaluation' in the last paragraph is superficial. Level 2 ('a poor answer but some understanding is shown'). 7 marks.

In my opinion, I don't think that the government should play any part in the housing market at all, and that they should encourage the private sector to build more houses. This is because I believe that if the government was to start building houses, then this would result in more government expenditure and an increase in household taxation. I don't agree with this because, if the government was to charge households more on their taxes, it would feel to them that they are paying the government to build houses and spend their money on something that isn't going to be any use to them.

This backs up my point because the housing market is not a public market as it isn't providing a public good or service and so this is why the government should not get involved as they are only useful in providing goods and services to the public that everyone is available to make use of.

I think that it is fair to let the public sector carry on in producing houses, as they can then receive all the money for the houses and don't need to worry about the government intervening in their market.

If the government was to take some action in the housing market, then all I believe they should do is to create subsidies on the firms in the housing market to help them produce their products.

All in all, I don't think the government should have any part in the housing market due to the worry of having an increase in household taxations and government expenditure, which would then result in inflation and a deficit on the balance of payments within the economy.

Hot tips

General advice

AQA Economics at AS uses two types of exam question: multiple-choice and data-response. We give you some tips on tackling multiple-choice items below, and some tips on answering data-response questions in the Exam Café section in Part Two. Please note that all this advice is equally applicable to both papers, Econ-1 and Econ-2.

In all exams, you should always pay full attention to the following advice.

● Keep an eye on the clock. Reserve some time for:

   O   reading through the paper at the start (and while you are doing this, marking bits that you need to pay particular attention to with a highlighter pen)

   O   reading through your written answers at the end (you might be surprised how many little written errors you can make while working under the pressure of exam conditions).

● Read the front cover of the exam paper and follow AQA advice on how to divide your time between the objective-test and data-response sections of the paper.

● Spend time on questions in proportion to the mark allocations. Do *not* spend half an hour on a question worth 5 marks, and only two minutes on a question worth 25 marks.

● Write clearly in ink (preferably black, but blue is okay as well). Do *not* use red, green or purple ink.

● *Never* use correction fluid. Cross out any mistakes and write the correct version again.

● Use *pencil* (with a ruler, if appropriate) to draw diagrams. Write labels in ink.

● Follow the *RUBRIC*. Do *not* answer *fewer* or *more* questions than required.

● Pay attention to **command words** (refer to advice on these in Part Two of this book – see page 179)

● Remember that examiners have to allocate some marks for the 'quality of written communication' (known as QWC). Write neatly and clearly, communicate in good clear English, and spell correctly.

Objective tests (multiple-choice)

AQA papers Econ-1 and Econ-2 both contain 25 multiple-choice **items** (they are often described as items rather than questions, because they do not always contain a question mark).

Be aware of the following features of a multiple-choice item.

● Each item has a **'stem'** which poses a problem or asks a question.

● This is followed by four **options** (A,B,C,D).

● One of these options is the **'best answer'** or **key.**

● The other three answers are incorrect, and are called the **'distractors'**.

● You get 1 mark for each key that you choose correctly.

● You do *not* have marks subtracted for 'wrong' answers.

It follows that:

● You should *always* attempt *all* of these items.

● Remember: even if you have to guess, you have a 1 in 4 chance of guessing correctly (ideally, of course, you should not need to guess at all).

● Sometimes, you can use your economic knowledge to eliminate some wrong answers, giving yourself a 1 in 3 or 1 in 2 chance.

Before you enter your choice on the answer sheet:

● Consider each option carefully, to convince yourself that you know:

   O   *why* your chosen key is correct, *and*

   O   *why* each of your identified distractors is *in*correct.

1. Which one of the following is a normative statement?

   A Petrol is more expensive than bottled water.   B Bottled water costs more to produce than petrol.
   C Petrol is more useful than bottled water.   D Bottled water has a bigger market than petrol.

2. The idea of opportunity cost suggests that all of the following are limited in supply *except* people's:

   A time   B wants   C resources   D incomes.

3. A mixed economy is said to exist when there is a combination of:

   A different types of goods and services on sale   B economic goods and free goods available
   C capital and labour used in production   D government and markets allocating resources.

4. When a market is at equilibrium:

   A all consumers can afford the product   B there is no shortage or surplus at the equilibrium price
   C all producers are equally efficient   D the equilibrium quantity is at its highest possible level.

5. The demand for season tickets at a railway station rose from 800 to 1,000 a month following a 10 per cent increase in the price of bus travel. The cross elasticity of demand of train season tickets with respect to the price of bus travel is:

   A −2.5   B −0.4   C +0.4   D +2.5.

6. Which one of the following is *not* a scarce economic resource?

   A land   B labour   C money   D enterprise.

7. Ambridge Parish Council needs to re-lay the village cricket pitch and extend the village hall. The council receives £25,000 from National Lottery funds and spends it on extending the village hall. As a result, the hall is used more frequently by villagers, some of whom were previously using the Scout Hall. The opportunity cost of the council's decision is:

   A zero, since lottery funds are not public money   B £25,000
   C earnings lost by the Scout Hall   D the improved cricket pitch.

8.
   > Borchester Council wants to double the number of cars using its car parks. It has decided to halve the price of car parking.
   >
   > –*Borchester Evening Echo,* 1st May 2003

   We may conclude from the statement that Borchester Council assumes that the price elasticity of demand for car parking (defined as a positive number) is:

   A equal to 0   B greater than 0 but less than 1
   C equal to 1   D greater than 1.

9. The table shows average incomes and the number of mobile phones purchased in a certain country. All the numbers shown are index numbers, with 1990 as the base year.

	1995	2000
Income	100	120
Number of mobile phones purchased	200	1,000

From the data it may be concluded that the income elasticity of demand for mobile phones between 1995 and 2000 was:

A 0.01   B 0.2   C 25   D 40.

10. Economists usually argue that the existence of a monopoly is likely to have undesirable effects on each of the following *except*:

A prices   B competition   C economic efficiency   D economies of scale.

Data-response question

HEALTH AND EFFICIENCY

Many economists would argue that efficiency in the NHS cannot be measured in quite the same way as in the world of business, and would put forward several reasons why the idea of a 'market' cannot easily be applied to health.

1. Unpredictability. With most goods and services, consumers can plan their purchases ahead. The family car, for example, usually wears out gradually. An individual or family can plan ahead and budget for a replacement. It is much more difficult to predict and budget for a broken bone or a sudden serious illness. There is a lack of knowledge. Market theory suggests that consumers have plenty of knowledge about what they are buying. In health care, however, the patient is very much in the hands of the specialised knowledge of the doctor.

2. Externalities. Health care often tends to benefit not only the user, but also the non-user. Many types of health care are neither public goods nor private goods. They are clearly 'merit goods'.

3. Unusual elasticities. In countries where health is dominated by the private sector, people pay for health insurance. The insurance policy to some extent breaks the link between a spending decision and the cost of treatment. There is some evidence from the USA that there is a temptation for doctors to prescribe over-expensive medicines and even perform unnecessary operations, believing that insurance companies will pay the bill.

When treatment is a matter of life and death, from the patient's point of view the price elasticity of demand for treatment might be very low or even zero. At the same time, health insurance becomes more affordable as incomes increase, and consumers will demand the latest high-tech, most expensive treatments. High income elasticity coupled with low price elasticity makes medical provision more and more costly as time goes on. Spending as a percentage of GDP in the UK, where everyone is entitled to health care free at the point of use, is lower than it is in the USA, which relies very much on the private sector, but where 30 per cent of the population have no health insurance.

(a) Define the term 'public good'.   (5 marks)

(b) Give an example of a type of health care that is clearly a 'merit good' and explain its 'externalities'.   (8 marks)

(c) In 2007, the Welsh Assembly government abolished prescription charges in Wales. Using a supply and demand diagram to help you, predict what would be likely to happen to the market for prescription medicines in England if the UK government were to make a similar decision affecting patients there.   (12 marks)

(d) Examine the case for government involvement in the provision of health care, and evaluate the idea that having a National Health Service is more 'efficient' than relying on the private sector.   (25 marks)

PART 2

The National Economy

INTRODUCTION

Macroeconomics

As you will have learned in Part 1, microeconomics is about how individual markets might work and not work. The focus was on the smaller units which together make up a whole economy. Hence you will have worked on firms, and markets and customers. Macroeconomics is about the bigger picture – the whole economy – and involves having a better understanding of topics such as inflation, employment levels, national income, investment and the balance of payments. You may think you know what these terms mean, but economists have very precise definitions and, as ever, particular ways of analysing and evaluating a range of factors that have an impact on us all.

Chapter 6 is all about the data which economists use to measure the performance of an economy. These are the indicators, such as growth rates, inflation levels and unemployment, which appear regularly in newspapers and on television. Crudely, they indicate whether or not a national economy is doing well or badly. They also enable us to compare the performance of the UK economy with that of other countries.

These economic indicators can also be used to understand changes in the performance of the UK economy over time. Economic activity can be seen to fluctuate from boom to bust and back again. Such historical changes are often referred to as the business or economic cycle. Chapter 6 will also give you an understanding of why these cycles might occur, and how they might affect the different economic indicators identified earlier.

Chapter 7 is more theoretical and concerns two models which economists use to develop a better understanding of how the macroeconomy actually works. The circular flow model is a visual representation of the economy and aggregate demand and aggregate supply analysis is also a graphical representation. You will have to learn and use these graphs when you take your Unit 2 examination.

When you have developed an understanding of how the macroeconomy might work, you will be able to understand the what, why and the hows of government economic policy. This provides the content for Chapter 8, which involves knowing about possible policy objectives including economic growth, inflation, employment and the balance of payments, and how these potential objectives might clash.

Finally, Chapter 9 introduces a range of policy measures that governments can use. These include fiscal, monetary and supply-side policies. Each is explained and you will be helped to assess their potential effectiveness in relation to different policy objectives. By this stage you will not only be ready for your Unit 2 exam but also able to advise the Chancellor of the Exchequer.

Again, each chapter includes definitions, learning tips, activities and a series of Economics in context case studies designed to illustrate how our understanding of macroeconomics has developed over time.

At the end of Chapter 9 there is another Exam Café to help you prepare for the Unit 2 examination. A list of suggested further reading can be found at the end of the book.

6 The measurement of macroeconomic performance

On completion of this chapter, you should be able to:

- understand how economists use national income, inflation, unemployment and the balance of payments to measure the performance of different economies
- compare the performance of different economies
- understand the economic cycle
- be able to use a range of economic indicators – such as GDP, the rate of inflation, unemployment and investment – to identify the various phases of the economic cycle
- distinguish between demand-side and supply-side shocks
- distinguish between positive and negative output gaps.

Macroeconomic indicators

One of the important jobs that economists do is to try to have a better understanding about how well individual economies are doing. Most of us have some notion about whether the economy is going well or badly and politicians are always claiming to have the right answers.

Economists try to take a more balanced and objective view and they use a number of key indicators to make judgements about the performance of the macroeconomy. These include:

- gross domestic product (GDP)
- gross domestic product per capita
- economic growth
- inflation as measured by consumer price index (CPI) and retail price index (RPI)
- unemployment and employment
- the balance of payments on current account.

Not only are these data sets used to measure the performance of the UK economy, they are also used to make international comparisons. These can be particularly important in helping us understand how the world economy is likely to change in the future.

ACTIVITY ····⁝

'China's economic growth has averaged 9.5 per cent over the past two decades.'

What does this statistic mean? Is it significant? Justify your answer.

 learning tip Watch out when it comes to international comparisons. Although different countries are moving towards common measures of economic performance, different countries may record similar data in different ways.

GROSS DOMESTIC PRODUCT

This data provides the single most important basis for measuring the performance of an economy. Gross Domestic Product refers to the total value of goods and services produced in an economy in a given period of time. **GDP** is a widely used, if rather crude, measure of how much income has created in an economy in a given period of time. It is worked out by adding up the values of new goods and services that are produced. This is a relatively easy task for government statisticians but GDP misses out putting a value on areas of economic activity which are not officially recorded. For example, some families employ nannies to look after their children. The income that nannies receive for their services represents a contribution to GDP. However, if the same work is undertaken by a parent, they do not get paid and their contribution to GDP is not recorded. Similar arguments apply to illegal economic activity and all those willing to work for 'cash on the side'. Moreover, this official statistic also misses out the value of wealth created by those who work as volunteers, and does nothing to distinguish between economic activity which is socially destructive and socially beneficial. Thus, cleaning up after the floods of 2007 actually added to GDP.

However, knowing the estimated GDP for the UK in 2006 was $2.14 trillion (a million million) does not mean much. Statisticians and economists often have to do things to data or make comparisons in order to bring out different meanings.

One simple comparison that can be made is to compare the GDPs of different countries. Table 6.1 shows the world's top ten when it comes to this measure of economic performance.

There should be little surprise as we all know that the USA has the most powerful economy in the world, and you may have heard politicians talk about the UK as the fourth largest economy. However, the value of these statistics is limited as is explained in the following sections.

GROSS DOMESTIC PRODUCT PER CAPITA

GDP data is made much more useful when it is changed to take account of the population of a country. Thus, if this data is recalculated to take account of the size of each country's population some strange things happen. Who comes out on top? – Luxembourg. The USA drops to number 7 and the UK falls out of the top ten chart. This calculation is simply a matter of dividing the GDP of each country by its population to work out the **GDP per capita**.

This data is now much more meaningful and when it comes to taking into account our population the

Table 6.1 Economic performance by gross domestic product (GDP) (million $)

1	USA	11,667,515
2	Japan	4,623,398
3	Germany	2,714,418
4	UK	2,140,898
5	France	2,002,582
6	Italy	1,672,302
7	China	1,649,329
8	Spain	991,442
9	Canada	979,764
10	India	691,876

Source: Nationmaster

Table 6.2 GDP per capita (£)

1	Luxembourg	66,463.78
2	Norway	54,467.23
3	Switzerland	47,999.07
4	Ireland	45,707.17
5	Denmark	44,742.82
6	Iceland	41,720.45
7	USA	39,452.74
8	Sweden	38,480.78
9	Japan	36,285.57
10	Finland	35,726
27	UK	31,755.83

Source: World Bank Data via Nationmaster

UK becomes the 27th richest country in the world. It appears that those living in 26 other countries might be better off. Moreover, you might be tempted to conclude that the standard of living for the average person in Luxembourg is almost twice that of a Finn. However, it is dangerous to leap to conclusions.

DEFINITIONS

GDP: gross domestic product: the total value of goods and services produced within an economy in a given period of time.

GDP per capita: GDP divided by the population of a given country.

Both these terms are often referred to as national income – as you will learn later, the total value of what is produced in an economy should be the same as the total value of all incomes.

learning tip For up-to-date data on GDP, economic growth inflation of different countries (and the source used to find data in this chapter), go to www.heinemann.co.uk/hotlinks, insert the express code 2223P and click on 'GDP data'. For one of the easiest currency converters to use, click on 'currency converter'.

You still need to be cautious about reading too much into this data. It appears that on average each person living in Luxembourg has an annual income of $66,463.78 or £32,760 but it could be that income in Luxembourg is very unevenly distributed, so knowing the GDP per capita gives only a rough idea how well off the population of a given country is. Of the countries listed above, the USA has the most unequal distribution of income so this averaged-out figure hides significant poverty and hardship, especially for minority groups in the USA.

Another thing to bear in mind before reading too much into this kind of statistic is that it can be a

There is much poverty as well as much wealth in the USA

mistake to equate the standard of living as expressed by this data and the actual quality of life experienced in a given country. Economic data like this does not directly measure the quality of the environment, incidence of crime or other measures of wellbeing. GDP data provides an indication, not hard evidence, about living standards.

ECONOMIC GROWTH

Economic growth is a key macroeconomic indicator which is also based on GDP as it involves looking at percentage changes in GDP over time. In many ways this is a far more useful measure as it clearly indicates whether or not an economy is expanding or contracting. A positive figure indicates that incomes are rising and that an economy is growing while a negative figure shows that an economy is contracting and that incomes are falling. The current top ten in terms of economic growth are shown in the diagram below.

Table 6.3 Economic growth (%)

1	Azerbaijan	34.5
2	Equatorial Guinea	18.6
3	Maldives	18.0
4	Angola	15.0
5	Mauritania	14.1
6	Armenia	13.4
7	Kuwait	12.6
8	Latvia	11.9
9	Trinidad and Tobago	11.9
10	Estonia	11.4

162	UK	2.8

Source: World Bank Data via Nationmaster

DEFINITION

Economic growth: the positive percentage change in GDP over a given period of time – usually a year.

Even more caution is needed in interpreting these figures, which are probably the result of one-off benefits that will not necessarily last. Thus, Azerbaijan, Equatorial Guinea, Angola and Kuwait are all significant oil producers that will have benefited from the recent significant increases in the price of oil. If any of these countries were to maintain these growth rates over a number of years, their economies would be changing at an amazing rate. Output in Azerbaijan would double in value in less than three years. You have to go a long way down this table to find the UK, which, according to this data set, is in one-hundred-and-sixty-second position with a growth rate of 2.8 per cent, 0.1 per cent ahead of Germany. Interestingly, only four countries show negative growth rates. It's not surprising that they include Lebanon and Zimbabwe.

ACTIVITY ····⁝›

Use the links suggested in the previous activity, or similar, to look at growth rates over the last 10 years in different parts of the world. What do your findings tell you about the economic performance of different regions?

Economic growth rates over time are a very significant statistical measure of the performance of any macroeconomy. If even low rates are sustained, their cumulative effect can be considerable. In the years following World War II, the UK economy grew at an annual rate of around 2 per cent over a 25-year period. This doubled per capita incomes and changed many people's lives for the better. Chinese growth rates over the last decade have been between 7 and 11 per cent per annum. Over a 10-year period, GDP has increased by a factor of 2.5. Regular visitors to China are often staggered by the rate of changes they see over short periods of time.

Caution also needs to be exercised before reading too much into economic growth data. Unless inflation effects are stripped out, high rates of economic growth can be illusory, and growth rates are almost always adjusted to take out the effects of inflation. Economists often use the terms *real* or

ECONOMICS IN CONTEXT

CHINESE ECONOMIC GROWTH

The Chinese economy is now the fourth largest in the world when measured by nominal GDP, and is predicted to surpass Germany to assume third place in early 2008. In 2006 its per capita income was approximately US $2,000, which is still relatively low. But it is rising rapidly. Around 70 per cent of China's GDP was in the private sector. The smaller public sector was dominated by about 200 large state enterprises concentrated mostly in utilities, heavy industries, and energy resources.

Since 1978, the Chinese government has been reforming its economy from a Soviet-style centrally planned economy to a more market-oriented economy. Since 1978, these reforms have helped lift millions of its citizens out of poverty, bringing the poverty rate down from 53 per cent in 1981 to 8 per cent in 2001.

The Chinese government has replaced collective farms with family-run units, increased the authority of local officials and plant managers in industry, permitted a wide variety of small-scale enterprise in services and light manufacturing, and opened the economy to increased foreign trade and foreign investment.

The government also has focused on foreign trade as a major vehicle for economic growth. Chinese officials claim the result has been a tenfold increase in GDP since 1978.

The two most important sectors of the economy have traditionally been agriculture and industry, which together employ more than 70 per cent of the labour force and produce more than 60 per cent of GDP. The focus in development has been on the industrial sector and this has lead to an economic/cultural/social gap between the rural and urban – a major division in Chinese society.

ACTIVITY ····>

Research the development of the Chinese economy in greater depth and assess the contribution made to rapid economic growth by:

(a) infrastructure improvements

(b) foreign capital

(c) education

(d) foreign trade.

at constant prices to indicate that growth or other data has been adjusted to account for inflationary effects.

As noted earlier, growth data is derived from looking at changes in GDP, and these statistics may not include the value of goods and services, which are not recorded in official data.

INFLATION

Inflation refers to increases in the price level over time, and as with other data, these are usually expressed on an annual basis. The inflation top ten is given in the Table 6.4.

> ### DEFINITION
>
> **Inflation:** increase in the price level over time, usually a year.

Table 6.4 Countries with the highest inflation (%, annual)

1	Zimbabwe	976.4
2	Iraq	64.8
3	Guinea	29.0
4	Burma	21.4
5	Congo, Democratic Republic of	18.2
6	Afghanistan	16.3
7	Venezuela	15.8
8	Iran	15.8
9	Serbia and Montenegro	15.5
10	Liberia	15.0

142	UK	3.0

Source: CIA World Factbook via Nationmaster

This data shows that there appears to be a close correlation between high rates of inflation, war and civil unrest: 7 of the 10 countries listed above fall into this category, and this data indicates that none of these economies could be described as in good shape.

Lower levels of inflation are also an aim for economists, governments and the general population for a number of reasons:

● From a personal point of view, if prices are rising more quickly than your income is, you will become worse off.

● If prices rise more quickly in the UK compared to other countries, it will be more difficult for UK-based firms to compete with foreign-based competitors.

● Inflation can distort the *price mechanism*, which relies on changes in prices to indicate changes in demand and/or supply.

Relatively low levels of inflation are not considered to be a major worry for governments and economists, but they are always concerned that inflation might start accelerating out of control.

 learning tip Students who have a limited understanding of economics often think that the government sets the rate of inflation. Do not make this mistake. They do not. Governments will try to influence rates of inflation and their efforts might or might not be successful.

MEASURING INFLATION

Inflation is quite difficult to measure. As noted earlier, inflation refers to changes in the price level. This begs the question, prices of what? The short answer is that economists in the UK try to measure the changes in prices of a typical collection of goods and services bought by the typical family. Immediately, you should realise that rates of inflation are different for different people. Prices of different goods change at different rates, and we all purchase different combinations of goods and services. Economists try to get round the problem by measuring changes in the prices of a 'basket' of goods bought by the typical household. All measures of inflation are based on a series of weighted averages which are designed to indicate what a typical or average member of the public will experience in terms of inflation. Periodically, the contents of these 'baskets' are changed to reflect changing patterns of expenditure. Currently, the government uses two measures of inflation.

● The **Consumer Price Index (CPI)** is the official measure of inflation used by the government to shape macroeconomic policy. This basket does not include owner-occupied housing costs. This is to enable international comparisons to be made. It is argued that volatility in house prices distorts the measurement of inflation, especially as most people buy and sell houses very infrequently.

DEFINITION

Consumer Price Index (CPI): an index of retail price changes that excludes the prices of 'owner-occupied housing costs'.

● The **Retail Price Index (RPI).** This is the oldest measure and includes owner-occupied housing costs. As shown in the table below, inflation measured in this way tends to be above the CPI.

> ### DEFINITION
>
> **Retail Price Index (RPI):** an index of price changes that does include expenditure of owner-occupied housing costs.

Changes in inflation are shown in Figure 6.1, which shows an upward trend in inflation for much of 2006, but after reaching a peak in February 2007, prices grew less rapidly.

ACTIVITY ⋯⋯

Use the UK Office of National Statistics website to find out three examples of goods and services which have been added to or excluded from the 'typical basket of goods'. Explain why these decisions were made. (You can go to www.heinemann.co.uk/hotlinks, insert the express code 2223P and click on 'Office of National Statistics'.)

INDEX NUMBERS

Statisticians use **index numbers** to make it easier to make year-on-year comparisons. Knowing that a given basket of goods cost £750 one month and £785 a year later indicates that prices have gone up, but it is not immediately obvious whether or not this change is significant or not. You would need to work out the percentage change, which comes out at 4.7. Data such as this are easier to interpret if presented as index numbers. A base year, say 2002, is chosen

> ### DEFINITION
>
> **Index numbers:** a means by which the percentage change year on year can easily be understood as numbers are expressed in terms of a base year value of 100.

to which the value of 100 is given. If prices have risen in 2003 by 4 per cent, the index given to that year is 104. If they fall the next year by 2 per cent, the index would fall to 102.

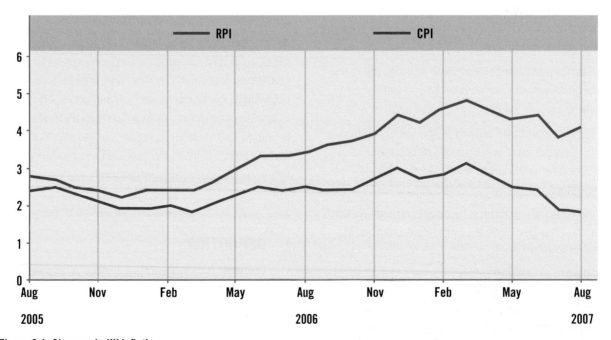

Figure 6.1 Changes in UK inflation

You should by now get the picture that all statistics are at best approximations of actual phenomena. Don't get too cynical and take up the view that 'statistics can prove anything', but always remember that, as good as they are, statistics won't necessarily tell the whole story.

UNEMPLOYMENT

Unemployment is a key measure of economic performance, as it is something that can directly affect everyone in society. Not having a job usually means having to accept a lower standard of living. Unemployment is not only about having less because it also often affects people's self-esteem and sense of worth. For those lucky enough to be in work, rising unemployment is usually associated with

High levels of unemployment are bad for everyone in a society

lower levels of economic activity, which can mean smaller pay packets and less overtime. Many political commentators believe that ultimately elections are won and lost in voters' pockets. In other words, if electors are reasonably optimistic about their employment prospects, they will vote in the party in power. If they are insecure, then the opposition stands a better chance of winning.

> ### DEFINITION
>
> **Unemployment:** the numbers or proportion of the workforce who are not working in paid employment but would like to do so.

As with the other measures of economic performance, defining unemployment is not quite as straightforward as it first might appear. Common sense tells us that those people looking for work who can't find work should be defined as unemployed. Should this be expanded to include those who are not working and are *not* looking for work? Do parents who stay at home work? What about students? Defining who is actually unemployed is not easy. Currently, the UK government uses two measures of unemployment:

● **Claimant count,** which is limited to those seeking work who are eligible for benefit. This measure clearly excludes those seeking work who do not qualify for benefits (for example, those leaving school and college, and women returning to work). It is calculated by looking at the number of people actually on benefit, and as such it tends to underestimate the number of people who would consider that they are unemployed.

> ### DEFINITION
>
> **Claimant count:** a measure of unemployment using records of those formally registered as entitled to unemployment benefit.

● **The International Labour Organisation (ILO)**. This unemployment measure is wider, as it is based on surveys that include those who have been seeking work in the last four weeks but who are not necessarily eligible for welfare benefits. This definition, used in other countries, enables comparisons to be made between the UK and other European countries.

Both measures are usually expressed as a percentage of the whole available workforce and in absolute terms. In late 2007, the UK claimant count stood at 852,900 whereas the ILO measure showed that 1.65 million were unemployed.

The government prefers to focus on employment rather than unemployment figures and currently boasts that there are now more people in work (29.1 million) than at any time since comparable records began in 1971. This statistic tends to indicate that the UK economy is performing well. However, it masks the fact that some of these employed people are doing part-time and/or temporary jobs, while others may not be fully using their skills and qualifications.

ECONOMICS IN CONTEXT

THE GROWTH OF A GENERATION OF 'NEETS'

The government is becoming increasingly concerned about a growing army of young people in Britain being left behind. That's the conclusion of a recent report by the Prince's Trust, which exposed the crisis of 'neets' – young people aged 16 to 24 not in education, employment or training.

Relatively low unemployment masks almost 1.3 million 'neets', a lost generation that has grown by 15 per cent since 1997. The failure to tap their potential undermines social cohesion, damages the economy, and puts a growing strain on the exchequer. The report estimates the cost at £3.65 billion a year.

Recent estimates indicate that 45,000 16-year-olds leave school each year functionally illiterate and/or innumerate. This forgotten generation can only look forward to a future of unemployment, as demand for unskilled labour plummets.

ACTIVITY ⋯⋗

Find out more why this group of young people exists. Talk to other students, parents, carers and teachers and assess the economic impact of the growth in numbers of 'neets'. Will the raising of the school leaving age to 18 solve this problem?

THE BALANCE OF PAYMENTS

The balance of payments is an account which is meant to record all flows of money in and out of a given economy. As you will learn in Chapter 8, it is divided into different sections, but the part which is most commonly used as a macroeconomic indicator is called the **balance of payments on current account.** This is worked out on a monthly basis by adding up the total value of goods and services that are exported and setting it against the value of all **imports** of goods and services. This leaves a balance. A positive balance indicates that more has been spent on **exports** from the UK than has been spent on imports and this is called a **current account surplus**, whereas a negative balance is called a **current**

DEFINITIONS

Balance of payments on current account: a record of the value of exports of goods and services set against the value of imported goods and services.

Imports: goods and services that come into a country or economy.

Exports: goods and services sold to people living outside a country or economy.

Current account surplus: in the balance of payments, when the value of goods and services exported from a country exceeds the value of imports.

account deficit and it indicates the reverse. The most recent balance of payment accounts are shown in Figure 6.2.

These statistics show that we owe people in other countries more than they owe us. By the end of 2006, this country was £14 billion in the red. It is also useful to note that the data was revised in September 2006 and that the balance of payments is not quite as bad as it was previously thought to be.

On the surface, it would seem that it is more desirable for the balance of payments on current account to be in surplus rather than deficit. This would appear to indicate that the UK plc is being more successful in terms of world trade than many of its competitors. A deficit, on the other hand, may well indicate that we are choosing to buy more goods and services made in other countries or that those in other countries are spending less on goods and services we provide, or a combination of the two.

Economics, being economics, means that things are not necessarily what they seem to be. First, there is nothing to guarantee that the balance of payments on current account will actually balance. There are millions of buying decisions in this country and abroad, most of which are taken independently of each other: there is no way that the balance of payments will automatically balance. Therefore, at any one time a deficit or surplus is almost inevitable. However, there could be problems if either surpluses or deficits persist in the long run.

If the UK is in long-term surplus it follows that other countries are in long-term deficit and will be in debt to us. This can cause them long-term problems which may result in falling exports. Long-term deficits can also be a problem because they mean that this country is building up debts to other countries. Economists do not make speedy judgements about the performance of an economy on the basis of a superficial examination of the balance of payments account. They try to analyse why a country is in deficit or surplus in order to understand the underlying reasons.

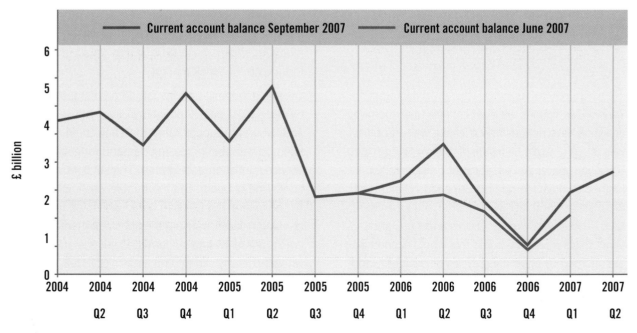

Figure 6.2 Current account balances

Economic cycles

Economists have long been aware that the performance of most macroeconomies tends to fluctuate in a cyclical pattern over time. These are called business or **economic cycles**. Over a long period of time, it appears that macroeconomic indicators of GDP, growth, inflation, unemployment and the balance of payments go through peaks and troughs, and there appears to be a relationship between these indicators as they change over time.

DEFINITION

Economic cycles: fluctuations in economic activity over time.

These observations are not confined to economists, as we all have notions about feeling well off or less well off. You might be aware of the 'swinging sixties' – ask your parents – as a time of prosperity. You might also have learned about periods of economic depression when jobs were scarce and times were hard. These were times of boom and bust, and economists have long noted that whole economies are affected by alternating cycles of prosperity and depression. This is illustrated in a very simplified way in Figure 6.3 below, which shows an imaginary economy in which time is measured on the horizontal axis and changes in GDP on the vertical axis.

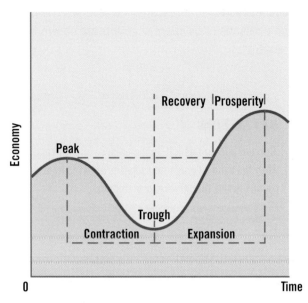

Figure 6.3 The economic cycle

In the period of boom, such as the 1920s in the USA, GDP was rising, unemployment was falling; inflation was accelerating, and imports growing, as domestic suppliers could not keep up with demand. In boom periods consumer confidence is likely to increase, and when people feel optimistic about the future, borrowing is likely to rise, leading to even more demand for goods and services. If economies are expanding in this way, business profits will rise and investment in new plant and machinery is also likely to increase. Boom times are often associated with rising stock market prices, and in the later 1920s many Americans believed that they could make a fortune on the stock market.

Overall, economic activity carried on increasing, but by early 1929 the US economy began to overheat and, when producers found that they could not keep up with the increasing demand for goods and services, inflation accelerated. The stock market continued to boom. But the bubble was finally burst by the failure of a German bank, which led to other banking failures, causing the US stock market to crash. Some investors committed suicide and the whole economy slid into recession. GDP fell, people become poorer, jobs were lost, prices fell (deflation), imports probably fell and the economic growth became negative. It took 10 years and another world war before the USA returned to prosperity.

Boom and bust in the 1920s and 1930s affected most of the world and had a big influence on economists and governments. The severe depression in Germany is seen as providing the conditions for Adolf Hitler's rise to power, and, therefore, as a contributory factor to World War II. As a consequence, governments try to intervene in order to smooth out economic activity. Much of what you are about to study in macroeconomics is designed to give you a better understanding of different approaches to the management of economic activity.

ECONOMIC CYCLES IN THE UK ECONOMY

The extremes seen in the 1920s and 1930s have not been repeated in the UK, although economic performance has fluctuated over time. Figure 6.4 shows how GDP in this country has changed over time. Two things should be apparent. First, over time, GDP has followed an upward trend. Second, there are fluctuations over time in national income. In the real world these fluctuations are the actual economic cycle.

So, over a long period, UK GDP has been rising – although if you look closely at the data, GDP fell in 1952, 1975, 1981 and 1991 – but the overall trend is upward.

Fluctuations in the economic cycle are easier to see if economic growth is used as a macroeconomic

indicator. It is like putting the performance of the economy under a microscope. Most of the time economic growth is positive, but there are times when growth is greater than others. This is illustrated in Figure 6.5, in which rates of growth are plotted on the vertical axis and time on the horizontal. This shows that in more recent years there have been fluctuations in economic growth, but at all times

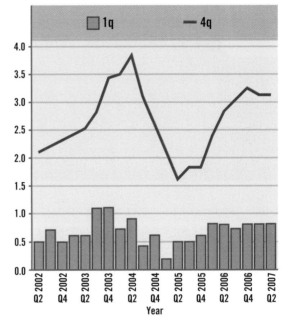

Figure 6.5 UK economic growth

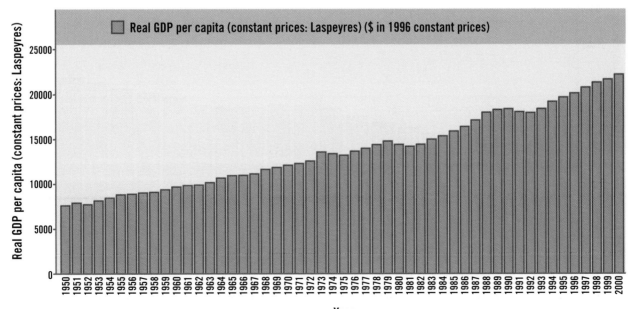

Figure 6.4 UK GDP 1950–2000

in the last five years economic growth has been positive. There have not been periods of 'boom and bust', but rather variations in the rate of growth in the economy. These variations are around an average rate of growth of around 2.5 per cent over the last five years, peaking in the summer of 2004 at around 3.7 per cent and dropping to 1.6 per cent a year later.

> **learning tip**
>
> Understanding relative rates of growth for the first time can be confusing but you have to get your head round it – remember that if you read that in the first quarter of 2006 economic growth stood at 2.6 per cent whereas in the second quarter it fell to 2.1 per cent, that this does not mean that growth rates have fallen; rather it means that the rate of growth has fallen.

This data can be looked at over a longer period of time, as shown in Figure 6.6, which shows data from 1979 to 2000.

This shows an upward trend. Usually, economists measure the state of the economic cycle in relation to what they call the **trend rate of growth**, that is, the

annual change in national income. In this case the trend rate is around 2.5 per cent, which means that the economy is becoming better off at an average rate of 2.5 per cent. Periods in which the growth rate exceeds this can be classified as having a **positive output gap** and those periods in which the growth rate is lower as having a **negative output gap**.

> **DEFINITIONS**
>
> **Trend rate of growth:** the averaged-out rate of growth over a period of time.
>
> **Positive output gap:** occurs when actual economic growth is above the trend rate.
>
> **Negative output gap:** occurs when actual economic growth is below the trend rate.

If the actual rate of growth of the economy is above this trend of 2.5 per cent, the threat of increasing rates of inflation is greater, as there is less spare productive capacity in the economy. The converse is

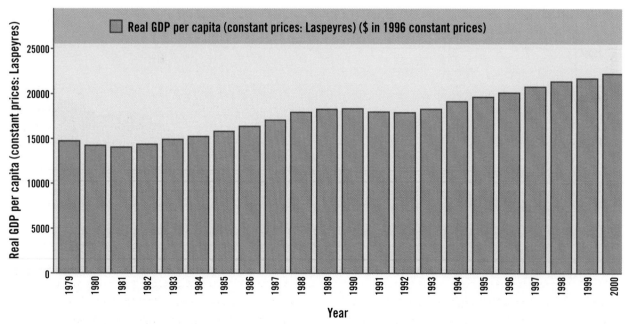

Figure 6.6 UK GDP per capita 1979–2000

also likely, that if actual rates are below trend, then it is likely that rates of inflation will be lower, as there is spare productive capacity in the economy. Similarly, there is less potential for economic growth when the actual data is above trend and greater potential when below trend.

This data shows that the last **recessions** occurred between 1979 and 1981 and between 1990 and 1992, and that since then the economy has been growing steadily. There is considerable debate between economists as to whether or not these trends will continue. Some argue that government management of the economy has become more sophisticated and that we will not lurch from boom to bust. Others argue that globalisation is having a big positive effect on the UK economy. There are no definitive answers, but when you have completed this unit you should be in a better position to analyse what might be happening to the economy, and to evaluate the likely effects of different economic policies. Good analysis and evaluation are the prerequisites for a top grade in AS Economics.

ACTIVITY ····❖

Research the possible causes of either the 79–81 or the 90–92 recessions. Explain why they occurred and assess whether they are likely to be repeated.

DEFINITION

Recession: technically, when economic growth in the economy is negative for more than two or more successive quarters (for six months or more).

WHAT DETERMINES ECONOMIC CYCLES?

There is no real consensus between economists as to what actually determines economic cycles. Some have argued that they are random. Marxists believe

that they are an inevitable by-product of capitalism. Others blame governments for over-stimulating and over-correcting the economy. What we do know is what you have probably already worked out for yourselves: one good thing can lead to another, in that if an economy is growing, and its population are feeling better off, they will spend more, producers will produce more, investment will increase creating a virtuous cycle of economic expansion. This process is called an **upward multiplier** and is explained more fully on pages 132–3.

In a recession, the converse is likely to happen, consumers will feel worse off, they will spend less, less will be produced, investment will fall and unemployment will rise. This is called a **downward multiplier**.

DEFINITIONS

Upward multiplier: the mechanism by which growth in an economy stimulates further growth in that economy.

Downward multiplier: the mechanism by which negative growth, or contraction, in the economy stimulates further decline.

Further study of macroeconomics will improve your understanding of these processes and help you judge the strength and usefulness of different arguments. One thing that there is broad agreement about is that economies might be subjected to shocks which will trigger booms or slumps.

Shocks

Changes in the economic cycle might be triggered by shocks that can trigger a chain reaction in macroeconomic variables. The most dramatic external shocks are those associated with extremes in weather or war. Steady economic growth in an economy might be brought to a virtual standstill by

Expenditure on troops and equipment in Iraq directly affects the UK economy

hurricane, earthquake or flood. Thus, the conflict in Iraq will have direct effects on UK economy. The UK government is spending an estimated £7 billion on the war, which could represent a positive shock to the economy if it represents additional demand for goods and services produced in the UK. This represents a **demand-side shock**. This is not the only shock to stem from the war. Conflict in the region has limited the supply of crude oil, which could lead to higher energy prices which in turn could be classified as a **supply-side shock** as they may lead to increases in the costs of production for many UK businesses and have an adverse effect on the UK economy. It is possible that an external event such as this could push an economy into recession.

ACTIVITY ····⫶

Analyse the effects of a bird flu epidemic on the UK economy.

ACTIVITY ····⫶

Use the Internet to show how far it is possible to use the concept of shock to explain the variations in the economic cycle in Russia between 1996 and 2003 shown in Figure 6.7.

DEFINITIONS

Demand-side shocks: those external events which are likely to affect the demand for goods and services from a given economy.

Supply-side shocks: those which will be first felt on the costs of supplying goods within a given economy.

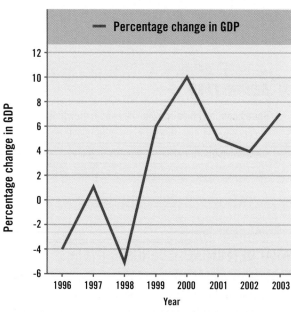

Figure 6.7 Variations in the economic cycle in Russia

ACTIVITY ····﹖

Update the data below to assess the relative performance of the UK and US economies.

USA	
GDP	$13.13 trillion (2006 est.)
GDP growth	3.2% (2006 est.)
GDP per capita	$44,000 (est.)
GDP by sector	agriculture (0.9%), industry (20.4%), services (78.6%)
Inflation (CPI)	2.5% (2006 est.)
Population below poverty line	12% (2006 est.)
Labour force	151.4 million (includes unemployed) (2006)
Unemployment	4.4% (2007)
Trade	
Exports	$1.024 trillion (2006 est.)
Export goods	agricultural products (soybeans, fruit, corn) 9.2%, industrial supplies (organic chemicals) 26.8%, capital goods (transistors, aircraft, motor vehicle parts, computers, telecommunications equipment) 49%, consumer goods (automobiles, medicines) 15% (2003)
Main export partners	Canada 23%, Mexico 14%, Japan 6%, Mainland China 6%, UK 3.5%
Imports	$1.869 trillion (2006 est.)
Import goods	agricultural products 4.9%, industrial supplies 32.9% (crude oil 8.2%), capital goods 30.4% (computers, telecommunications equipment, motor vehicle parts, office machines, electric power machinery), consumer goods 31.8% (automobiles, clothing, medicines, furniture, toys) (2003)
Main import partners	Canada 17%, China 16%, Mexico 11%, Japan 8%, Germany 5%

UK	
GDP (PPP) ranking (2006)	6th
GDP (PPP) per capita ranking (2006)	11th
GDP (2006)	$2.1 trillion
GDP growth (2006)	2.75%
GDP per capita (2006)	$35,000
GDP by sector (2006)	agriculture (1%), industry (26%), services (73%)
Inflation (CPI) (2006)	2.3% (2006)
Poverty rate (2002)	17%

Labour force (2006)	31 million
Labour force by occupation (2006)	services (81%), industry (18%), agriculture (1%)
Unemployment rate (2007)	5.4%
Main industries	machine tools, industrial equipment, scientific equipment, shipbuilding, aircrafts, motor vehicles and parts, electronic machinery, computers, processed metals, chemical products, coal mining, oil production, paper, food processing, textiles, clothing, and other consumer goods
Trade	
Exports (2006)	$470 billion
Main partners (2004)	USA 15%, Germany 11%, France 10%, Ireland 7%, Netherlands 6%, Belgium 6%, Spain 5%, Italy 4%
Imports (2006)	$600 billion
Main partners (2004)	Germany 14%, USA 9%, France 8%, Netherlands 7%, Belgium 6%, Italy 5%, China 4%, Ireland 4%

ACTIVITY ⋯⋗

Choose a European country and collect data on its performance over the last 20 years. Analyse the data you collect and write a brief report assessing economic performance, identifying key internal and external shocks and predicting future trends. If you are able to, compare your findings with others in your class.

learning tip

You should always know the current indicators of economic growth, unemployment, inflation and the balance of payments on current account. For the UK government's official site, you can go to www.heinemann.co.uk/hotlinks, insert the express code 2223P and click on 'UK economic indicators'.)

7 How the macroeconomy works

On completion of this chapter, you should be able to:

- understand how the circular flow model can be used to illustrate how the macroeconomy works
- use aggregate demand and aggregate supply analysis to explain macroeconomic problems and issues
- identify the determinants of aggregate demand
- understand the significance of the interaction between aggregate demand and aggregate supply in influencing the level of economic activity
- understand the multiplier process
- define and explain short-run aggregate supply
- discuss the determinants of long-run aggregate supply
- Explore how changes in aggregate demand and supply will affect national income, output, employment, economic growth and inflation.

Introduction

This chapter is devoted to increasing your understanding of how the macroeconomy works. You will be introduced to two ways of modelling the economy:

- the **circular flow model**, and
- **aggregate demand** and **aggregate supply**.

Both models can be used to predict how national income, output, employment, inflation and economic growth respond to changes in a range of different variables, such as consumption, investment and exports.

These models are both relatively simple to understand but they are also powerful. They provide a graphic way of understanding the significance of different economic forces that shape our lives. Never forget, however, that they are models, and as such they present a simplified way of looking at and

understanding an extremely complex set of inter-relationships.

There is a direct link between the content of this chapter and the description of economic cycles contained in the previous one. In this chapter you should develop a much better understanding of what causes booms and slumps, and this will provide you with an introduction to looking at the success, or otherwise, of government policies to promote economic growth and avoid the damaging effects of high rates of inflation.

The circular flow of income

Your analysis of economic cycles will be improved when you have developed an understanding of the circular flow of income. This is a simplified model of economic activity within the economy. The following sections show:

- how this model is constructed

- how it might be used to explain economic cycles, and macroeconomic equilibrium

- possible limitations of it.

BUILDING THE CIRCULAR FLOW MODEL

All models consist of a number of building blocks and the circular flow starts by suggesting that it is reasonable to divide the economy into two areas of activity. First, it helps to think about the four factors of production, identified in Chapter 1 – land, labour, enterprise and capital – in the sense that they are all owned by individuals and groups of individuals within a given economy. Landlords own land, companies and others own capital, those who take risks and make decisions own entrepreneurial skills and we all own our own labour. For the purposes of this model,

ECONOMICS IN CONTEXT

WALL STREET CRASH

The Circular Flow of Income features a simple yet very powerful model of the economy developed by John Maynard Keynes in the 1930s. At the time, UK and many other economies were in deep recession. The prevailing economic wisdom was that a prudent government should behave in much the same way as a prudent household. It should also strive to balance its budget. In a recession, government revenue from taxation will fall, so it followed that governments should also cut their expenditure to keep budgets balanced. As shown in the previous chapter, the Wall Street Crash of 1929 triggered worldwide economic depression. Many businesses in the UK went bust and unemployment in 1932 peaked when one in five of the workforce were out of work. Government revenue from taxes declined and many argued that the government should also cut its spending to match its income.

This conventional wisdom was turned on its head by Keynes, who argued that the government should actually increase spending to help cure the recession. Keynes, an academic and an adviser to the UK government, argued against this in his *General Theory of Employment, Interest and Money*, published in 1936. President Roosevelt of the USA reluctantly agreed over a period of time to follow Keynes's advice to use government spending to cure the depression.

Keynes died in 1946 but his economic ideas still have a major influence on economic policies today. Ideas and concepts such as the circular flow, multiplier and output gaps, all discussed in the text, are largely underpinned by Keynesian theory.

all are grouped together under the generic term **households.** Second, all those responsible for actually producing goods and services are lumped together as firms. This is illustrated in Figure 7.1.

> ### DEFINITION
>
> **Households:** collective term for the owners of factors of production.

In this model, firms and households interact with each other. If firms wish to produce goods and services, they will have to purchase factors of production from households. This can be represented by the arrow *A* depicting flows of land, labour, capital and enterprise moving from households to firms.

Households don't freely give up what they own. Land, labour, capital and enterprise have to be paid for by the firms demanding them. This flow of payments can be added to Figure 7.1 and *B* represents different types of income to households: rent, wages/salaries, interest and profits.

In the simplest form of this model, it is assumed that households spend all they earn. They use all their income to buy consumer goods and services. Together these are called **consumption**. This flow *C* is

directly linked to firms as they produce all goods and services in an economy.

> ### DEFINITION
>
> **Consumption:** current spending on goods and services.

Finally, it is assumed that firms produce goods and services in response to demands from consumers and this reaction to consumption can be represented by flow *D* – output from firms to households.

THE CIRCULAR FLOW AND ECONOMIC CYCLES

The circular flow model can now be used to show different stages in the economic cycle. Suppose for some reason households demand more goods and services than firms plan to produce. We would expect them to respond by increasing production. In order to do so they will have to pay out more in rent, interest, wages/salaries and profits. Households will now receive an increase in their income and the economy will grow as in the boom phase of the economic cycle.

On the other hand, if customers don't purchase all the goods and services produced by firms, then output, employment and incomes will fall as in the recession phase of the economic cycle. Employment levels will also be linked to this cycle. As has been noted, rising levels of output will normally be associated with increases in the demand from firms for factors of production. Labour is one of these factors and it is easy to understand that if output in an economy is increasing so will the demand for labour. Any increase in the demand for labour should lead to an increase in the numbers employed, which is also likely to result in a fall in unemployment and vice versa.

This model of the circular flow of income will be in equilibrium when planned consumption equals planned output, a situation shown in Figure 7.1 when the consumption flow going into firms is equal to the production flow coming out of firms.

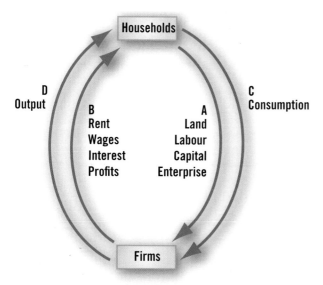

Figure 7.1 Circular flow of income in a simplified economy

SAVINGS AND INVESTMENT

The circular flow model presents a simplified model of the actual economy. Only in subsistence economies is everything that is earned in terms of income spent immediately on goods and services. Most of us at some time in our lives manage to save money. We all are faced with a simple choice between spending and saving. If our income is unchanged and we choose to save more, we have to reduce the amount we spend on the consumption of goods and services. The opposite is also true.

Savings represent a **withdrawal** or **leakage** from the circular flow. In Figure 7.2 they are represented by an arrow coming away from households. **Investment** occurs when firms expand their productive capacity by replacing worn-out machinery and/or increasing the scale of their production. This represents an **addition** or **injection** to the circular flow. An increase in investment represents an increase in demand for those firms producing investment goods or services, for example, machines to produce machines, or improved software to enable speedier processing of information.

An increase in savings, other things being equal, will depress income, output and employment, whereas an increase in investment will cause these macroeconomic indicators to increase. The reverse is also true.

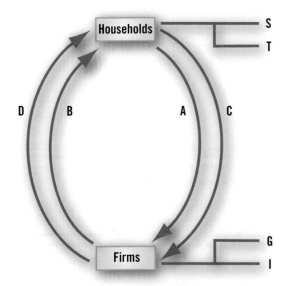

DEFINITIONS

Savings: proportion of income not spent on consumption, imports or taken in taxation.

Withdrawal: income not passed on in the form of consumption in the *circular flow*; sometimes called **leakage**.

Investment: spending by firms to increase productive capacity.

Injection: an addition to the revenue of a firm that does not normally arise from the expenditure of households; also known as an **addition**.

GOVERNMENT SPENDING AND TAXATION

An additional 'player' or economic agent can be factored into the circular flow model: the government. Actions of all governments have a significant effect on economic activity. Thus, all governments levy taxes. In the model this is presented by an outflow from households. The act of *taxation* is treated as a withdrawal and, as should be clear from Figure 7.3,

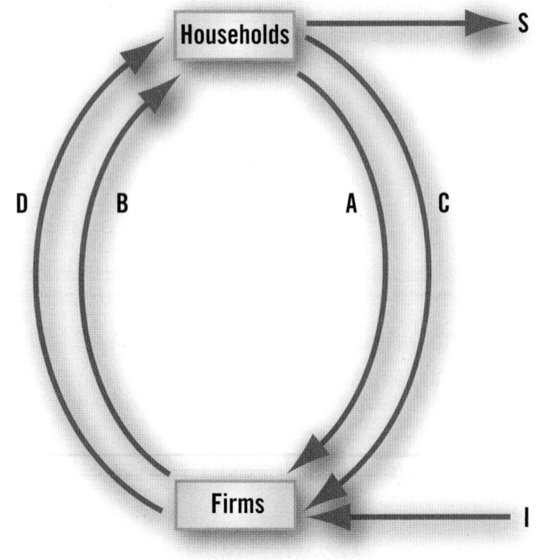

Figure 7.2 Circular flow including savings and investment

Figure 7.3 Circular flow including government spending and taxation

will result in falling levels of consumption, output and incomes, and rising unemployment.

Governments don't usually hide all their taxation revenues away, they also spend. Government spending, whether it is on making war or building hospitals, is treated as an injection or addition to the circular flow. Other things being equal, an increase in government spending will lead to expansion in the economy and growth in incomes and output levels.

ACTIVITY ⋯⋙

Use the circular flow model to illustrate and explain why Keynes urged governments to spend more to reduce unemployment in the 1930s.

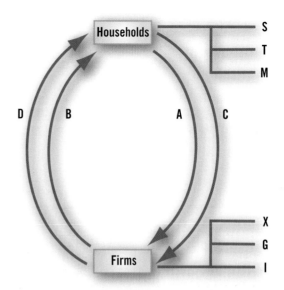

Figure 7.4 Circular flow including imports and exports

IMPORTS AND EXPORTS

The circular flow model outlined so far represents a **closed economy** – one which does not trade with other economies. The model can be further developed to account for the impact of imports and exports. This is called an **open economy.** If we choose to spend income on a good or a service which is produced in another economy, some, perhaps all, of that element of our expenditure will flow out of our economy into another. Imports are a withdrawal from the circular flow in the same way that savings and government taxation are and they can be added to the diagram as shown in Figure 7.4.

If on the other hand, those living in other economies decide to purchase or consume UK-made goods or services then, other things being equal, our economy will expand. *Exports* are, therefore, an addition or injection to the circular flow as illustrated above. The impact of imports and exports can also be added to the equation for the equilibrium of the circular flow.

THE CIRCULAR FLOW AND MACROECONOMIC EQUILIBRIUM

The circular flow model can be used to explain **macroeconomic equilibrium.** The model has been expanded to include savings, taxation and spending on imports. These are collectively known as withdrawals. Similarly, government spending, investment and exports represent injections. The macroeconomy will be in equilibrium when these two flows are equal. This can be represented by the equation

$$S + T + M = I + X + G \text{ (where S = savings,}$$
T = taxation, M =imports, I = Investment, X = exports, and G = government expenditure)

This is the same as saying that the macroeconomic equilibrium requires that the total value of

DEFINITIONS

Closed economy: a *circular flow* model that does not include the effects of foreign trade, that is, imports and exports.

Open economy: a *circular flow* model that does include the effects of foreign trade (imports and exports).

DEFINITION

Macroeconomic equilibrium: a state when national income is neither rising nor falling.

withdrawals is equal to the total value of injections, or:

W = J (where W stands for withdrawals and J for injections)

ACTIVITY ····⋗

How and why might employment levels in the UK be affected by:

(a) a decrease in income tax

(b) a fall in business confidence

(c) the widespread outbreak of foot and mouth disease in the UK?

LIMITATIONS OF THE CIRCULAR FLOW MODEL

The circular flow model illustrates a contribution by J.M. Keynes to our understanding of how the government might use its spending and taxation policy to influence the macroeconomy, in particular, in the context of the 1930s, to solve unemployment. For a long period both right- and left-wing governments in all the industrialised countries adopted Keynesian demand management policies. The logic was simple: if macroeconomic indicators implied that the economy was heading for recession, governments could increase their spending or cut taxes. This, it was argued, would lead to increased injections, rising incomes, rising consumption, lower unemployment and higher levels of prosperity. What would there be to stop the economy from expanding and expanding?

Remember what economics is meant to be all about – unlimited wants and finite resources. If consumption continues to carry on rising, firms will find it more and more difficult to purchase the factors

of production required to expand production. Some will offer higher wages, rents and rates of interest and greater shares of profits to attract resources. At some stage, the process of growth and expansion will break down and this will probably be associated with rising rates of inflation. Resources will be depleted, some firms will go out of business and the whole process described earlier will go into reverse, associated with falling incomes, production, consumption and output, and rising unemployment – the slippery slope of recession.

Adopting Keynesian demand management policies meant stimulating the economy when depression threatened and slowing it down when it began to overheat. But Keynesian approaches were really questioned in the 1970s, when high rates of unemployment were associated with high levels of inflation – largely caused by a four-fold increase in the price of crude oil.

> **learning tip**
>
> The circular flow model is relatively easy to understand and it presents a simplified illustration of what is actually going on within an economy. It should help you to understand how economic decisions by different agents are linked. The model can be used to analyse the effects on employment, output, income and expenditure of changes in key variables such as government spending, saving and investment. It has also provided governments with a better understanding of how they might try to reduce the harmful effects of unemployment and avoid shortages and higher price levels associated with periods of boom. However, the model presents a simplified picture of how an economy works, and governments using it as the basis for economic policy have not always been successful.

Aggregate demand and aggregate supply

Models of aggregate demand and aggregate supply provide another way that economists explain macroeconomic problems such as inflation, unemployment and economic growth. The sections that follow explain the determinants of both aggregate demand and aggregate supply. These are then put together to illustrate macroeconomic equilibrium and enable you to predict what might happen if key variables change.

THE DETERMINANTS OF AGGREGATE DEMAND

Aggregate demand refers to the total demand for goods and services in an economy. In Figure 7.5 the focus is put on a section of the circular diagram on page 127.

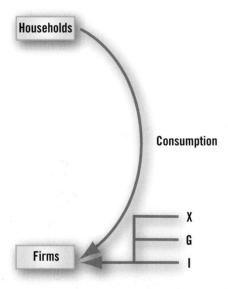

Figure 7.5 Circular flow and aggregate demand

The flows of consumption, investment and government spending represent three elements of the total demand for goods and services in a closed economy. This total demand is referred to as *aggregate demand* and can be expressed as

aggregate demand = C + I + G

This equation can be modified to apply to an open economy by taking account of exports and imports of goods and services. Thus:

aggregate demand = C + I + G + (X–M)

Aggregate demand can be illustrated graphically. In Figure 7.6, the level of national income is measured on the horizontal axis and the price level on the vertical. Consumption, investment, government spending, exports and imports are all likely to increase if the price level falls and they are all likely to decrease

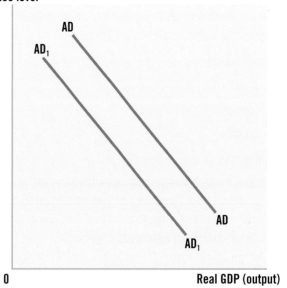

Price level

Figure 7.6 Aggregate demand diagram

if the price level rises. Aggregate demand can, therefore, be drawn as a schedule falling from left to right. If any of its components rises, other things being equal the aggregate demand schedule will shift to the right; if any fall then the reverse will happen.

> **learning tip** When you take your Unit 2 exam, there is a very good chance that you will be asked questions which require you to use some version of the aggregate demand and aggregate supply diagram. Make sure you can reproduce this accurately. You would be surprised at how many students get muddled up between this diagram and the demand and supply diagrams used in microeconomics.

ACTIVITY ⋯⋯⋮

Practise your understanding of aggregate demand by showing the effects of the following:

(a) businesses reduce their planned levels of investment

(b) government abolishes inheritance tax

(c) the US economy goes into recession

(d) the Monetary Policy Committee of the Bank of England cuts interest rates.

THE DETERMINANTS OF AGGREGATE DEMAND

The previous section illustrated how aggregate demand is made up of five components:

- consumption
- government spending
- investment
- exports
- imports.

If any of these change, aggregate demand will shift up or down. It is, therefore, important for you to have an understanding of the factors that influence each of the determinants of aggregate demand.

CONSUMPTION

The biggest single influence on aggregate demand is what we currently spend on goods and services. This is called *consumption* and it is likely to change in response to changes in:

- income
- consumer confidence
- cost and availability of credit
- savings.

Income

The most important factor affecting consumption is *income*. If our incomes increase, most of us will go out and spend more. When we are hard up, we are likely to spend less. Economists are particularly interested in how we respond to changes in our income. This is measured by the **marginal propensity to consume (MPC)** which is the percentage of any change in income that is spent on consumption of goods and services. Economists assume that people on low incomes have higher MPCs that those on high incomes.

> ### DEFINITION
>
> **Marginal propensity to consume (MPC):** the percentage of any change in income that is spent on the consumption of goods and services.

Consumer confidence

The level of income is not the only factor to influence consumption, as our expectations and perceived level of happiness have been shown to affect consumer spending. Economists use the short-hand term **consumer confidence** to describe this influence, but it is often hard to identify the factors which increase or decrease this 'feel-good' factor.

> ### DEFINITION
>
> **Consumer confidence:** consumers' perceptions of their future well-being.

ECONOMICS IN CONTEXT

HAS THE 'WORLD CUP' EFFECT SAVED THE HIGH STREET AFTER ALL?

It certainly seems as though it has made a difference, at least. Comet owner Kesa Electricals saw sales jump 11.3 per cent in its first half. Like-for-like sales – that is, excluding new or refurbished stores – at Comet rose 8.6 per cent in the six months to July 18th. Sales were boosted mainly by strong demand for flat-screen televisions in the run-up to the football tournament.

Meanwhile, official statistics showed that retail sales rose for the fifth month in a row between May and June. For the three months from April to June sales were 2.1 per cent ahead of the previous quarter. That's the highest quarterly growth rate since February 2004.

Cost and availability of credit

The cost and availability of credit also have a large effect on consumption, especially on more expensive elements of spending such as housing and cars. Most home buyers in the UK take advantage of mortgages – large loans which are repaid over a long period of time.

Small changes in interest rates can have a large effect on mortgage repayments, and this can have a big impact on spending on other goods and services. Similarly, the lending policies of banks and building societies change. Clearly, if it is relatively easier to borrow money, consumption levels are likely to be higher than in those times when it is harder.

Savings

Savings, as we have seen, are the flip side of consumption. If, other things being equal, we decide to save more, we have less to spend. If our incomes have not changed and we choose to save less, consumption will increase.

The **savings ratio** measures the proportion of income that is saved. Savings are primarily related to income. Those on low incomes are likely to save a smaller proportion of their income than those on higher incomes. They will also be affected by changes in the rate of interest. An increase in interest rates is likely to lead to an increase in savings and vice versa. Consumer confidence will also affect savings.

> **DEFINITION**
>
> **Savings ratio:** the proportion of income that is saved.

ECONOMICS IN CONTEXT

PRICED OUT?

The number of first-time home buyers fell to a 25-year low in 2005, research has revealed.

Halifax, Britain's biggest mortgage lender, said an estimated 320,000 people took their first step on to the property ladder last year, 10 per cent fewer than in 2004 and 40 per cent down on 2002.

It said numbers fell to their lowest level since 1980, although there were signs of a slight pick-up during the second half of the year.

One problem for first-time buyers is the massive deposit required to buy property. The average house buyer must save £23,967 – more than double the £9,894 they needed five years ago.

A typical first-timer takes five years to save this sum, up from the three years it took to build a deposit in 2000. People are now 33 years old on average when they buy their first home.

Soaring house prices in recent years have left first-time buyers priced out of the market in many UK regions.

Source: financial news website thisismoney.co.uk

learning tip
Be precise when you use the terms savings and investment. The first refers to setting aside income that would otherwise be spent. This could involve putting money in a coffee jar, safe, building society or pension fund. In general usage these last two might be referred to as investments. Economists also use the word investment to describe spending by firms that increases their productive capacity.

GOVERNMENT SPENDING

You may think that when government revenues are high, government spending is likely to be high and vice versa, but influences on the level of government spending are more complex and also affected by different political perspectives. Although some elements of government spending on essential services such as the police, education and armed forces are relatively stable and not usually controversial, others such as welfare payments, transport subsidies and the NHS generate considerable debate. Government spending depends, therefore, on political priorities. Those adopting Keynesian approaches to the management of the economy are likely to consider spending more in times of recession and less in boom times, to try to keep the economic cycle on a more even keel. Those who subscribe to more right-wing approaches may be anxious to cut levels of spending to reduce the impact of government on people's lives.

INVESTMENT

Investment is a form of specialised spending by firms and is primarily influenced by expected levels of national output. Firms are more likely to invest if business is expected to grow, hence there will be a positive relationship between investment and national income. Firms will also be sensitive to changes in the cost and availability of credit.

Increases in investment can be particularly beneficial to the economy as they not only lead to increased aggregate demand but also can result in expanded productive capacity. When the economy is expanding, investment tends to grow more quickly than national output. The reverse, however, is also true: investment tends to fall at a faster rate than national income in a period of recession. This **accelerator effect** is why any change in investment is likely to have an especially significant effect on the state of the economy.

> ### DEFINITION
>
> **Accelerator effect:** the proportionally bigger effect on investment that is likely to be caused by a given change in demand.

EXPORTS

Generally speaking, people living in other countries will buy UK-produced goods and services if they are cheaper than those produced by other countries or if they are perceived to be better value for money in terms of technological advancement and/or quality. The relative price of *exports* will be influenced by

rates of inflation in different countries and by the exchange rate, while quality and technological advance are more likely to be influenced by levels of investment in the UK economy.

IMPORTS

Spending by UK residents on *imports* will be influenced by similar factors. Demand is likely to rise if import prices fall, and likely to be greater if foreign-produced goods are perceived to be better value because of quality or technological advancement.

> ### ACTIVITY ····➤
>
> Use appropriate graphs to show how aggregate demand might be affected by:
>
> **(a)** a fall in government spending
> **(b)** a fall in interest rates
> **(c)** a fall in the exchange rate.

The multiplier

Before we move on to consider aggregate supply, it is important to understand that the effect of any change to aggregate demand is likely to have a larger proportional effect on national output. This **multiplier effect** is very important because it means governments can use relatively small changes in government spending or taxation to bring about much larger changes in national output. The easiest way of understanding how and why the multiplier effect actually works is to use the circular flow model in Figure 7.7.

> ### DEFINITION
>
> **Multiplier effect:** an effect, analysed by the economist John Maynard Keynes, whereby any change in aggregate demand has a proportionally bigger eventual effect on national output.

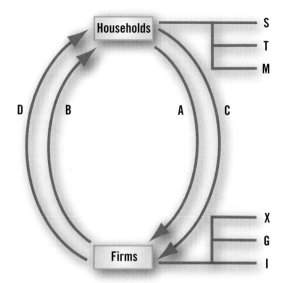

Figure 7.7 Circular flow model

Suppose the government and private sector agree to accept proposals to build a Severn Barrage. This massive engineering project would cost in excess of £15 billion and this would require a mixture of government spending and private sector investment. This would mean that the demand for surveying, construction, generation and other equipment would rise by £15 million. This increase in aggregate demand would lead to an increase in output, and payments to factors of production would rise by £15 billion. Household incomes would rise by the same amount, leading to an increase in consumption, savings, government revenues and imports.

Suppose 60 per cent of the extra income is spent on consumption of UK-produced goods, this would lead to an increase in aggregate demand of £9 billion, which in turn would end up in an extra £9 billion of income. If the process were to repeat itself, a further £5.4 billion of consumption would be generated. So far the initial increase in aggregate demand of £15 billion has led to a £29.4 billion increase in national income and the process will continue with ever-decreasing amounts being added to national income. The process will come to an end when the outflows of savings, taxation and spending on imports equal that original increase in aggregate demand of £15 billion.

learning tip
Although at AS level you are not required to calculate the size of the multiplier, it is useful to have an understanding of how this might be determined. Just to remind you – the exam will not ask you to calculate the value of the multiplier, but knowing this can improve your understanding of the significance of the multiplier.

CALCULATING THE MULTIPLIER

By now you should have developed an understanding that the size of the multiplier will be determined by the proportion of additional income devoted to consumption expenditure. This is called the *marginal propensity to consume*. In the Severn Barrage example, we assumed that 60 per cent of additional income would be spent on consumption. This would give an MPC of 0.6. If all extra income was spent on consumption, the MPC would be 1, whereas an MPC of 0.4 would indicate that 40 per cent of additional income would be spent on consumption.

Working out the size of the MPC is really a matter of logic. If we know what proportion of additional income is saved, taken by the government in the form of taxation or spent on imported goods, what is left will be the MPC. Economists recognise this and often focus on the **marginal propensity to withdraw** when assessing the potential impact of any change in aggregate demand on economic performance.

DEFINITION

Marginal propensity to withdraw (MPW): the proportion of any change in income which is *not* spent on consumption.

Determinants of short-run aggregate supply

Aggregate supply focuses on the output side of the economy and refers to the total value of goods and services that are produced in an economy at a given level of prices. In the short run it is assumed that the overall capacity of the economy is fixed, whereas in the long run the productivity capacity can change. This means that output can only be increased in the short run if there is spare productive capacity in the economy. Capital inputs are usually regarded as fixed in the short run. Firms are likely to increase their output of goods and services if prices and therefore profits are rising. This will be achieved in the short run by making better use of productive capacity and/or taking on more labour. Hence, a rising price level is likely to lead to an increase in short-run aggregate supply. On the other hand, falling prices in the short run will result in falling profits and falling output. Therefore the short-run aggregate supply curve is drawn sloping upwards from the left to right. This is shown in Figure 7.8.

SHIFTS IN SHORT-RUN AGGREGATE SUPPLY

The main influence on short-run aggregate supply will be costs of production. If, for example, wages rise, the profitability of production will fall and

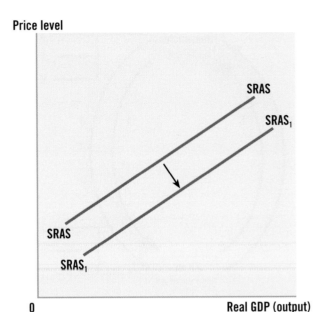

Figure 7.9 Shifts in short-run aggregate supply

output is likely to fall, shown by a movement to the left from *SRAS* to *SRAS₁*. On the other hand, if costs of raw materials fall, falling costs of production are likely to lead to increased output at each level of prices. In other words, the *SRAS* will shift to the right if costs of production fall. This is illustrated in Figure 7.9 above.

Other factors which can change the costs of production in the short run include changes in government taxation on companies, trade union activity and the availability of incentives to encourage greater productivity.

Short-run equilibrium between aggregate demand and aggregate supply

The diagrams representing aggregate demand and short-run aggregate supply are drawn using the same horizontal and vertical axes and therefore superimposed one on top of the other. This is shown in Figure 7.10. This graphical analysis enables us to predict the equilibrium level of national output and the relative level of prices. Aggregate demand is equal to short-run aggregate supply at *x* and this occurs when national output stands at *OY* and the price level at *OP* by *ab*. Below *x* aggregate demand exceeds aggregate supply. Households would be demanding more goods and services than firms were producing. Shortages

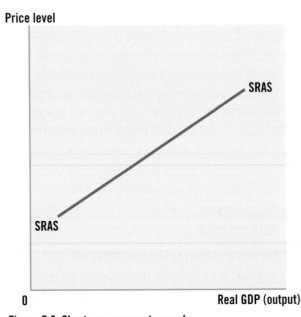

Figure 7.8 Short-run aggregate supply

Price level

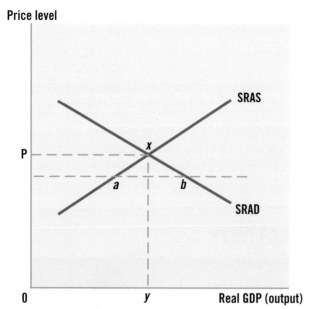

Figure 7.10 Equilibrium between aggregate demand and aggregate supply

would occur and it would be expected that prices of goods and services in short supply would rise. This increase in the price level would encourage firms to expand production and in order to do so they would increase their demand for factor inputs, a movement along the short-run aggregate supply curve resulting in increasing employment levels and incomes. At the same time, rising price levels would choke off some of the excess demand, shown by a movement along the aggregate demand curve. These two sets of changes in the economy would come to a halt when equilibrium is reached at x.

ACTIVITY ···

Use aggregate demand and supply diagrams to explain what might happen in an economy if aggregate supply were greater than aggregate demand.

USING AGGREGATE DEMAND AND SHORT-RUN AGGREGATE SUPPLY

This model can be used to predict what will happen to macroeconomic indicators if any of the variables determining aggregate demand or short-run aggregate supply change.

Suppose, other factors being equal, there is an increase in demand for UK exports. These are one of the components of aggregate demand, and an increase in exports means that there will also be an increase in aggregate demand. This is shown by the shift in that curve to the right as illustrated below in Figure 7.11 by the movement from AD_1 to AD_2. Prior to the boost to UK exports, the price level is represented by OP_1 and the level of national output at OY_1. If the price level were to be unchanged, this increase in aggregate demand would mean that aggregate demand would be greater than aggregate supply, creating shortages of goods and services in the economy, leading in turn to a rise in prices. This would, as has been shown earlier, lead to firms increasing production and result in an increase in national output and also increases in income and employment levels. These changes would continue until a new equilibrium is reached with the price level rising to OP_2 and national output standing at OY_2. Hence this model predicts that an increase in exports by UK-based firms will result in an increase in both national output and the price level. In other words, both the rate of inflation and the numbers employed would rise.

Suppose households choose to increase the proportion of income which they save. This would represent a fall in consumption, shown in the

Price level

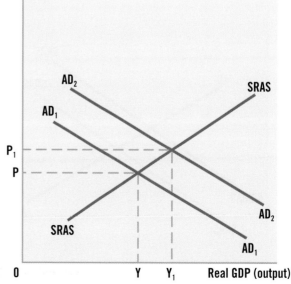

Figure 7.11 Increasing aggregate demand

Price level

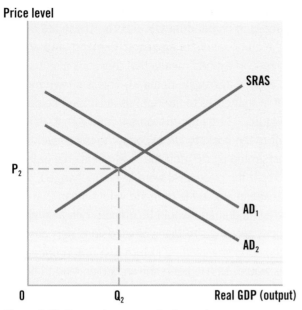

Figure 7.12 Decreasing aggregate demand

diagram above by a shift in aggregate demand from *AD₁* to *AD₂*. In analytical terms, aggregate supply would be greater than aggregate demand, leading to a falling price level and a drop in national income and employment levels until a new equilibrium is established with prices at *OP₂* and output *OQ₂*. The outcomes would be a fall in the price level and a cut in national income and employment levels.

Price level

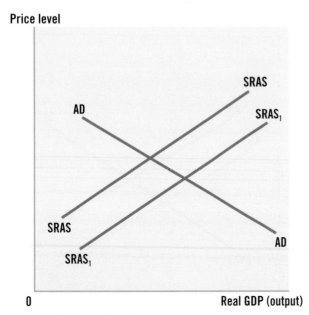

Figure 7.13 Increasing short-run aggregate supply

Finally, changes in production costs will have an effect on short-run aggregate supply. Reductions in costs will boost production, as shown by a shift to the right of aggregate supply. This would create excess supply which would result in falling prices leading to increased output, income and employment levels.

If production costs rise in the short-run, aggregate supply will shift to the left, leading to rising prices, and lower output, income and employment levels.

ACTIVITY ⋯⋗

Use aggregate demand and short-run aggregate supply to analyse the impact on employment, incomes and prices of:

(a) rising crude oil prices

(b) a cut in interest rates

(c) increases in government spending within an economy approaching full employment.

INFLATION

Inflation (see page 110) refers to a period in which prices are rising, and is usually measured in terms of the annual rate of change. Inflation data for the last 13 years is shown in Figure 7.14 below. Currently, the Consumer Price Index (CPI) stands at 1.8 per cent and the Retail Price Index (RPI) at 4.1 per cent. Over the last 13 years in the UK, inflation has always been positive, but annual rates for CPI have ranged from just under 1 to 3 per cent. The relatively low rates contrast with data from the early 1990s, when the RPI peaked at 9.5 per cent.

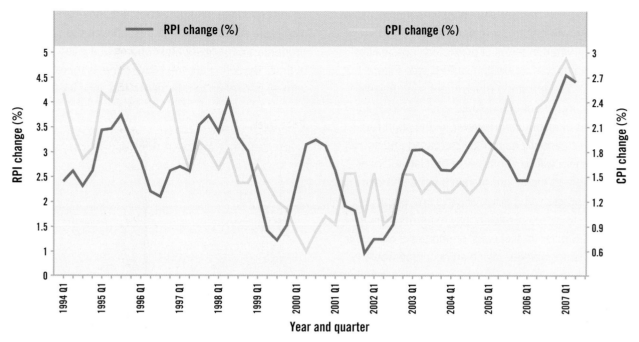

Figure 7.14 Inflation in the UK

national income but acceleration in the price level, that is, an increase in the rate of inflation. Should the government be foolhardy enough to continue its programme of expansion to AD_4, national income would not change but the rate of inflation would continue to increase.

Aggregate demand and short-run aggregate supply curves can be used to provide a possible explanation for variations in the rate of inflation. Figure 7.15 represents an initial equilibrium in an economy which could be in the depths of depression, with relatively low levels of national income and widespread unemployment of factors of production. Under such conditions, the government might well decide to increase its spending to stimulate economic recovery. This is illustrated in Figure 7.15, where a comparatively modest increase in government expenditure will cause AD to shift to the right from AD_1 to AD_2 and lead to the establishment of a new equilibrium at b with higher levels of national income, reduced levels of unemployment and a slight increase in the price level. A further increase in government spending as represented by AD_3, would lead to a further but relatively smaller expansion in

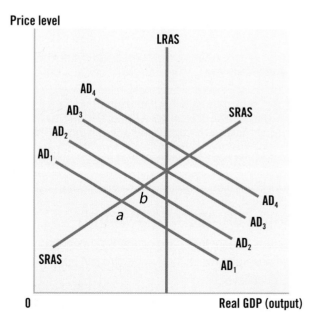

Figure 7.15 Effect of successive increases in AD

In this situation the government started its process of expansion when there were unused resources in the economy, when in terms of production possibilities the economy was well within its PPC (see Figure 1.3, page 11). The growth in government spending will cut the numbers of unemployed and lead to a better utilization of resources. However, in the short run, productive capacity cannot be increased and sooner or later there will be shortages of crucial factors of production. In the labour market it will be harder to recruit workers with particular skills and employers are likely to increase rates of pay to attract scarce workers. Similar 'bottlenecks' or shortages will occur in other factor markets. Such an economy would be approaching full employment – a theoretical situation where it is not possible to increase output in the short run. As the diagram shows, further stimulus to the economy has only one outcome – pushing up inflation.

ACTIVITY ⋯⟫

Assume an economy is at the point of full employment. Use aggregate demand and supply diagrams to illustrate the short-run effects of:

(a) increases in interest rates

(b) increases in the exchange rate

(c) panic buying.

ACTIVITY ⋯⟫

Use the Internet to find out rates of inflation in three different countries over the last ten years. Assess the economic significance of the data you have collected.

Long-run aggregate supply

Different economists have different views on the relationship between long-run aggregate supply and the price level.

Classical economists argue that if markets are allowed to work freely there will be no unused resources in the long run. Thus, the long-run aggregate supply (LRAS) is the same as the total productive capacity of an economy at a given point of time. By definition, the LRAS curve is therefore vertical in relation to changes in the price level.

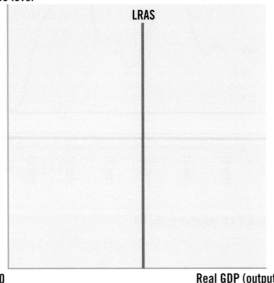

Figure 7.16 **LRAS (classical)**

DEFINITION

Classical economists: those who believe that without government intervention, changing prices ensure that markets clear. In other words, if the supply is greater than demand at a given price, falling prices will bring about *market equilibrium*. They believe that the labour market works in the same way: if unemployment exists, wages will fall until the demand for labour is equal to the supply, that is, until unemployment disappears. This can be applied to all factor markets.

Keynesians *do not* believe that markets always clear, which could mean that even in the long-run there might be unused resources in the economy. Thus, long-run aggregate supply could still potentially change in response to changes in the price level.

Price level

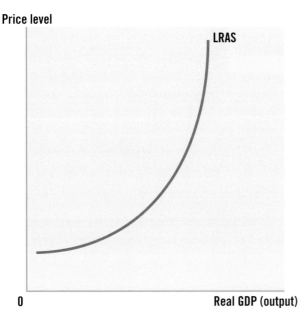

Figure 7.17 LRAS (Keynesian)

The two different perspectives are illustrated in Figures 7.16 and 7.17. These show that classical economists believe that in the long run, any increase in aggregate demand is likely to be inflationary, whereas the Keynesian position is similar to that in the short run – where an increase in aggregate demand can lead to increases in both national income and inflation – until the point of full employment is reached, after which prices carry on rising while output does not change.

ACTIVITY ····⫶

Why do classical economists and Keynesians disagree as to the gradient of the long-run aggregate supply? Is this disagreement important? Justify your answer.

DETERMINANTS OF LONG-RUN AGGREGATE SUPPLY

Any increase in the productive capacity of an economy will shift the long-run aggregate supply curve outwards to the right. Increases in the supply of factors will boost the productive capacity of the economy. Thus, workers from other countries may be attracted to this country, boosting the supply of labour and increasing productive capacity.

The quality and productivity of existing factors can also be improved. Better training and education could increase the skill levels of the labour force, technological improvements can make capital more productive, and increasing competition might lead to improved allocative and productive efficiency.

There is a wide range of other factors that can shift the long-run aggregate supply curve outwards, indicating that an economy is experiencing economic growth. Increasingly, advanced economies focus on improving the quality of human capital by encouraging the development of improved enterprise skills. All students in the UK are meant to have elements of enterprise education as part of their studies in years 10 and 11. This is meant to encourage more initiative, develop team-working skills and give students confidence when it comes to taking risks. It is believed that the development of these skills will eventually benefit all of us by expanding the productive potential of the economy.

The effects of any of these factors are illustrated in Figure 7.18 by the rightward shift in the LRAS curves. Both Keynesians and classical economists would agree that the result would be an increase in national income and a reduction in the price level.

Long-run aggregate supply would shift to the *left* if the quantity and/or quality of factors of production were to be reduced. Thus, an aging workforce, cuts in skills training, and relatively low levels of spending on research and development can all lead to a reduction in productive capacity and falling economic growth.

Economic growth in some less developed economies can be held back if key elements of the infrastructure are missing. Poor transport, ill-developed banking facilities and a lack of confidence in legal and judicial process can all act as brakes on economic growth. Should any of these factors worsen, for example as in Zimbabwe, economic growth goes into reverse with falling incomes and rampant inflation. This, as shown in Figure 7.19, will result in falling national income and an increasing price level.

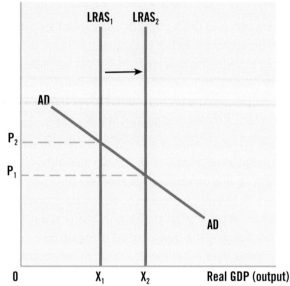

Figure 7.18 Increases in LRAS

ACTIVITY ⋯⫶

Use production possibility curves, the circular flow of income and short- and long-run aggregate demand and supply to illustrate the possible outcomes of the following:

(a) increased expenditure by the government on the NHS

(b) reduction of inheritance taxes by $1.4 billion

(c) cutting civil service jobs

(d) a fall in the value of the US dollar.

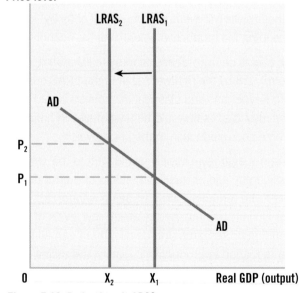

Figure 7.19 Reductions in LRAS

ACTIVITY ⋯⫶

One of the particular problems of the UK economy is that we have a relatively high propensity to import. In boom times, when incomes are rising, we tend to spend relatively more on imported goods and this means that the UK economy tends to suck in imports. What implications might this have for:

(a) UK manufacturers

(b) the balance of payments

(c) the government?

8 Economic performance

On completion of this chapter, you should be able to:

● understand the objectives of government economic policy
● analyse and evaluate policies to promote economic growth
● understand demand-pull and cost-push influences on inflation
● Analyse and evaluate different causes of unemployment
● know what the balance of payments on current account consists of
● understand what is meant by a deficit and surplus on the balance of payments
● learn that the government might be faced with conflicts in attempting to achieve different economic objectives.

This chapter aims to give you a deeper understanding of all these concepts mentioned briefly in the preceding chapter. You will have further opportunity to apply and develop the following models of how aspects of the economy work:

● the circular flow
● aggregate demand and supply
● production possibility curves.

learning tip Make sure you can produce the basic diagrams associated with each of these models.

Economic growth

In the section which follows you will learn about the differences between long-run and short-run economic growth, and how these can be shown using both production possibility curves and aggregate demand and supply, You will also be introduced to those factors that are likely to determine economic growth, and have an understanding of the long-term trend rate in economic growth.

As noted on page 000, economic growth refers to increases in real output in the economy over time. *Real*

means that the effects of inflation on growth have been accounted for. Thus, if output had grown by 5 per cent but inflation was running at 2 per cent, the actual or real rate of growth would have been 3 per cent.

learning tip When looking at any data or graphs of economic growth rates, check whether inflation has been allowed for, or 'stripped out'. The use of the terms 'real' or 'at constant prices' indicates that allowance have been made for inflation. If you see the terms 'current prices' or 'market prices', no account has been taken of the effects of inflation.

SHORT-RUN ECONOMIC GROWTH

The production possibility curve illustrated in Figure 8.1 below shows all those combinations of two sets of goods – beef and wheat – that could be produced in an economy if all available factors of production were being used. However, should there be unused resources, as presented by any point to the left of *PPC*, for example *y*, it would be possible to increase the production of both beef and wheat by making better use of available factors of production. This could happen in the short run and is illustrated in

Beef

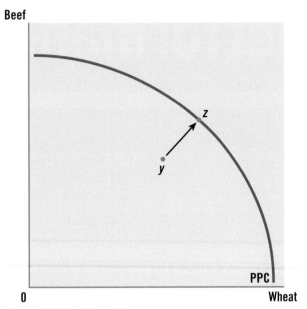

Figure 8.1 Actual growth

Price level

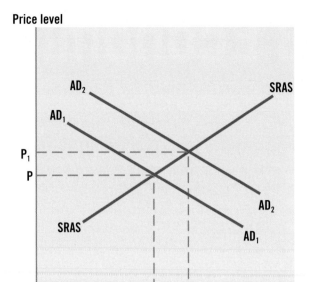

Figure 8.2 Increasing aggregate demand

a movement from *y* to *z*. Economists use the term **actual growth** for short-term economic growth, to differentiate it from long-term economic growth that involves an outward shift in the **production possibility curve (PPC)** (called **potential growth**).

DEFINITIONS

Actual growth: an increase in real output in the short term.

Production possibility curve (PPC): a line showing all the different combinations of two goods that can be produced using all available resources (see page 11).

Potential growth: a long-term increase in productive capacity indicated by an outward shift of the PPC.

Short-run economic growth can also be illustrated using aggregate demand and aggregate supply diagrams. Figure 8.2 features a short-run aggregate supply curve. If there were unused resources in the economy, an increase in aggregate demand from *AD₁* to *AD₂* would result in an increase in national output from *OY* to *OY₁*.

Economic growth can also occur in the short run if costs of production fall. This could happen if imported raw materials became cheaper, if workers became more productive, or if the government were to reduce taxation on firms. If any of these were to happen, the *SRAS* curve would move downward to the right, which could result in both short-term economic growth as national output grows and a reduction in the price level. This is illustrated in Figure 8.3.

Price level

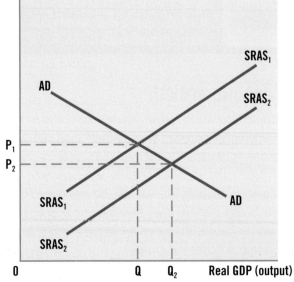

Figure 8.3 Falling cost of produce

LONG-RUN ECONOMIC GROWTH

Long-run economic growth can be illustrated by use of both:

● production possibility curves, and

● aggregate demand and supply analysis.

Production possibility curves

Economic growth in the long run can be achieved by changes in all factor inputs, and if these result in an expansion of productive capacity, this will be illustrated by an outward shift in the production possibility curve (PPC). Thus, in Figure 8.4, an increase in long-run economic growth is illustrated by the movement from PPC_1 to PPC_2, showing that it would be possible to increase production of both capital and consumption goods.

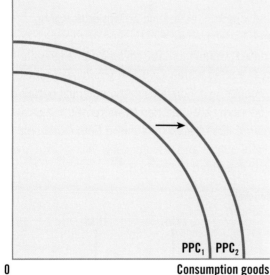

Figure 8.4 Long-run economic growth

Aggregate demand and aggregate supply analysis

Aggregate demand and aggregate supply analysis can be used to illustrate long-run economic growth. This is shown in Figure 8.5 below by the movement from $LRAS_1$ to $LRAS_2$. These long-run curves have been drawn vertically to illustrate classical economic analysis that falling factor prices will always result in full employment of resources in the long run. This indicates that if productive capacity is increased, it

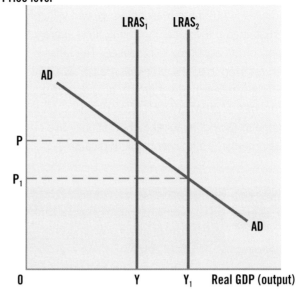

Figure 8.5 Long-run economic growth

is possible to have positive economic growth and a falling price level at the same time.

ACTIVITY ⋯⬩

Use PPC and aggregate demand and supply diagrams to illustrate the differences between a short-run fall in the rate of economic growth and a long-term reduction.

FACTORS AFFECTING SHORT-RUN ECONOMIC GROWTH

Once you have an understanding of aggregate demand and aggregate supply, you have the means to explain why economic growth might change in the short run. Aggregate demand is made up of consumption, investment, government spending and exports less imports. Hence, if any of these factors were to increase, aggregate demand would shift to the right and, providing there is excess capacity in the economy, short-term economic growth would occur. This was shown earlier in Figure 7.11 in which aggregate demand shifts from AD_1 to AD_2, causing shortages in the economy, which should stimulate firms to increase output from OY to OY_1.

As noted earlier, this boom phase cannot be sustained in the short run as, sooner or later, full employment will be reached. In this context, further increases in output and economic growth will only be sustained if the capacity or long-term aggregate supply of the economy is increased. The latter is often referred to as the *potential growth rate*, which is the long-run trend rate of growth as distinct from the *actual rate of growth*, which is simply the short-term change in level of national output, usually used by governments as a key economic indicator.

> **learning tip**
>
> The government, through the Monetary Policy Committee (MPC) of the Bank of England, uses the interest rate as the principal means of influencing short-run economic growth. Reductions in the interest rate will tend to increase growth in consumption, leading in turn to increases in aggregate demand. If the MPC is fearful of the build-up of inflationary pressures, it is likely to increase interest rates, in an attempt to reduce growth in consumption, leading to a fall in aggregate demand, resulting in reduced inflationary pressures.

ACTIVITY ···⟫

Why might economists be more interested in the potential than in the actual rate of growth in the economy?

Currently, economists consider that the potential growth rate in the UK economy is 2.75 per cent. The actual rate for 2006 was estimated at 3 per cent and the forecast for 2007 is 2.8 per cent. This indicates that economic growth is currently above the long-term trend and is unlikely to be sustained at this level in the future. For this reason, the UK Treasury is predicting a growth rate for 2008 at 2.2 per cent. The differences between potential and actual rates are illustrated in Figure 8.6. Any differences between actual and potential levels of GDP are referred to as output gaps. When output is above trend, a positive gap exists, whereas a negative gap exists when output is below trend.

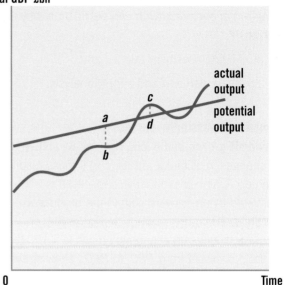

Real GDP £bn

Figure 8.6 Growth in potential and actual output

FACTORS AFFECTING LONG-RUN ECONOMIC GROWTH

In the long run, economic growth rates will be primarily determined by changes in aggregate supply. As noted earlier, increases in long-run aggregate supply lead to increases in the potential output of the economy. If increases in the potential output of the economy are matched by increases in aggregate demand, it is possible to achieve both increased national output and, theoretically, falling price levels. This is illustrated in Figure 8.7.

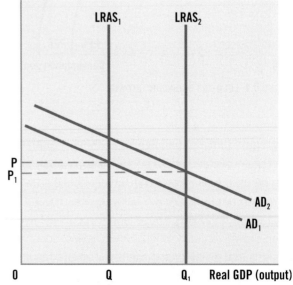

Price level

Figure 8.7 Matching increases in LRAS with increasing AD

There are many factors that are likely to affect long-run aggregate supply. They are usually referred to as **supply-side factors** and can be grouped together into two categories:

- quantity of factors of production, and
- quality of factors of production.

Increases in either one or both of these variables are likely to increase the productive capacity of the economy.

> **DEFINITION**
>
> **Supply-side factor:** a variable that can influence the productive capacity of an economy.

QUANTITATIVE CHANGES

There have been times in history when the abundance of land, labour, capital and enterprise have led to massive spurts in long-run aggregate supply. Historically, increasing birth rates and decreasing death rates have led to changes in the size and age structure of populations. This can provide significant increases in the supply of labour, which can in turn result in outward shifts in the long-run aggregate supply (LRAS) curve.

Wall Street in the late 19th century, when the US economy boomed

Immigration can also result in an increase in long-run productive capacity. In the second half of the 19th century, vast areas of the USA were settled by Europeans who literally took over thousands and thousands of acres of land rich in a whole host of raw materials. Immigration from Europe ensured that there was a growing and enterprising workforce. Little wonder that investment funds also flowed across the Atlantic and the US economy grew rapidly.

Similarly, immigration to the UK from the Indian subcontinent and the West Indies in the 1950s and 1960s, and in more recent years from eastern Europe, has boosted the productive capacity of the UK economy.

High rates of economic growth in China have been fuelled by a combination of rapid capital accumulation and a large labour force.

However, economic resources in the long run appear to be finite. Even the changes mentioned above have an opportunity cost of reduced availability of resources in other countries. The loss of skilled and productive workers from India, Pakistan and Bangladesh acted as a brake on economic growth in those countries.

QUALITATIVE CHANGES

There are a number of supply-side factors that can increase productive capacity by improving the quality of factors of production so that a given factor becomes more productive. These include:

- technology
- investment
- productivity
- attitudinal factors
- factor mobility.

Technological changes

Technological changes can have a major impact on the productivity of capital. Translating the outcomes of research and development into more efficient ways of producing goods and services (**innovation**) can reduce costs of production and increase productive capacity. While economists may disagree as to the

ECONOMICS IN CONTEXT

TECHNOLOGY CORE TO 'FOURTH INDUSTRIAL REVOLUTION':

Economist says technological innovation is no longer enough in world economy

The world economy is entering its fourth industrial revolution and technology will be at the heart, says a leading economist.

According to Klaus Schwab, executive chairman and founder of the World Economic Forum, the world is shifting from being an information society to one that uses data more intelligently.

Technological innovation is no longer enough. Countries, companies and individuals will need to exploit their knowledge more smartly if they are to succeed in the new 'Intelligence Society', he says.

'We are moving into a society which will be driven by well networked individuals, where people are empowered. It's not just intelligence in the sense of technological innovation, it's also about empowering people so that they become a lot more creative than in the past,' Schwab told delegates at the SAS Forum International in Geneva today.

Schwab says the IT industry – and more broadly the global economy – will undergo major changes in the next ten years as economic and political power shifts away from the United States to China and India.

'There are 4 million university graduates coming out of China and India each year and there are 13 times more students graduating in engineering and science in these countries than in the US, where the numbers are decreasing,' he said.

With 140,000 software engineers located in Bangalore alone, regions like California's Silicon Valley, with just 120,000 developers, will be hard pushed to keep the crown for IT leadership unless it innovates, says Schwab.

Source: VNU

DEFINITION

Innovation: the introduction of new inventions of products or processes.

extent to which ICT developments have contributed to economic growth, there is broad consensus that the so-called computer revolution has led to an increase in productive potential in many economies. Improved communication has led to much quicker transfer of modern technologies and a speeding up of the time taken to innovate.

Investment

Economists tend to agree that the single most important factor contributing to long-term economic growth is the level of investment in an economy. Increases in investment not only boost aggregate demand in the short run, they have the potential for increasing the long-run productive capacity of an economy. Implementing technological change, improving the quality of human and physical capital and raising productivity all require investment.

Investment in human capital by improved training and education is another means of promoting economic growth. Getting workers to be more collaborative and to show initiative is thought to be as important as the development of more practical skills. Poor literacy and numeracy skills in the UK workforce hinder productivity and limit the acquisition of further skills.

ACTIVITY ····⊹

It has been suggested by a number of economists that relatively low levels of investment in the UK limit long-term economic growth. How might you interpret the following data?

Productivity and capital per hour, 1999 (UK=100)

	France	Germany	USA
GDP per hour worked	123	111	125
Capital per hour worked	154	126	133

Productivity

Productivity, as noted on page 51, refers to the output per period of time of factors of production.

Performance stars can motivate workers

Particular attention is paid to labour productivity. Both governments and private sector firms are constantly looking at ways of increasing productivity. This can range from simple exhortations – to work harder, to take shorter breaks, to move from task to task more quickly – to more subtle approaches focusing on developing good team-working skills and trying to increase the motivation of workers.

ACTIVITY ···⋗

Talk to other students and those in employment to find out and assess the effectiveness of different techniques used by employers to raise productivity of workers.

Attitudinal factors

These are another means of raising productivity of workers by trying to change attitudes to working practices. Typically, these involve trying to get workers to take on new roles, and to respond positively to tasks that they are given.

Other measures include changing the attitudes of employers, discouraging discrimination against women and minority ethnic and social groups. If these efforts are successful, it is possible for businesses and the economy as a whole to benefit from greater productive potential.

Schools are also used to encourage the development of more positive attitudes to enterprise and work. This can involve activities such as Young Enterprise, Key Skills and the Duke of Edinburgh awards – all designed to promote initiative, team work and problem solving.

Factor mobility

As noted in the section on the housing market on page 86, unavailability of affordable housing in areas in which the demand for labour is high presents a barrier to factor mobility. The government may intervene to subsidise housing in such areas. Also, the government seeks to encourage occupational mobility by encouraging more young people from working-class backgrounds to go to university.

Institutional changes can also make capital more mobile. Banks and other institutions have their role to play by being prepared to lend to businesses taking risks and trying out new ways of producing goods and services.

Is economic growth good?

The main benefit of economic growth is that it enables many people to enjoy a higher standard of living. Economic growth over the last two centuries in the UK has transformed the lives of many and, although there are still problems of poverty and deprivation, these are not on the scale experienced by our parents and their parents. In the developing world, economic growth can contribute to better nutrition, clean and safe water, lower rates of infant mortality and longer lives.

However, as you will have learned when studying market failure, economic growth is also associated with negative externalities, which may in the long term threaten the continuation of life as we know it. Climate change is a direct outcome of continued economic growth, as is the depletion of the world's resources.

ACTIVITY ···⋗

Use the Internet to compare and contrast economic growth rates between two members of the EU over the last ten years. Explain your findings.

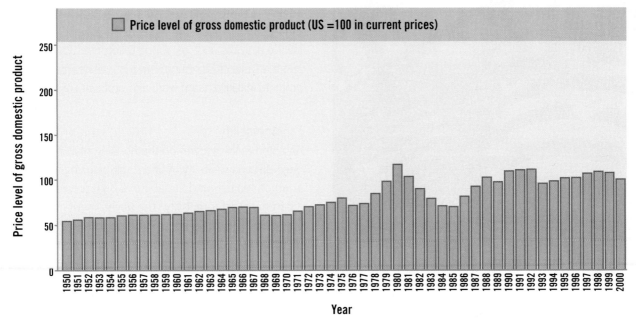

Figure 8.8 Inflationary pressures

Inflation and disinflation

Inflation refers to a sustained rise in the general price level and **disinflation** to a sustained fall in the general price level. The graph in Figure 8.8 shows that over the last 50 years in the UK inflation has been far more common than disinflation.

> **DEFINITIONS**
>
> **Disinflation:** a sustained fall in the general price level.

> **learning tip**
> Deflation is not the 'opposite' of inflation. The term 'deflation' is used by economists to refer to a period of time in which demand and output in an economy are falling. This can be associated with disinflation, that is, with falling prices.

DETERMINANTS OF INFLATION

There are two sets of factors that are likely to stimulate inflation in an economy:

- demand-pull, and
- cost-push.

Demand-pull

Aggregate demand and aggregate supply analysis enables us to understand how changes in macroeconomic variables can lead to **demand-pull inflation**. In Figure 8.9 below, an increase in aggregate demand leads to accelerating inflation as an economy approaches full employment. In this example, aggregate demand can be said to be increasing more rapidly than aggregate supply and, as noted earlier, shortages of goods and services will occur. Moreover, firms will offer higher returns in order to attract more factors of production. Increases in income are likely to lead to further increases in

> **DEFINITION**
>
> **Demand-pull inflation:** rising price levels attributable to excess demand in the economy.

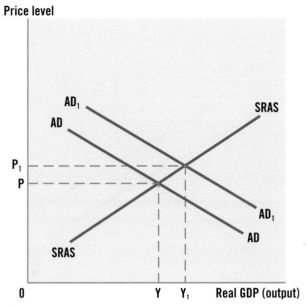

Figure 8.9 Demand-pull inflation

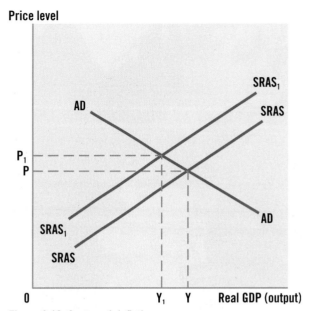

Figure 8.10 Cost-push inflation

consumption and aggregate demand. Sooner or later, some businesses won't be able to meet the needs of customers or recruit workers with particular skills.

Economists refer to **bottlenecks** in the economy. These are like pinch points: longer delivery times of some resources will generally slow up production. Excess demand will, therefore, lead to rising prices as shown by the rise in price level from OP to OP_1. The impact of demand-pull influences on inflation is likely to intensify as an economy approaches full employment.

Cost-push

Another cause of inflation relates to increases in the costs of production. This is sometimes called **cost-push inflation.** If firms are faced with increases in the

costs of production, they may well attempt to pass on these increases to customers. This will be easier for those firms with a degree of monopoly power or when there are relatively few unused resources in the economy. In the 1970s, much attention was focused on trade unions, which were said to use their bargaining power to push up wage rates. More recently, increases in the cost of crude oil have been seen as having a potential to create cost-push inflation. This is shown in Figure 8.10, where increases in the price of oil push up costs faced by producers who in turn increase their prices, shown by upward movements in the $SRAS$ curve to $SRAS_1$, leading to an overall increase in the price level from OP to OP_1 and a fall in the national output.

COST PRICE SPIRAL

Irrespective of the original trigger for inflation, once prices start rising they can have a tendency to continue rising at an accelerating rate. Thus, if the demand for goods and services increases, this not only pushes up prices but also leads to an increase in incomes, which can lead to further increases in prices. If firms and households come to expect inflation to continue, they might try to safeguard their profits and standards of living by pushing up prices even further and demanding higher

DEFINITIONS

Bottleneck: a shortage of particular products, services or factors of production associated with demand-pull inflation.

Cost-push inflation: an increase in price level attributable to increases in the costs of production.

In Germany in the 1920s it was cheaper to burn money than buy fuel

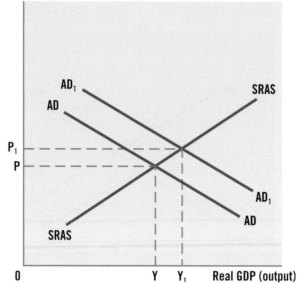

Price level

Real GDP (output)

Figure 8.11 Effects of falling AD

incomes. The fear of inflation spiralling out of control is one that haunts governments. Rampant inflation, or **hyperinflation** to give it its proper name, is associated with economic and social breakdown as seen in Germany in the 1920s, some Latin American countries in the 1960s and in Zimbabwe today. The UK has also experienced periods of relatively rapid inflation in the early 1980s and again about a decade later.

> **DEFINITION**
>
> **Hyperinflation:** very high levels of inflation usually involving daily changes in the prices of goods and services.

DISINFLATION

Disinflation and a fall in the price level can happen together. This is illustrated in Figure 8.11, where falling levels of aggregate demand result in a falling price level from OP_1 to OP_2. The same outcome is predicted if there is an increase in short-run or long-run aggregate supply not matched by changes in aggregate demand.

Periods of deflation are far less common in the UK economy than periods of inflation. They are, however, associated with periods of recession in the economic cycle. The last period of significant deflation, between 1920 and 1935, was associated with the 'Great Depression', which culminated in very high levels of unemployment and widespread social hardship. Falling rates of inflation in the 1990s led to a fear that deflation would again occur but, so far so good, inflation has held relatively steady between 2 and 3 per cent and fears of both high inflation and deflation have been held in check.

ACTIVITY ⋯⋮

Use the Internet to compare and contrast inflation rates in two members of the EU over the last ten years. Explain your findings.

Employment and unemployment

You will be familiar with the everyday notions of employment and unemployment but in the previous chapter you will have learned that actually defining unemployment and the directly related concept of employment is not so straightforward. To an economist, any activity that contributes to the creation of wealth within an economy is a form of employment. Yet, as you will have noted, not all actions of wealth creation are recorded formally. For example, the contribution of carers of the young, old and disabled is hard to quantify, as is the 'contribution' to the nation's wealth from illegal activities. As noted earlier, two official statistics are used to measure unemployment:

● the claimant count, and

● the Labour Force Survey.

In terms of the aggregate demand and supply model, national output or income as measured on the horizontal axis is taken as a proxy or measure of the level of employment in an economy. It is assumed that, if national income is rising as indicated by any movement in the equilibrium to the right of *OY* in Figure 8.12, more people will be employed and unemployment will fall. Any move to the left indicates the opposite. These changes in employment levels can be triggered by changes in aggregate demand or aggregate supply, but they will not occur if the economy is running at full employment.

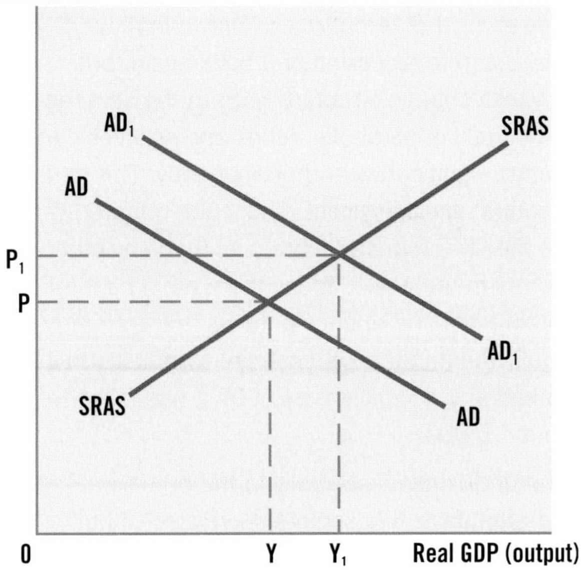

Price level

Figure 8.12 Output and employment

> **ACTIVITY ····⫶**
>
> Use production possibility analysis to show possible increases and decreases in employment levels in both the short run and the long run.

TYPES OF UNEMPLOYMENT

Economists are generally agreed that it is possible to categorise unemployment according to its possible cause. Understanding the possible cause as being

● cyclical

● frictional

● seasonal

● structural

is useful to governments if they wish to choose polices to minimise the harmful effects of unemployment.

Cyclical unemployment

Cyclical unemployment refers to changes in employment levels that are directly related to the economic cycle described in the previous chapter. The demand for labour is likely to be higher in the boom part of the cycle and lower at times of recession. It is likely that full employment will be reached at the peak of a boom period in the economic cycle. If boom is to be followed by recession, falling aggregate demand would mean that firms would not be able to sell as many goods and services, causing their outputs to fall, leading to a fall in demand for labour. In the short run this might be met by cutting overtime, but sooner or

> **DEFINITION**
>
> **Cyclical unemployment:** unemployment attributable to fluctuations in the economic cycle leading to a fall in demand for labour.

later some people would lose their jobs. Loss of income and jobs is likely to lead to the *multiplier effect*, which in this case would deepen the depression. This was the kind of unemployment identified by J.M. Keynes in the 1930s. He argued that unemployment could be caused if aggregate demand and aggregate supply were in equilibrium at a lower level than full employment. Such a situation was described as demand deficient, and it followed from this analysis that unemployment would be 'cured' by a revival in the economy, which could be triggered by some form of stimulation to aggregate demand.

Frictional unemployment

Although most people regard unemployment as a 'bad thing', **frictional unemployment** can be associated with a dynamic and healthy economy. Many of you will face temporary unemployment as you move from job to job. Similarly, you may make choices about your lifestyle that involve changing jobs or even removing yourself from the labour market to travel or to return to education. Movements between jobs create frictional unemployment, but as long as new employment opportunities are opening up as others may be closing down, the existence of frictional unemployment can be an indicator of a growing and developing economy.

However, frictional unemployment can become more problematical if those who are faced with losing one job are ignorant of new opportunities or if the labour force is particularly immobile. In situations such as this, there is a danger that what would normally be a short time without a job becomes a more extended wait – in which case this form of unemployment could become 'structural' (see below).

DEFINITION

Frictional unemployment: unemployment of a short duration associated with people moving from job to job.

Seasonal unemployment

This is straightforward, as the demand for some goods and services can be seasonal, as can the production of some goods and services. **Seasonal unemployment** is traditionally associated with jobs in the primary sector that may be dependent on the weather or seasonal conditions. In the UK the trend is for employment in this sector to be declining over time, as employment opportunities in the service sector are tending to be relatively more significant. However, those dependent upon seasonal work tend to be more vulnerable to unemployment and in the case of migrant agricultural workers much more at risk of exploitation by unscrupulous employers. To be more positive, seasonal employment can be particularly attractive to students and those prepared to travel looking for work.

DEFINITION

Seasonal unemployment: unemployment attributable to seasonal variations in demand for particular forms of labour.

Structural unemployment

Economies, as has been noted, are dynamic. They grow at different rates. They can move from boom to recession and back again, but they also change structurally. Both the demand and supply of particular goods and services can change significantly and permanently. This causes **structural unemployment**. Thus, one hundred years ago the UK produced more coal than any other country in the world. Today there are a handful of working pits and opencast mines in the country. Employment in the UK coalmining industry in 1920 peaked at 1.25 million; by 2007 it had fallen to around 5,000.

Other industries, especially in the primary and manufacturing sectors, have also all but disappeared. Those workers who have skills and experiences that are no longer in demand can be faced with long-term unemployment as the basic

Coalmining was once an important industry in the UK

IS UNEMPLOYMENT A PROBLEM?

The focus in the earlier sections has been unemployment and its causes. The impact of the loss of jobs for seasonal, frictional, cyclical or structural reasons can be reduced and even offset by the creation of new employment opportunities. As implied earlier, a dynamic and growing economy will be characterised by fluctuations in employment. In an ideal state, new jobs would be created to replace those that have been lost. Recent UK government statistics indicated that 132,000 new jobs had been created over a 12-month period. Does this mean that unemployment is no longer a problem? As ever in economics, the answer to this is both a yes and a no.

DEFINITION

Structural unemployment: unemployment associated with a fall in demand for labour related to the long-term decline of particular industries.

structure or make-up of the economy changes. Structural unemployment is clearly much more of a problem if a large percentage of the workforce in a particular region or area is dependent on employment in an industry that is in decline. In the UK, the decline of textile manufacture, coalmining, fishing and agriculture, and of low added-value manufacturing has had a disproportionate effect on the north and west of the UK, creating what some have called a north–south divide. While it is dangerous to over-generalise, the Midlands and south-east of the country have been less dependent on declining industries and structural unemployment tends to be less of a problem there.

ECONOMICS IN CONTEXT

INEQUALITY 'RISING' UNDER LABOUR

The Institute for Public Policy Research (ippr) says inequality in Britain has continued to increase since Labour came to power in 1997.

Although fewer people are living in poverty than in 1997, the proportion of wealth held by Britain's richest 10 per cent rose from 47 per cent to 54 per cent during the 1990s, it said.

The study shows that women are more likely to be living in poverty and that people's lives are largely determined by parents' social class and skin colour.

New jobs have replaced some of those lost through structural unemployment; knowledge about vacancies and opportunities has been improved by the use of the Internet; some areas of the country have recovered dramatically from the closure of significant employers. However, as you will study in greater depth for A2, the divide in the UK between the rich and the poor has widened and there is a hard core of the employed who tend to be concentrated in particular areas and within particular ethnic groups. Unemployment is closely linked to other aspects of relative deprivation, which in turn creates other social costs, not least those associated with illegal drug use and criminal behaviour. These social effects of unemployment are a cost to society as is its failure to fully use all potential sources of labour.

Balance of payments

The balance of payments refers to accounts used to record flows of expenditure that are generated by UK residents purchasing foreign-produced goods and services, and similar flows generated by foreign residents if they choose to buy UK-produced goods and services. The first set of transactions is commonly referred to as *imports* and the second set as *exports*. The relative size of these two flows can have a significant effect on the major macroeconomic indicators of economic performance. This can be shown using the circular flow model.

ACTIVITY ····⫶

Use the circular flow model to predict what will happen to income, output and employment if the value of UK exports changes relative to changes in the value of UK imports.

learning tip Be precise – again! Note the activity refers to the value of UK imports and not the amount – as far as the balance of payments is concerned it's the value that is important not the actual amount.

If you have been successful in undertaking the above task, you will have demonstrated that, other things being equal, a rise in the value of exports relative to the value of UK imports should lead to an increase in production, rising incomes and falling unemployment. The opposite effect will be felt if the value of imports is rising relative to the value of exports.

Similar analysis can be undertaken using aggregate demand and aggregate supply analysis. In Figure 8.13, an increase in the value of exports is represented as an increase in aggregate demand from AD_1 to AD_2. This is described as **export-led growth** and in this case national income rises from OY_1 to OY_2. The price level also rises from OP to OP_1. In this case a rise in exports can contribute to demand-pull inflation.

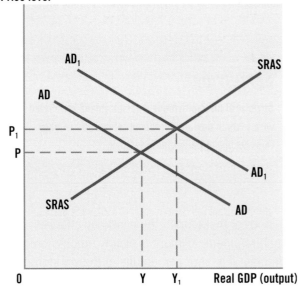

Figure 8.13 Export-led growth

DEFINITION

Export-led growth: economic growth attributable to an increase in the value of exports.

ACTIVITY ····⟩

Use aggregate demand and aggregate supply analysis to predict what might happen if there is an increase in the value of UK imports not accompanied by a similar increase in the value of UK exports.

THE BALANCE OF PAYMENTS ACCOUNT

The previous section should have confirmed the common-sense notion that rising exports will have a beneficial effect on the economy whereas a relative rise in the value of imports might reduce inflation but is also likely to cut incomes and employment levels. This is a rather simplistic view of the contribution that international trade might have on our welfare. The remainder of this chapter will help you obtain a more detailed understanding of the make-up of the UK balance of payments and the importance of **international competitiveness**. In A2 considerable attention will be given to understanding the negative and positive effects of **globalisation,** which is another context in which international trade is particularly important.

DEFINITIONS

International competitiveness: the trade effectiveness of a given economy in comparison to others.

Globalisation: the development of worldwide markets and production.

The balance of payments account has two parts:

- the current account, and
- the capital account.

BALANCE OF PAYMENTS ON CURRENT ACCOUNT

This is broken down into four components:

- trade in goods account
- trade in services account

- investment income flows
- transfers.

The trade in goods account

This includes all payments for the import and export of physical goods – things which we can see and touch. Exports of goods generate a positive flow of money into the UK economy and are known as credits. Imports of goods result in negative flows of money and are treated as debits. The balance between these inflows and outflows is called the balance of trade in goods. If the value of exports of goods is greater than the value of imports, this country has a **trade surplus**. If the opposite is the case, as it usually is for the UK, this country is said to have a **trade deficit**.

DEFINITIONS

Trade surplus: when the value of exported goods exceeds the value of imported goods.

Trade deficit: when the value of exported goods is less than the value of imported goods.

The trade in services account

This is the record of credits and debits created by imports and exports of *services*, such as banking, insurance, transport and tourism. If the value of exported services exceeds that of imported services, which is usually the case for the UK, this account will be in surplus. As far as the UK is concerned, the fact that the trade in services account is usually in surplus helps reduce the impact of a deficit in the trading account, which tends to be the norm with the UK.

These two balances are often put together and called the **balance of trade**.

DEFINITION

Balance of trade: the balance between the trade in goods account and the trade in services account, in the balance of payments on current account.

The investment income account

These two accounts do not cover all transactions generated between the UK and other countries. UK residents who own property abroad or shares in foreign companies benefit when they earn interest, dividends and profits and this creates an inflow into the UK accounts. Foreigners owning assets in the UK may generate outflows as they receive interest, dividends and profits.

Current transfers

These are transactions such as those generated by giving aid to foreign countries, income brought to this country by immigrants, and transfers of funds to and from the EU (for example, aid to depressed areas from the European Social Fund). Current transfers can be both inflows and outflows.

The current account balance is the overall balance of these four subdivisions of current transactions between UK residents and abroad. The table below shows a summary of the UK balance of payments for 2006.

THE CAPITAL ACCOUNT

This account is concerned with recording the value of the purchase and sale of assets in other countries by UK residents that create inflows and outflows, as do similar transactions carried out by foreigners in the UK economy. These transactions include **foreign direct investment (FDI),** which occurs when a foreign company buys or expands plant in this country. This counts as an inflow, whereas if UK residents purchase assets held in another country, an outflow will be created.

DEFINITION

Foreign direct investment (FDI): investment in a given economy by residents of another economy.

learning tip

The balance of payments are a complex set of accounts that record all payments to and receipts from foreign countries. The imports and exports of physical goods are the most obvious element of these accounts: fluctuations in these will have an impact on the performance of the UK economy. Changes in any of the other components will also have an impact on the UK economy. Thus, a decision of a UK-owned company to invest abroad leads to an outflow of funds from the UK but, if the investment is successful, will lead to a long-term inflow of funds in the form of interest, dividends and profits. For this reason, it is sometimes helpful to distinguish between the short- and the long-term effects of changes in the balance of payments.

There might be long-term deficits or surpluses in individual components of the balance of payments, but in the long term the whole account must balance. There are, as you will learn in the following chapter and on the A2 part of your course, different ways of bringing the balance of payments into balance, each with different side effects on the rest of the economy. Governments are, therefore, keen to encourage a 'healthy balance of payments' and to avoid the problems associated with persistent deficits.

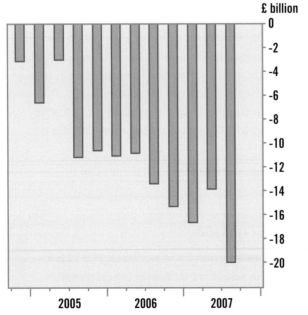

Table 8.14 UK balance of payments for 2005–2007

ACTIVITY ···:·

How might the balance of payments be affected in the short and long term by:

(a) a renewed outbreak of foot-and-mouth disease in the UK

(b) increased debt relief by the UK government to poorer countries

(c) higher rates of inflation in the UK compared to other members of the EU

(d) increased productivity of UK aerospace workers?

ACTIVITY ···:·

Use the Internet to compare and contrast the balance of payments on current accounts of two members of the EU over the last ten years. Explain your findings.

Policy conflicts

At the beginning of the chapter, we identified four broad objectives that governments might well have in terms of macroeconomic policies. They can be summarised as:

● increasing and achieving the growth potential of the economy

● price stability

● minimising unemployment

● improving the external performance of the economy as reflected in the balance of payments on current account.

While it is not impossible for governments to achieve all four of these objectives, there are many potential conflicts. For example, greater economic growth is likely to lead to the creation of more jobs but could lead to higher rates of inflation and a worsening balance of payments.

Maintaining price stability might involve reducing inflationary pressures by raising interest rates. This could result in slower rates of economic growth and lengthening dole queues. However, there could be an improvement in the balance of payments as slower rates of economic growth might be associated with lower incomes. Lower incomes will reduce the demand for imports, and lower growth could release productive capacity to sell more abroad.

Policies to minimise unemployment could lead to excessive growth, which might contribute to inflation and could lead to deterioration in the balance of payments as this country consumes more imported goods.

In the following chapter, you will get a better idea of how the UK government has tried to find a balance between different objectives. It should help you assess the overall effectiveness of government macroeconomic policies.

ACTIVITY ···:·

Compare and contrast the macroeconomic performance of two EU countries over the last ten years.

9 Macroeconomic policy

On completion of this chapter you should be able to:

- know the differences between fiscal, monetary and supply-side policies
- understand how fiscal polices can have both macroeconomic and microeconomic effects
- analyse the use of fiscal policies in terms of aggregate demand and aggregate supply
- know that monetary policy can involve the use of interest rates, the money supply and exchange rates
- understand how and why the Monetary Policy Committee (MPC) of the Bank of England sets interest rates
- evaluate how supply-side polices may increase the trend rate of growth, unemployment, inflation and the balance of payments on current account
- understand that supply-side changes can occur independently of government.

You need to remember that there are four principal objectives of macroeconomic policy. These are:

- increasing and achieving the growth potential of the economy
- price stability
- minimising unemployment
- improving the external performance of the economy as reflected in the balance of payments on current account.

This chapter is devoted to different policy measures that governments can use in an attempt to meet these objectives, and how to reconcile possible conflicts in trying to meet these objectives. You will also start to get an insight into differences that different economists and political parties might have about economic objectives and the attractiveness, or otherwise, of particular policies.

Fiscal policy

Fiscal policy refers to the use of taxation and government spending to affect macroeconomic variables. For more than 1,000 years, UK governments have levied taxes on all or some of the population. The raising of revenue in this way can be seen to have three possible functions:

- to raise revenue to pay for public spending
- to change the distribution of income
- to influence levels of aggregate demand.

DEFINITION

Fiscal policy: government use of taxation to influence macroeconomic variables.

RAISING REVENUE

The scale and scope of the government's desire to raise revenue is illustrated in the UK government's budget, which is published in March of each year. Planned spending and expected receipts contained in the 2007 budget are contained in Table 9.1.

Most of the items of expenditure and revenue are self-explanatory The government is now using categories of spending in line with international

Table 9.1 Planned spending and expected receipts, UK government (2007 budget)

Government spending	£ billion	Government revenue	£ billion
Social protection	161	Income tax	157
Health	104	National insurance	95
Education	77	Others	84
Others	59	VAT	80
Public order and safety	33	Corporation tax	50
Defence	32	Excise duties	41
Debt interest	30	Council tax	23
Personal social services	28	Business rates	22
Housing and environment	22	**Total**	553
Industry, agriculture, employment and training	21		
Transport	20		
Total	587		

Source: HM Treasury. Crown Copyright material reproduced with the permission of the Controller of HMSO and the Queen's Printer for Scotland.

standards. These mean that spending on recreation, culture, sport and overseas development are contained within the 'other' category. Spending on welfare, such as job seeker's tax allowance, pensions and other benefits, are contained within 'social protection'. 'Personal social services' refers to spending on social services. On the revenue side, 'others' includes capital gains tax, stamp duties, death duties and vehicle excise duties.

GOVERNMENT EXPENDITURE

It is worth looking more closely at how the government spends its revenue. It is a common misconception for students at an early stage in their studies of economics to imagine that the government pumps vast sums of investment into businesses. The table above shows that government spends just under 3.6 per cent of its total budget on 'Industry, agriculture, employment and training'. Social services, health and education constitute over 58 per cent of government spending.

The structure of the budget tends to indicate a range of government objectives. Spending on health and social services can show that the government sees these as merit goods and is trying to reduce inequalities. Defence, public order and safety can be seen as spending on public goods that the market system would not supply. It could be argued that spending on education and transport helps us all benefit from the positive externalities by having a better educated workforce and improved communications.

If this is actually the case, then this form of spending will also have an effect on long-run aggregate supply as these infrastructure improvements should increase the productive capacity of the whole economy. If these objectives were to be achieved, successful fiscal policies could lead to increases in national output and reductions in the price level. This win–win situation is illustrated in Figure 9.1.

This shows that spending on education could increase the productive potential capacity of the economy from $LRAS$ to $LRAS_1$. This would lead to a fall in rates of inflation from OP_1 to OP and an increase in national output from OX to OX_1.

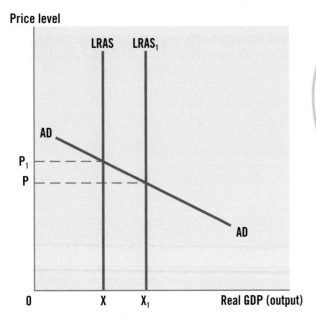

Price level

Figure 9.1 Possible effects of educational spending

learning tip
Students who have a poor understanding of economics often confuse the government's budget with the balance of payments. They muddle up government expenditure and taxation with imports and exports. Make sure you don't fall into this trap, by knowing the difference between the two concepts.

GOVERNMENT REVENUE

Looking at the revenue side of the government's budget, it should be clear that the government is heavily reliant upon national insurance and income tax for its revenue. The latter is called a **progressive tax** as those who earn more pay proportionately more in income tax. Currently, if you are single and you earn £12,000 a year, you would pay around £1,130 in tax – 9.4 per cent of your income. If you were single and earned £50,000 a year, you would pay around £11,500 in income tax – nearly 23 per cent of your income. The amount you actually pay depends on a number of other factors, but one of the principles underlying income tax is that the rich pay relatively more. Other taxes such as value added tax (VAT) don't discriminate between the rich and poor in the same way – we all have to pay a sales tax of 17.5 per cent on purchases of a wide range of goods and services irrespective of our earnings. Such taxes are called **regressive** as they are proportionately greater for those on low incomes.

The fact that changes in fiscal policy can not only affect macroeconomic policy objectives but also have redistribution effects means that government decisions about fiscal policy are very finely judged.

CHANGING THE DISTRIBUTION OF INCOME

Government spending accounts for around 40 per cent of total spending in the economy. How it raises taxes and how it spends its revenue can have an effect on the overall distribution of income. Thus, switching revenue raising from regressive taxes to those that are progressive should shift income away from the better off to those on lower incomes. For example, if VAT was reduced and income tax increased, the poor would benefit at the expense of the rich.

Changing spending priorities can also have an influence on the distribution of income. Increased spending on social housing tends to favour the less well off, whereas increased expenditure on road building tends to benefit the better off.

INFLUENCING AGGREGATE DEMAND

You will have noticed in Table 9.1 that the two sides of the government's budget are not equal. The government plans to spend £587 billion and expects to receive £553 billion in revenue. In other words, there is a **budget deficit** of £34 billion which the government will need to borrow in order to bring the budget into balance. If planned revenue exceeds planned expenditure, the government would be said to have a **budget surplus**. Equality between planned revenue and expenditure is a called a **balanced budget**. The UK government sets out a balanced budget over a period of time. This **golden rule** of fiscal policy means that the government attempts to ensure that over the period of the economic cycle there is either a surplus or a balanced budget. The government no longer uses fiscal policy as a lever to stimulate or to deflate aggregate demand.

DEFINITIONS

Budget surplus: occurs when the government plans to raise more in revenue than it plans to spend.

Balanced budget: occurs when planned government spending is equal to planned revenue.

Budget deficit: occurs when the government plans to spend more than it plans to raise in revenue.

Golden rule: government target of keeping government revenue in line with government expenditure over the period of the economic cycle.

ACTIVITY ····⫶

Currently there is some debate as to whether or not the government will be able to stick to its golden rule of fiscal policy. Use aggregate demand and supply analysis to show what might happen if government spending exceeds government revenue over the economic cycle.

learning tip
Using aggregate demand and supply diagrams as indicated above provides you with a good opportunity to score marks in your examination for evaluation. Diagrams can be used to show the possible effects of fiscal policy failures.

ACTIVITY ····⫶

Use the data given in the table above and assume that the government wishes to balance its budget, that is, make planned expenditure equal to planned revenue. Choose up to five changes that you would make to the budget. Evaluate both the economic and political impacts of your proposals.

THE EFFECTIVENESS OF FISCAL POLICY

There is little doubt that changes in government spending and taxation can have a direct effect on macroeconomic objectives. We can be reasonably certain that if taxes are reduced, aggregate demand will grow and incomes and employment will increase with possible inflationary side-effects. To some extent fiscal policies can act as an **automatic stabiliser** in respect to changes in the economic cycle. In times of recession, government expenditure is likely to increase automatically as growing unemployment is likely to lead to increased welfare payments, while tax revenues are likely to fall with a decline in economic activity. Both changes could lead to an increase in aggregate demand, which could promote recovery from recession. Moreover, in times of boom, welfare expenditure will fall and tax revenues increase. Both factors should lead to a reduction in aggregate demand and, therefore, fiscal policies have the potential to automatically iron out the worst of fluctuations in the economic cycle.

DEFINITION

Automatic stabiliser: fiscal policies that may automatically reduce fluctuations in economic activity associated with the economic cycle.

Governments have attempted to avoid short-term changes to fiscal policy and to publish more long-term plans for government spending and revenues. This longer-term planning may have contributed to one of the longest periods of economic growth of the UK economy as shown in Figure 9.2. But as with many major economic issues, different economists

Figure 9.2 Economic growth in the UK

have different views on why the economy seems to have done so well over the last 15 years.

There are, however, three major problems with more proactive fiscal policy:

● timing

● flexibility

● political unpopularity.

Timing

It often takes time for changes in government taxation and/or expenditure to take effect. Thus, consumers may take time to adjust their spending plans in response to cuts in income tax. These delays are often referred to as 'time-lags'. Other factors could therefore increase short-run economic growth before the fiscal measures to boost consumption take effect. In this context, fiscal policy will worsen the fluctuations associated with the economic cycle, and may contribute to increasing inflation.

Flexibility

Much of government spending is designed to protect the worse-off in society, and also to improve the environment, education and health. Changing spending on these can be difficult, for example, changes half-way through a programme to improve the NHS. Similarly, changing tax rates on a regular basis to regulate the economy is disruptive and

provides additional risks to both households and firms. Fiscal policy, though powerful, is not the most flexible of economic policies.

Political unpopularity

Changes in *fiscal policies*, especially those relating to raising additional revenue or cutting expenditure, are not usually popular with the electorate. Raising taxes in the past has resulted in civil unrest. Both the main political parties fear the political backlash that would be associated with some fiscal policy decisions. In the UK both Labour and the Conservatives say that they do not plan to raise income tax. At the same time, they also

Fiscal policies can cause civil unrest, such as the Poll Tax riots of 1990

both claim that they will stick to budget changes that should lead to increases in spending on both health and education. These commitments reduce the scope which UK governments have to use fiscal policies to achieve macroeconomic policy objectives. It could be argued that these political constraints make monetary and supply-side policies more attractive alternatives.

> **ACTIVITY** ····⁙
>
> Use the Internet to access the government's budget for a different year to 2007. Compare the two sets of data. What can you work out about priorities in government policies? Have they changed?

Monetary policy

In addition to fiscal policy, governments can also use the influence they have over the banking systems to:

- change interest rates
- affect the money supply
- change exchange rates.

This is known as **monetary policy**. This different set of policy levers also can affect macroeconomic objectives: economic growth, the price level, employment and the balance of payments on current account. For example, if it becomes harder for households and firms to borrow money, consumption and investment are both likely to fall. If this happens, aggregate demand will fall, leading to a fall in the rate of inflation and a drop in national output and employment.

> **DEFINITION**
>
> **Monetary policy:** the use of interest rates, money supply and exchange rates to influence macroeconomic variables.

> **ACTIVITY** ····⁙
>
> Use aggregate demand and aggregate supply analysis to illustrate the possible effects of making it easier to borrow money.

INTEREST RATES

Interest rates represent the cost of borrowing money and also the return that might be received from depositing savings in a bank, building society or other financial institution. Interest rates are always expressed as a percentage, usually on an annual basis. Thus, at the moment a savings deposit with the Coventry Building Society will earn you 6.4 per cent interest: if you save £100 for a year, you will receive a return of £6.40. As you would expect, the interest rate on loans is higher, and at the time of writing ranged from 7.4 per cent for a loan from Northern Rock to 29.7 per cent for one from the Ulster Bank. In the latter example, it would cost you £29.70 to borrow £100 for a year.

> **DEFINITION**
>
> **Interest rates:** the cost of borrowing, or the benefit of lending or depositing, money, usually expressed as a percentage.

> **learning tip**
>
> This is another plea to be precise – remember you **borrow**, the bank **lends**. Students often use these terms interchangeably and this makes it harder for examiners to make sense of your answers.

You will study how the banking system works in much greater detail in the A2 part of your course, but at this stage you need to realise the importance of a stable and honest banking system to the functioning of both the economy and society as a whole. Banks rely on the trust of both borrowers and lenders and in order to try to ensure trust and stability, all economies have some form of **central bank.** Although they work in different ways, they usually act as the bankers' bank and the interest rate charged to individual banks, should they need to borrow, will have a direct influence on rates charged to borrowers or received by lenders. The interest charged to individual banks is often called the **bank rate**.

In some countries, the central bank is directly controlled by government, in which case it is possible for governments to set the bank rate. In other countries, including the UK, bank rates are set by an independent body set up for that purpose. In the UK the central bank is the *Bank of England* and, although it is technically owned by the government, its *Monetary Policy Committee (MPC)* is meant to be free of government influence to set the bank rate. Its members meet on a monthly basis and in March 2008 they confirmed the UK bank rate at 5.5 per cent.

The MPC is made up of economists working for the Bank of England, together with four appointments from academic and commercial organisations. It was set up in 1997 by the newly elected Labour government, which wanted to create greater stability in interest rate policy. Its remit is to ensure that inflation is held within a range of 1 to 3 per cent – the actual target being 2 per cent. Although meeting this target is the prime responsibility of the committee, it is also required to be mindful of the impact of changes in interest rates on incomes, employment and the rate of exchange.

THE MONEY SUPPLY

In the past, the Bank of England has been used by the government to try to regulate how much credit is available to borrowers. This pool of potential funding is called the **money supply**. Some economists

have argued that changes in the money supply lead directly to changes in the rate of inflation. This controversial economic issue is studied in greater depth in the A2 part of your course.

Economists tend to agree that if it is easier for households and firms to borrow money, aggregate demand will be boosted, leading to potential increases in both incomes and the price level. However, there is less agreement as to the ability of a government directly to restrict the growth in the money supply in order to fight inflation. In the past, governments have tried to use direct controls to limit the ability of banks to lend. These direct controls were never particularly effective, as both banks and borrowers could find ways of evading them. For this reason, the central banks of most developed economies do not attempt directly to regulate the money supply, preferring to concentrate on using changes in interest rates to keep inflation in check, although not at the expense of limiting long-term economic growth.

Another reason for not focusing on the money supply is shown by the performance of the UK economy during the 1980s. In 1979, the incoming Conservative government was committed to fight inflation by cutting the money supply. Because direct controls had been shown to be ineffective, they used a variety of measures, including raising taxes and interest rates and cutting government expenditure. The result was the deepest depression since the 1930s, with unemployment reaching 12.4 per cent of the working population in 1984. With hindsight, the social costs of this type of monetary policy might be seen to be too high.

THE EXCHANGE RATE

The **exchange rate** refers to the rate at which one currency can be exchanged for another. Thus, at the time of writing £1 is worth US$2.01 or €1.45. Twelve months ago, the pound sterling was worth $1.80. This means that the value of the pound has risen in relation to the value of the US dollar. These changes in the exchange rate are likely to have an impact on macroeconomic objectives. In 2006 US residents would have had to pay $1.80 to buy each pound needed to purchase a UK-produced good or service. As the value of the pound has risen, US residents now have to pay more in terms of dollars to purchase UK-produced goods. On the other hand, the falling value of the US dollar means that US-produced goods appear to UK residents to be cheaper. Therefore, if the value of the pound rises in relation to the dollar, exports to the USA become relatively dearer, whereas imports into the UK priced in US dollars, such as oil, become relatively cheaper. If the exchange rate against the dollar were to fall, UK-produced goods and services in the USA would become cheaper and imports priced in dollars more expensive.

Changes in exchange rates (see Figure 9.3), especially for a country such as the UK, which is heavily dependent upon international trade, can have a significant impact on macroeconomic performance.

A falling exchange rate will tend to boost exports and reduce imports, leading to an increase in aggregate demand for domestically produced goods and services, with a consequent increase in national output, employment and prices. This is shown in Figure 9.4 by the shift in aggregate demand to the

ECONOMICS IN CONTEXT

BRITS GO BARGAIN-HUNTING IN NEW YORK

For the first time since 1982 the pound is worth two dollars, and British shoppers are flocking to New York for what is effectively a city-wide half-price sale. Weekend shopping breaks in the city have become so popular that British Airways and Virgin Atlantic have laid on extra daily flights – but how long can the bonanza last?

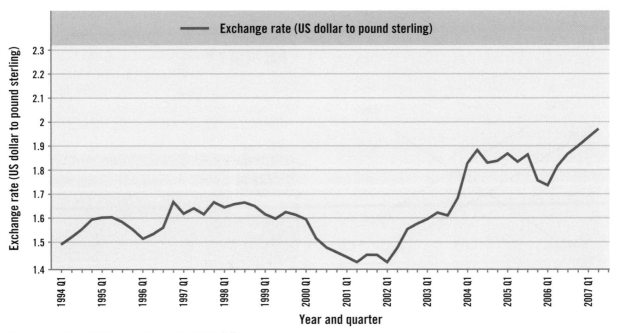

Figure 9.4 Value of the pound in terms of US dollar

right, leading to an increase in national output of *OY* to *OY₁* and an increase in the price level from *OP* to *OP₁*, dependent on the availability or otherwise of spare capacity in the economy.

It follows that increasing exchange rates are likely to lead to a fall in national output, employment and output and a reduction in the rate of inflation.

The preceding analysis gives lots of clues as to why governments might be tempted to try to influence the exchange rate as a means of achieving different economic objectives. These could include:

● improving the balance of payments by encouraging a fall in the exchange rate

● encouraging domestic expansion by the same means

● reducing the rate of inflation by raising the exchange rate.

In the past, exchange rates have actually been set by governments, but this form of direct control, as was the case with the money supply, was never particularly effective.

An alternative policy to influence the exchange rates involves the use of reserves of foreign currency held by central banks, which can be manipulated to influence exchange rates. Thus, if the Bank of England releases holdings of US dollars onto foreign exchange markets, this could decrease the value

of the dollar and improve the value of the pound. Alternatively, increasing holdings of US dollars will boost the value of the dollar and reduce the value of the pound.

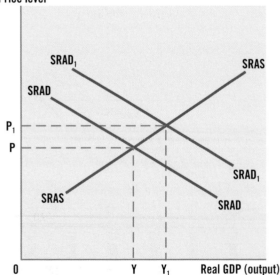

Price level

Figure 9.5 Effects of falling exchange rates

ECONOMICS IN CONTEXT

BLACK WEDNESDAY

In UK politics and economics, Black Wednesday refers to 16th September 1992, when the Conservative government was forced to withdraw the pound from the European Exchange Rate Mechanism (ERM) due to pressure by currency speculators – most notably George Soros, who made over US$1 billion from this speculation. In 1997 the UK Treasury estimated the cost of Black Wednesday at £3.4 billion, but it is now known that the Treasury spent £27bn of reserves in propping up the pound.

Black Wednesday has been a major event in shaping monetary policy in the UK. Until the enormous embarrassment in 1992, the government used its reserves of gold and foreign currency in an effort to influence the exchange rate. UK governments now take the view that it is better to leave the determination of the exchange rate to market forces, and monetary policies are no longer used to influence the exchange rate.

ACTIVITY ····⫶

Find out more about Black Wednesday. Why were speculators like George Soros so successful?

learning tip Although the government does not intervene to change the value of the pound, its actions in terms of macroeconomic policies can still affect the value of the pound.

THE EFFECTIVENESS OF MONETARY POLICY

It appears that the UK government and the Bank of England have learned much about the

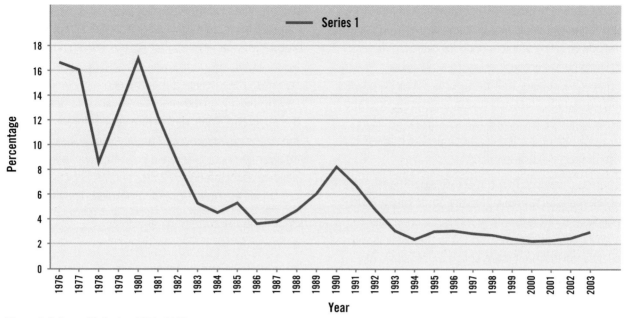

Figure 9.4 Annual inflation 1976–2003

effectiveness or otherwise of monetary policy in influencing macroeconomic objectives. It might be an exaggeration, but it now seems clear that attempts to control the money supply and the exchange rate can both go seriously wrong. On the other hand, using the interest rate to keep inflation within targeted levels appears to have worked very well. The use of the terms 'seems' and 'appears' is deliberate, as there is some level of debate between economists as to why inflation appears, as shown in Figure 9.5, to have been tamed. Is this the result of the work of the MPC, or could other factors be significant?

Supply-side policies

When monetary and fiscal policies are used by governments to help to effect macroeconomic objectives, they are primarily aimed at influencing aggregate demand. **Supply-side policies** are, as the term implies, aimed at boosting aggregate supply by increasing the productive capacity of the economy.

> **DEFINITION**
>
> **Supply-side policies:** government policies designed to increase the productive capacity of the economy.

Their potential impact is illustrated in Figure 9.6 by the rightward shift in aggregate supply leading to a rise in national incomes from OX_1 to OX_2 and downward pressure on price levels from OP_1 to OP_2.

You will have learned in your studies for the first module of your economic course that more competitive markets can be associated with a more efficient economy; a *lack* of competition can have the opposite effect.

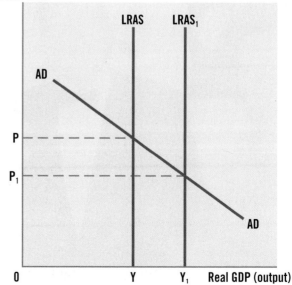

Figure 9.6 Successful supply-side policies

There are many ways in which governments have tried to encourage markets to be more competitive. These include enacting anti monopoly legislation, outlawing collusion between businesses, making it easier to start up new businesses, making sure consumers are better informed, reducing tariffs and quotas on imports, and privatisation of state-owned assets. Economists tend to agree that promoting more competitive markets is a useful supply-side approach.

There is, however, much more disagreement about the effectiveness of many other supply-side policies. At one extreme are those economists who argue that markets are best left to themselves with as little government intervention as possible. At the other extreme are economists who consider that government intervention is needed because a market-based system produces socially unacceptable outcomes. For this reason supply-side policies can be placed into two categories:

● market oriented, and

● interventionist.

MARKET-ORIENTED POLICIES

These supply-side policies are often associated with right-wing economists who were particularly influential in the 1980s on UK governments under the leadership of Margaret Thatcher and on US governments led by Ronald Reagan. In their most extreme form, economists such as Arthur Laffer and Robert Mundal argued that governments should cut taxes, especially on the well off, and decrease welfare benefits. They believed that the economy would be improved if governments intervened far less in the economy. Their views were very different from those of Keynes, who *had* argued that government intervention could increase economic welfare. The policies associated with Laffer and Mundal are often described as market-oriented policies. They include:

● cutting marginal rates of taxation

● reducing government expenditure

● cutting welfare benefits

● reducing trade union power

● privatisation and deregulation

● encouraging the free movement of labour and capital.

Cutting marginal rates of taxation

Marginal taxes are the extra taxes paid on extra income, and if progressive taxes are used this means that a bigger and bigger proportion of additional incomes is taken in the form of taxation. Laffer argued that high **marginal rates of taxation** on the better off acted as a disincentive to work. He believed that tax cuts would increase the incentive to work. He argued that reducing the tax burden on the rich would encourage more entrepreneurial activity, and that there would be a **trickle-down effect** in that, if the better off became wealthier, their increased spending

Margaret Thatcher and Ronald Reagan in the 1980s

DEFINITION

Marginal rates of taxation: those paid on any addition to an individual's income.

Trickle-down effect: the suggestion that raising the incomes of the better off can lead to increases in the income of the less well off.

would help improve the incomes and living standards of the less well off.

In the UK, in 1979 the top rate of income tax was 83 per cent; this has now been reduced to 40 per cent. The effects of these tax cuts on the incentives to work are disputed by economists. It can be argued that reducing taxation could have the opposite effect, as it allows people to work less hours for the same amount of income.

Reducing government expenditure

Another, closely related, market-oriented supply-side policy has been to maintain balanced budgets. If tax rates are also reduced, this means that government spending has to be cut. This is seen as being desirable by right-wing economists who argue that the public sector is more bureaucratic and less efficient than the private sector. They argue that reducing the size of the public sector releases more resources for the private sector.

Cutting welfare benefits

It has long been argued that the existence of welfare benefits acts as a disincentive for some members of the population to work. Common sense tells us that if benefits from not working exceed those from working, some people will choose unemployment, thus reducing the size of the workforce. Some economists have gone so far as to argue that all welfare payments create disincentives to work, as they stop labour markets from clearing. They believe that unemployment will actually be cured if wages are allowed to fall to bring about equilibrium between the demand and supply of labour. The existence of welfare benefits provides workers with an alternative source of income to that derived from paid employment. Therefore, some supply-side economists argue, governments should not pay welfare benefits.

Reducing trade union power

It has been argued that powerful trade unions help create rigidities in the labour market that limit the flexible use of labour, push up wages, and lead to lost production should strikes or other forms of industrial action occur. Reducing trade union power was

another aspect of the economic policies followed by Conservative governments in the 1980s. They made it harder for workers to go out on strike and tried to make unions responsible for losses made by firms that could be linked to trade union activities.

Privatisation and deregulation

Privatisation refers to the transfer of the ownership of assets from state or public ownership to the private sector. This policy was vigorously pursued by Conservative governments in the 1980s and continued by successive Labour governments, leaving far fewer nationalised or state-owned businesses. It is agued that privately owned businesses have a greater incentive to innovate and to become more efficient. Forty years ago, many major businesses were state owned. They included:

- Thomas Cook
- The National Coal Board
- British Gas
- ports and airports
- British Rail
- British Leyland
- The Central Electricity Generating Board
- The Milk Marketing Board
- British Airways
- The Bank of England.

Today only the last of these is in state ownership, but economists tend to disagree as to the impact of privatisation on the promotion of competition and whether or not this has increased long-run aggregate supply. The privately owned businesses running the railways, selling gas, electricity and water businesses are not perceived to be particularly competitive.

Deregulation refers to the reduction of rules and regulations which might be seen to hinder the free working of markets. In the past, competition within particular UK industries has been limited. Thus, local bus services were often given to single suppliers, only chemists could sell particular drugs, and if you wanted your eyes tested you would have to go to a local optician. These regulations tended to create

> ### DEFINITIONS
>
> **Privatisation:** the transfer of ownership from the public to the private sector.
>
> **Deregulation:** the reduction of government rules and regulations that may hinder the free working of markets.

local monopolies and many have been removed. As with other aspects of supply-side policies, the effects of deregulation are debatable.

Encouragement of free movement of capital and labour

One of the very first policy changes made when Margaret Thatcher came to power in 1979 was to remove all exchange controls, which effectively meant that capital flows in and out of the country were no longer regulated by the government. More recently, the UK government has been much less restrictive than other European governments in response to the broadening of the EU to include countries like Poland, Slovenia and the Baltic States. Workers from these countries have been free to seek work in the UK.

INTERVENTIONIST POLICIES

It is a mistake to only associate supply-side policies with right-wing economists who were particularly influential in the 1980s. Interventionist policies tend to be associated with more left-wing economists who also argue for supply-side policies because they believe that markets do not always work to promote economic welfare. As noted earlier, John Maynard Keynes was an advocate of government intervention to cure long-term unemployment.

Interventionist approaches are still influential: former Prime Minister Tony Blair argued for a 'Third Way' in which market-based solutions were preferred but governments should still intervene in the interests of greater fairness and, crucially, to promote

macroeconomic stability and encourage growth in the productive capacity of the economy. Interventionist supply-side policies include:

- improved education and training
- subsidising investment in research and development
- infrastructure improvements
- promoting enterprise
- anti monopoly policies
- nationalisation.

Education and training

The importance of this policy has previously been identified when talking about economic growth. Improving the skills and productivity of the workforce through improved education and training is clearly a means by which the productive capacity of the economy can be increased. The Labour government with its emphasis on 'education, education, education' and other policies such as 'train to gain', the introduction of vocational courses, and investment in improving literacy and numeracy, has claimed that the UK work force is becoming more flexible, more multi-skilled, and therefore more productive.

Businesses also realise that education and training make a significant contribution to the development of a more skilled and productive workforce.

Research and development

Some government funds are used to support research and development in new technologies considered to improve international competitiveness. Such funding is often channelled through UK universities, which have a good record in terms of new inventions that should contribute to supply-side improvements.

Businesses are given tax breaks to encourage the adoption of new technologies and more efficient means of production.

Infrastructure improvements

The productive capacity of the economy can also be improved by investment in infrastructure such as roads, railways and ports. Such investment is often long term and can be less attractive to private sector investors. You may remember from the section on fiscal policies that the government currently spends £20 billion a year on transport – the bulk of it going towards road building.

Promoting enterprise

It has been noted earlier that the government seeks to increase the productive capacity of the economy by encouraging more entrepreneurial activity through education about enterprise, grants for business start-ups, and support for small businesses. In recent years the government has made it easier for those who have become bankrupt to go back into business. These policies link to those to promote more competition and are designed to encourage more risk taking in an effort to create a more dynamic economy.

The development of a more enterprising workforce is a goal to which many businesses contribute, both in respect of their own employees and through various projects to link businesses to school and community based activities. For example, Asda offers prizes to employees who show greatest skill in predicting sales of particular products or brands. Many businesses use various types of commissions and bonuses to reward enterprising behaviour by their employees.

Anti monopoly intervention

UK governments have legal mechanisms to intervene in order to limit the effect of monopoly power, and to promote competition with the objective of increasing the competitiveness of the economy and, therefore, contributing to conditions favourable to the long-term growth of the economy.

The Competition Commission is invested with powers to investigate monopolies and to judge whether or not they are acting in the **public interest**. This is the term used to describe the balancing up of advantages and disadvantages which may be attributable to the behaviour of monopolists. Typically, it is about the trade-off between consumers enjoying some of the benefits that are said to accrue from economies of scale, with other anti competitive practices. The

> **DEFINITION**
>
> **Public interest:** a measure against which an attempt is made to balance up the positive and negative effects of, for example, a monopoly, or other economic factor.

commission recently reported on a long investigation into the behaviour of the four leading supermarkets in the UK, and found that they were not exploiting customers, as prices were broadly competitive, but they were taking advantage of their monopoly power to delay payments to, and force down prices paid to, suppliers.

The EU has stronger anti monopoly legislation, with the power to levy fines on those companies guilty of uncompetitive behaviour. British Airways was found guilty in 2007 of colluding with Virgin to ensure that they both charged the same fuel surcharges. BA has been prosecuted in the USA for similar reasons.

> **ACTIVITY ····**
>
> Use the Internet to find out which firms have been investigated recently by the Competition Commission. Assess how far this body has increased competition.

Nationalisation

Nationalisation is the reverse of privatisation: assets are owned by, or placed in the ownership of, the state. In the past, governments have taken failing private sector firms such those in the coal industry, railways and steel production, into state ownership. This is

> **DEFINITION**
>
> **Nationalisation:** the transfer of ownership from the private to the public sector.

no longer pursued as government policy, with the exception of Network Rail, which has been virtually nationalised after a series of highly publicised rail crashes. More recently, there have been suggestions that Northern Rock should be nationalised.

THE EFFECTIVENESS OF SUPPLY-SIDE POLICIES

Since the 1970s, successive UK governments have used a variety of supply-side policies to increase long-run aggregate supply. These are potentially very attractive politically, as they offer the prospect of higher levels of income and employment with reduced inflationary pressures. Many of these policies have been developed by right-wing economists who believe that economies can improve if the role and influence of governments is reduced.

Market-based supply-side policies were applied vigorously in the 1980s in both the UK and the USA. In the 1990s they were 'forced' on many developing countries by the World Bank. There is an enormous debate between economists as to the effectiveness of these policies. Some see them as a smokescreen for redistributing wealth from the poor to the rich, while others believe that reducing the role of government and increasing the incentives to work have produced a supply-side revolution that has improved economic welfare.

As far as the UK is concerned, the Labour government elected in 1997 has maintained and developed many of the market-oriented supply-side policies first introduced by the Conservatives, but they have tended to avoid those that are more controversial, such as cutting welfare benefits, and further reducing tax rates. At the same time, they have increased government expenditure on health and education. They have paid particular attention to the development of policies to improve workforce productivity and increase the incentives to work for those who might otherwise choose to be unemployed. It has been argued that the UK has a more flexible workforce, which has increased the competitiveness of the UK economy, especially when compared to the rest of Europe.

There is little doubt that some successful supply-side policies lead to growth in industrial capacity, but it is also true that both monetary and fiscal policies have

their role to play to ensure that aggregate demand is managed effectively to promote economic growth and restrain inflation. It appears that governments need to rely on a range of policy measures to try to ensure that potentially conflicting policy objectives are met.

ACTIVITY ····⫶

(a) Choose three supply-side policies which you believe will be the most effective in increasing the productive capacity of the economy. Justify your choices.

(b) Choose three supply-side policies which you believe will be the least effective in increasing the productive capacity of the economy. Justify your choices.

THE MACRO POLICY MIX

The governments of all developed economies use a mixture of fiscal, monetary and supply-side policies to try to ensure that macroeconomic policy objectives are met. In the UK there appears to be a growing consensus between economists on the desirability of this approach of using a mixture of supply-side, monetary and fiscal policies to achieve macroeconomic policy objectives.

It is logical to argue that long-term economic growth will only occur if supply-side policies are successfully implemented that increase the productive capacity of the economy. Effective supply-side interventions should also improve the international competitiveness of the UK economy, leading to an improvement in the balance of payments.

Traditionally, fiscal policies have been used to promote economic growth, but the government is now constrained by EU rules designed to limit the proportion of GDP taken up with government expenditure. Government spending is more likely to be directed to the provision of merit and public goods in order to deal with potential market failures. Taxation policies are used to provide greater incentives for the unemployed to enter the labour market, and the present UK government appears to place less emphasis on using fiscal policies to redistribute income from the better off to the less well off.

Monetary policies involving the changing of interest rates remain the lever favoured by UK, US and EU governments to maintain short-term economic growth as close to long-term trend rates as possible, thus avoiding inflation and trying to minimise unemployment.

There is, however, far more controversy about which supply-side policies are most effective. Arguments as to the merits or otherwise of market-based or interventionist government policies never seem to go away. If you have enjoyed the story so far, carry on for a second year of economic debate, discussion and argument.

ACTIVITY ⋯⋮

The UK government and the EU appear to use interest rates as the main way of achieving macroeconomic policy objectives. Assess the advantages and disadvantages of this approach.

ACTIVITY ⋯⋮

Which macroeconomic policies could be used to deal with the three scenarios outlined below? Choose those which you consider most appropriate. Justify your choice.

Scenario 1: Economic growth has been negative for the last 3 quarters. Unemployment is rising rapidly. The balance of payments on current account is in surplus, as is the government's budget. Inflation is running at less than 1 per cent.

Scenario 2: Economic growth has been negative for the last 3 quarters. Unemployment is rising rapidly. The balance of payments on current account is in surplus, as is the government's budget. Inflation is increasing and has reached 5 per cent.

Scenario 3: Economic growth is running at 3.5 per cent per annum. Unemployment is below 1 million. The balance of payments is in serious deficit. The government has a balanced budget and inflation has increased from 2.2 to 2.9 per cent.

ExamCafé
Relax, refresh, result!

Relax and prepare

Definitions, diagrams and the news

Ashley

I noticed that economists like using diagrams, such as Production Possibility Curves and aggregate demand/aggregate supply analysis. The good news is that when I looked at past papers, I found that there are only a handful of diagrams that come up time and again. For example, if prices change, it is due to either an increase or a decrease in demand, or an increase or decrease in supply, so there are just four key diagrams, which can be applied to all sorts of different situations involving price changes, if you know which one to choose.

I have put together a couple of pages of diagrams and I practice drawing them, so that I can reproduce them easily under exam conditions. I also practice writing explanations of what's happening in the diagrams, so that I can do this quickly and efficiently in exams.

Nasima

I never studied economics before I started AS. I found that it was a lot like learning a new language, lots of new words, and lots of words from day-to-day speech that have a special meaning in economics, a meaning that's not always the same as the everyday one.

So I did what I do when learning any new language: I started a 'vocabulary book'. This is a little notebook where I split each page in half with vertical line. On the left I put the new word, the economic term, or piece of jargon. On the right I put the definition. Sometimes I copy the definition out of a textbook, but often I find that I have to 'translate' the definition into one I can understand. As I say, it is a bit like learning a language. And it pays off, because very often an exam question will ask you to define a term. My teacher said that many candidates lose marks because they can't define terms fully and accurately.

Lori

For data-response economics, especially for paper Econ-2, I think it's important to be interested in current affairs. If you know what's going on in the world, if you know your economic theory, and you can link the two, then you can make much better sense of the subject. When we started our AS, the teacher advised us to start taking an interest in the news and he was right. Before I started the course, I never took much interest in anything other than the fashion pages, but now I make sure that I go to the library at least once a week to have a good look at the serious newspapers. If I find an article that's related to a topic we've done in class, I photocopy it and keep it in a file.

I also watch the news on television more often than before. *Newsnight* on BBC2 is very good, and the news on BBC Radio 4 is very useful, for example, the programme on at 10 at night. You might say 'boring', but I say that getting the grades you want at A Level makes it 'interesting'. You certainly won't learn much for your exams from non-stop music shows or 'reality' TV. I've also set the BBC News website as my 'homepage' on my computer, so I can easily keep an eye out for what's going on.

I want to get into a very good university, so when I went for interview I found that my improved general knowledge was a huge help. Being more 'aware' doesn't just help with economics, it's important all round.

Refresh your memory

Revision checklist

Can you…?	Turn to page…	Can you…?	Turn to page…
Make a list of important economic indicators and explain what they indicate	106	Explain how these objectives can conflict with each other	157
Define the term 'economic cycle'	116	Use a production possibility diagram to explain short-run and long-run growth	141, 143
Use a diagram to explain how positive and negative output gaps occur in the economic cycle	118	Define inflation and distinguish between demand-pull and cost-push inflation	148
Define the 'multiplier' and explain how the multiplier process works	119	Explain how unemployment is measured	113
Explain the main components in the circular flow of income	124	List and explain the different types of unemployment; distinguish between demand-side and supply-side causes of unemployment	151
Explain why income = output = expenditure	125	Describe the balance of payments on current account; explain the meaning of surplus and deficit on current account	155
Explain how the circular flow of income can be in 'equilibrium'	127	Give examples of how strengths and weaknesses in the domestic economy can affect the balance of payments	156
Explain the influence of the multiplier and accelerator	132	Explain how changes in the exchange rate can affect the balance of payments, and how this in turn can affect the level of domestic economic activity	165
Use an AD and AS diagram to analyse changes in the macroeconomy	128	Distinguish between fiscal and monetary policy	158, 163
List the components of AD and explain how each of these components is determined	129	Explain why governments collect taxes and how government spending can affect the economy	159
Explain how AD affects the level of economic activity	130	Explain how modern fiscal policy is governed by 'budgetary rules'	159
Distinguish between short- and long-run aggregate supply and explain how each is determined	134, 139	Explain how the interest rate is used by the Bank of England to influence AD in the short run and achieve its inflation target	163
List the main objectives of macro policy	157	Make a list of 'supply-side policies' and explain how these are used to try to increase the long-run trend rate of non-inflationary growth	172

Key word quiz

Define:
1. aggregate demand and supply
2. gross domestic product
3. injections and withdrawals
4. equilibrium in the national income
5. the multiplier
6. output gap

These are answers to the following data-response question:

'UK inflation is mainly caused by rising costs in the economy.' Use the data to help you evaluate this statement (25 marks).

Armand's answer

Examiner comments:
Armand does well to refer to the data straight away, and this will help him score marks for analysis. We do not have sight of the data here, so this does not affect us, but the examiner might have found it helpful if Armand had indicated to which part of the data he was referring, e.g. 'Extract A', or 'line 25' (AQA extracts always have line numbers).

The data says that 'cost pressures' are strengthening. This can lead to cost-push inflation, where increased costs of production, e.g. higher labour or oil prices, force producers and suppliers to shift the burden onto consumers in the form of higher prices. The firm's ability to pass on these higher costs of production depends on what type of good or service they are providing, e.g. if it is a luxury good or a necessity. Hence the effects of cost-push elasticity can be limited by the price elasticity of demand. If a good is price elastic the producer will be limited in its ability to pass on the costs in the form of higher prices. However, the extract in the data says that there has been a 'steep rise in a number of goods', and this would suggest that cost-push inflation is a major problem.

Price increases of this sort can have wider repercussions. Following each round of inflation, the purchasing power of consumers (their real income' will effectively fall. This can lead to a wage-price spiral, where people look to reinstate the value of their real income by asking for higher wages (often via their trade union negotiating on their behalf). This again puts pressures on the costs of production, which producers might again pass on to consumers in the form of higher wages. However, one of the extracts says that productivity and competition among suppliers have both increased. This means that the effect of 'sharp increases in raw material costs' and 'record oil prices' will both be limited. Hence, the fairly constant inflation rates shown in the graph can be explained by economic growth, which has also meant that

Examiner comments:
The phrases 'luxury' and 'necessity' are rather vague, and some further explanation would help here.

Examiner comments:
Strictly speaking, 'goods' are not price-elastic. It is the **demand** for goods that has an 'elasticity' that can be measured with respect to price.

that demand-pull inflation is not really an issue, because increases in productivity will effectively cancel out some of the increases in production costs.

The extract also says that increases in UK inflation may 'force the Bank of England to raise interest rates.' Since interest rates are a cost on producers, who need to re-equip themselves regularly and usually borrow money for this purpose, and since interest rates affect the disposable income of consumers who have variable interest-rate mortgages, this statement strongly suggests that the Bank of England's view is that inflation is mainly demand led, rather than being caused by cost-push factors.

However, it does appear that the changes in costs can go some way to explain the trend of inflation in the UK. This is especially true when the price of oil is increasing. The price of oil affects the economy not only through the transport industry. Since so many of the products being transported depend heavily on oil as a raw material, the demand for oil is price-inelastic, and this cost factor can become far more significant than any demand factors.

Current anti-inflation policy, as used in the UK and the Eurozone involves the government setting a target inflation rate, then delegating control of interest rates to the central bank. This assumes that inflation is demand-led. Supply-side policy is then used to try to raise productive capacity, so raising the long-run trend rate of growth, and enabling higher growth rates to exist along side lower inflation rates. Costs are essentially a supply-side influence, so it would be surprising to find a government stressing costs as a major factor. In the UK, anti-inflation policy appears to have been working effectively since the independence of the Bank of England in 1997, and was working in a similar fashion for several years before that. It could be argued, however, that it has not yet been tested by a major external supply-side 'shock', such as a sudden and massive global oil-price hike, or a collapse in housing markets causing a catastrophic international collapse in capital markets and a large rise in international interest rates caused by a severe squeeze on credit.

Sara's answer

Examiner comments:
There is some confusion here. Sara has copied out a sentence from the data, but has not commented on it effectively. The CPI is a measure of inflation, it does not necessarily indicate the causes of inflation. The CPI will increase when the prices it tracks increase, for whatever reason. In other words, an increase in the prices that make up the CPI may or may not indicate an increase in costs.

Examiner comments:
This is a very good line of argument.

Examiner comments:
The supply and demand diagram has some relevance. However, an aggregate demand and aggregate supply (AD/ AS) diagram would be much more appropriate to this macro question.

Examiner comments:
The demand curve could have been drawn more steeply to signify a low elasticity of demand in the region of the line where the price changes. The reasons for the demand-inelasticity of oil could also have been mentioned, as could the reasons why oil prices affect costs and hence the inflation rate.

Examiner comments:
Overall: The answer is a bit on the brief side. Some relevant issues are touched upon, but points are not developed. There needs to be a clearer distinction between cost and non-cost factors. No evaluation. A poor answer but some understanding is shown. Level 2 (9 marks).

Changes in costs in the UK, for instance the cost of oil, can lead to inflationary pressures, as costs will rise, pushing prices up. In the extract it says 'steep price rises in a number of goods lifted the Consumer Price Index'.

If the Bank of England were to raise interest rates, this would bring the exchange rate up. The increased interest rates would encourage saving and people from other countries putting their money into UK banks. All this would increase the value of the pound. An increase in the value of the pound would mean that our exports would become less competitive and imports would become cheaper for UK buyers. Among these imports would be oil, which is usually priced in dollars, so this would reduce costs and cost-push inflation would fall.

The increased costs in oil can be shown in a diagram.

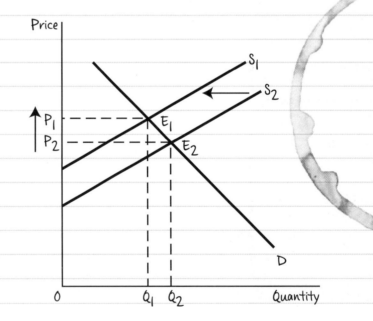

As you can see a cut in supply raises price hugely, as the demand for oil is inelastic, pushing prices up.

DATA-RESPONSE QUESTIONS

Re-cap on the 'General advice' in the Exam Café for Part One (see page 101).

AQA examination papers Econ-1 and Econ-2 are marked out of a maximum of 75. There are 25 objective test items (25 marks in total), so the data-response element is marked out of 50.

There are four parts to the data-response question, carrying 5, 8, 12 and 25 marks. Pay attention to the following points.

● You have a choice of question. Choose carefully, on the basis of the *whole* question. Don't be put off a question because a small part of it is difficult for you; don't be attracted to it if a small part appears easy. Remember that the final part carries the most marks.

● Label sub-questions clearly in the margin: (a), (b), (c), (d).

● Avoid the weakest approach, which is to simply copy out chunks of data without comment.

● Be aware of an 'incline of difficulty': as you move through the questions you should be using higher order skills...

● . . . and be aware of 'levels' of response. In particular, be aware that about half the marks for part (d) are awarded for this one important skill. So when answering this question *always* reserve some time and space to show your ability to evaluate, for example, by making judgements, justifying a policy, or assessing whether advantages outweigh disadvantages. Also pay attention to **command words** (see below).

● Use the data wherever possible, and refer to the data where appropriate.

● Use your knowledge of economic principles.

● Use your pre-existing economic awareness. (You can improve this from newspapers, television and radio.)

Command words

These are words that give you a strong clue as to the level and depth of treatment that the examiner wants. They are 'trigger' words that are closely linked to the levels of *skill* outlined in the 'assessment of objectives' of the AQA specification. Generally speaking, the higher the level of skill, the more marks are allocated, and the more time you should take on the question.

Some command words, such as **'discuss'** and **'explain'** can be interpreted differently, according to their context. AQA examiners, for example, tend to believe that the word 'discuss' is a very powerful trigger-word, asking for the highest skills (examiners on other boards might use it in a lower part of the skills incline). The word 'explain' can be interpreted as requiring a lower level of skill than 'analyse'. So to be on the safe side, we have placed these words at their highest level in the table below.

As a general rule, you will not go far wrong if you note *both* the command word(s) in a question *and* the time allocation, and always try to answer at as high a level of skill as you can, while devoting an overall amount of time to the question that is proportionate to the mark available. Refer back to notes on time management in the 'General advice' on exam technique in Part One of this book (see page 101).

Assessment objective	Typical command words
AO1: Demonstrate knowledge and understanding of the specified content	State, list, describe, outline
AO2: Apply knowledge and understanding of the specified content to problems and issues arising from both familiar and unfamiliar situations	Define, give examples, distinguish between
AO3: Analyse economic problems and issues	Analyse, explain
AO4: Evaluate economic arguments and evidence, making informed judgements	Evaluate, justify, discuss

Objective test items

1. Which one of the following is an expected result of an economic recovery?

   A lower taxation receipts
   C lower unemployment
   B higher government borrowing
   D higher business confidence.

2. In the circular flow of income, economic activity is most likely to rise if:

   A savings and investment both fall
   C investment rises and taxation falls
   B imports and investment both rise
   D savings rise and investment falls.

3. Which one of the following would cause interest rates to fall?

   A a relaxation of monetary policy
   C a budget surplus
   B higher levels of exports
   D lower industrial costs.

4. Which one of the following is most likely to reduce frictional unemployment?

   A an increase in the exchange rate of the pound
   C help for people with their re-training and re-location
   B expansionary monetary policy
   D a reduction in the school leaving age.

5. Which one of the following would be most likely to cause the measured level of gross domestic product to fall?

   A a reduction in 'do it yourself' activities
   C a reduction in the value of farm production
      consumed by farmers
   B an increase in interest rates
   D a devaluation of the pound.

6. Economic growth is best defined as:

   A an increase in short-run aggregate supply
   B a movement to the left within a production possibility curve
   C a shift to the left in aggregate demand
   D an increase in the long-run trend level of output.

7. Other things being equal, an increase in which one of the following is most likely to lead to a short-run increase in a balance of payments surplus?

   A government spending on goods and services
   C income taxes
   B the price level
   D the money supply.

8. An initial increase in investment leads to a greater increase in national income. This is known as the:

   A golden rule   B multiplier principle   C accelerator effect   D output gap.

9. If a government kept all other variables equal, it would be undertaking an expansionary fiscal or budgetary policy if it increased:

   A government expenditure   B interest rates   C taxation   D the exchange rate.

10. An output gap is likely to exist when there is:

   A a flexible workforce
   C heavy investment in productive capital
   B a surplus of skilled labour
   D spare capacity in the economy.

WHEN THE NORTH DOESN'T ROCK

In 2007 we began to hear stories about the 'sub-prime' mortgage market in the USA. What did this mean? It turned out that American mortgage companies were lending money to people with poor credit histories, and charging them a high rate of interest for the privilege. This fuelled a flurry of house-building activity. Television programmes in the USA encouraged speculators to indulge in the practice of 'flipping', buying a cheap house at auction, giving it a lick of paint, and selling at a profit. Many small investors saw this as a way of making a quick buck. Larger companies also bought up huge tracts of land in places like Florida, to build second homes for well-off Americans and Europeans. It began to seem that houses weren't just a place to live, but a useful money earner. However, when many of the 'sub-prime' borrowers found that (surprise, surprise!) they could not repay their loans, the market suddenly began to collapse.

That might have been the end of the matter, but in today's globalised money market, things are not always simple. It turned out that the American mortgage companies had spread their risks by 'bundling' their loans into financial packages that were traded around the world. In the UK, a company called Northern Rock got into serious trouble. It used to be a building society, which accepted short-term deposits from savers and turned them into long-term loans for house buyers. This business model moved too slowly for the impatient managers of Northern Rock and, to enable faster expansion, they turned themselves into a bank and began to raise finance on the international money markets. Unfortunately, their loans were no longer supported by bricks and mortar, but included many stocks and bonds from the uncertain and fragile sub-prime market. When news of the company's difficulties spread, there was a run on the bank when savers tried to withdraw their deposits, and the UK government had to step in.

Usually in the UK, we assume that the property market is driven by the real economy as opposed to the speculative economy. As incomes rise, so the demand for housing rises; when people lose their jobs, demand for houses falls. Two things are generally bad news for the housing market – high interest rates and high unemployment.

The strength of demand in the housing market influences whether the Monetary Policy Committee (MPC) of the Bank of England raises or lowers interest rates. The state of the housing market influences the demand for goods and services in the economy, and monetary policy affects the working of the housing market.

The 'north–south divide' in the UK is linked to house prices and interest rates. House prices and the share of owner-occupied houses vary a lot between regions. In a recession, when interest rates are high and exporting is difficult, exporters in the manufacturing regions suffer a disproportionate fall in demand for their output.

(a) What is meant by the term 'monetary policy'? (5 marks)

(b) Explain how changes in the housing market can have both upward and downward multiplier effects. (8 marks)

(c) With the help of an aggregate supply and aggregate demand (AS/AD) diagram, predict how a collapse in the 'sub-prime' market in the USA might affect output and prices in the UK economy. (12 marks)

(d) The Monetary Policy Committee (MPC) of the Bank of England appears to pay a lot of attention to the housing market. Explain why it does this and discuss whether it is possible to pay *too* much attention to house prices, rather than other economic indicators. (25 marks)

Further reading

It always pays to have access to other economics text books, especially when it comes to bits that you find difficult to understand.

Anderton, A. (2006) *Economics*, 4th edition, Causeway Press. A well written text in a new edition to match the new specifications

Sloman, J. (2006) *Essentials of Economics*, 6th edition, Prentice Hall Europe. An introductory text used at university level which is clear and very thorough but written at a higher level than is required for the AS examination

Powell, R. (2008) *AS Economics, C. AQA: Student Unit Guide to Unit 1*, Philip Allan. A clearly written revision guide

Bamford, C. and Munday, S. (2002) *Markets*, Heinemann

Smith, D. and S. Grant (2003) *UK Current Economic Policy*, Harcourt Heinemann

Munday, S. (2000) *Markets and Market Failure*, Heinemann

Economic Review. Available by subscription from Philip Allan Updates, four issues a year; includes a very useful update in September

Economics Today. Available by subscription from Anforme, four issues a year; accessible articles about economic issues

For useful **websites**, providing economic data, other useful links, and summaries of economic concepts, you can go to www.heinemann.co.uk/hotlinks, insert the express code 2223P and click on 'Bized' and 'Tutor2U'

Glossary

Accelerator effect: the proportionally bigger effect on investment that is likely to be caused by a given change in demand.

Actual growth: an increase in real output in the short term.

Aggregate demand (AD): the total demand for goods and services in a given economy.

Aggregate supply (AS): the total supply of goods and services in a given economy.

Automatic stabiliser: fiscal policies that may automatically reduce fluctuations in economic activity associated with the economic cycle.

Average cost (AC): the cost of producing each item of production – also called the unit cost.

Balance of payments on current account: a record of the value of exports of goods and services set against the value of imported goods and services.

Balance of trade: the balance between the trade in goods account and the trade in services account, in the *balance of payments on current account*.

Balanced budget: occurs when planned government spending is equal to planned revenue.

Bank rate: the rate of interest at which the central bank is prepared to lend to commercial banks.

Barriers to entry: factors that prevent firms entering or leaving an industry.

Bottleneck: a shortage of particular products, services or factors of production associated with demand-pull inflation.

Brand loyalty: a business term used by economists to indicate that customers may choose a particular product out of habit or belief that it is better in some way than others.

Budget deficit: occurs when the government plans to spend more than it plans to raise in revenue.

Budget surplus: occurs when the government plans to raise more in revenue than it plans to spend.

Buffer stocks: stocks held by a government or government agency that can be used in an attempt to stabilise prices.

Capital: machinery and plant that are used to help transform resources into production; a *factor of production*.

Central bank: a bank with the role of regulating a country's banks and implementing aspects of monetary policy.

Ceteris paribus (Latin: other things being equal): assuming other variables remain unchanged.

Circular flow model: a simplified representation showing how firms and households interact. It links the demand for goods and services, production, the demand for factors, and incomes.

Claimant count: a measure of *unemployment* using records of those formally registered as entitled to unemployment benefit.

Classical economists: those who believe that without government intervention, changing prices ensure that markets clear. In other words, if the supply is greater than demand at a given price, falling prices will bring about *market equilibrium*. They believe that the labour market works in the same way: if unemployment exists, wages will fall until the demand for labour is equal to the supply, that is, until unemployment disappears. This can be applied to all factor markets.

Closed economy: a *circular flow* model that does not include the effects of foreign trade, that is, imports and exports.

Command economy: an economy in which all economic decisions are taken by the state.

Common Agricultural Policy (CAP): European Union policies to protect farmers' incomes and encourage agricultural production within the EU.

Competitive demand: occurs when a buyer can choose between similar products or services.

Complements: goods or services that are often bought together.

Composite demand: occurs when a resource can be demanded for different purposes.

Constant returns to scale: these occur when long-run average costs do not change as firms grow larger.

Consumer confidence: consumers' perceptions of their future well-being.

Consumer Price Index (CPI): an index of retail price changes that excludes the prices of 'owner-occupied housing costs'.

Consumption: current spending on goods and services.

Cost-push inflation: an increase in price level attributable to increases in the costs of production.

Cross elasticity of demand ($^x\varepsilon_d$): a measure of the responsiveness of demand for one product to changes in the price of another product.

Current account deficit: in the balance of payments, when the value of goods and services exported from a country is less than the value of imports.

Current account surplus: in the balance of payments, when the value of goods and services exported from a country exceeds the value of imports.

Cyclical unemployment: unemployment attributable to fluctuations in the economic cycle leading to a fall in demand for labour.

Demand (more precisely **effective demand**): the demand for a good or service backed up by the ability to pay for it.

Demand curve: shows the likely relationship between the price of a good or service and the quantity demanded of that good or service. Demand curves usually slope down from left to right showing that price increases are associated with falling quantity demanded and price falls associated with increasing quantity demanded.

Demand-pull inflation: rising price levels attributable to excess demand in the economy.

Demand-side shocks: those external events which are likely to affect the demand for goods and services from a given economy.

Demerit good: something that is considered to be socially undesirable but is likely to be over supplied by the market system.

Deregulation: the reduction of government rules and regulations that may hinder the free working of markets.

Derived demand: a situation in which the demand for a good or service is determined by the demand for another good or service; usually relating to the demand for labour being determined by the demand for a final product or service.

Developed economies: economies with higher levels of national income that tend to have more highly developed service sectors.

Diseconomies of scale: increases in long-run average costs associated with the growth of firms.

Disinflation: a sustained fall in the general price level.

Division of labour: when different individuals, or wider groups, undertake different roles within the productive process.

Downward multiplier: the mechanism by which negative growth, or contraction, in the economy stimulates further decline.

Economic agent: an economic decision maker who or which recognises that different factors motivate and influence different groups.

Economic cycles: fluctuations in economic activity over time.

Economic growth: the positive percentage change in GDP over a given period of time – usually a year.

Economies of scale: decreases in *long-run average costs* attributable to the growing size of a firm.

Elasticity: a measure of responsiveness between one variable and another.

Enterprise: decision making and risk taking in terms of combining the factors of production to produce particular goods or services.

Equilibrium price: the price at which demand and supply are equal.

Excess demand: occurs when the demand for a good or service is greater than the supply.

Excess supply: a situation in which the supply of a product or service exceeds the demand.

Exchange: the trade in and exchange of goods and services.

Exchange rate: the rate at which one currency can be exchanged for another.

Export-led growth: economic growth attributable to an increase in the value of exports.

Exports: goods and services sold to people living outside a country or economy.

External costs: costs that have to be paid by third parties to a transaction.

External economies of scale: changes in *long-run average costs* which are attributable to changes in the size of an industry.

Factors of production: land, labour, capital and enterprise – the four inputs required to produce a good or service. Nothing can be produced without some element of each, and a good or service can usually be produced with different amounts of each.

Fiscal policy: government use of taxation to influence macroeconomic variables.

Foreign direct investment (FDI): investment in a given economy by residents of another economy.

Free market economy: an economy in which all economic decisions are made by the private sector.

Free riders: those who receive but don't pay for the benefits of a good or service.

Frictional unemployment: unemployment of a short duration associated with people moving from job to job.

GDP: gross domestic product: the total value of goods and services produced within an economy in a given period of time.

GDP per capita: GDP divided by the population of a given country.

Globalisation: the development of worldwide markets and production.

Golden rule: government target of keeping government revenue in line with government expenditure over the period of the economic cycle.

Households: collective term for the owners of *factors of production.*

Hyperinflation: very high levels of inflation usually involving daily changes in the prices of goods and services.

Imports: goods and services that come into a country or economy.

Incentive: usually regarded as a financial factor that motivates an economic agent to behave in a particular way. Thus, a retail assistant might work harder to make sales if s/he receives a commission on each sale.

Income elasticity of demand ($^y\varepsilon_d$): a measure of the responsiveness of demand to changes in income.

Indirect taxes: taxes levied on goods and services which only have to be paid by consumers purchasing such products.

Index numbers: a means by which the percentage change year on year can easily be understood as numbers are expressed in terms of a base year value of 100.

Inelastic: describes a variable that is not very responsive to changes in another.

Inferior goods: goods for which demand falls as income rises and increases as income falls.

Inflation: increase in the price level over time, usually a year.

Injection: an addition to the revenue of a firm that does not normally arise from the expenditure of households; also known as an **addition**.

Innovation: the introduction of new inventions of products or processes.

Inputs: resources required to produce goods and services.

Internal economies of scale: changes in *long-run average costs* that are attributable to changes in the size of an individual firm.

Interest rates: the cost of borrowing, or the benefit of lending or depositing, money, usually expressed as a percentage.

International competitiveness: the trade effectiveness of a given economy in comparison to others.

Investment: spending by firms to increase productive capacity.

Joint demand: a situation in which products or services are bought together.

Joint supply: occurs when a resource can be used for a number of different purposes.

Keynesians: economists who are in broad agreement with Keynesian theories which suggest that factor prices, especially that of labour, do *not* necessarily fall to ensure that all resources are fully employed.

Labour: the *factor of production* representing human effort and work in transforming *inputs* to *outputs.*

Labour productivity: output per worker over a given period of time – usually per hour.

Land: one of the four *factors of production* representing the primary resources involved in production.

Long run: the time taken to change inputs of all factors of production.

Macroeconomic equilibrium: a state when national income is neither rising nor falling.

Macroeconomics: is concerned with issues such as unemployment, inflation and growth – concepts which affect the whole economy.

Marginal propensity to consume (MPC): the percentage of any change in income that is spent on the consumption of goods and services.

Marginal propensity to withdraw (MPW): the proportion of any change in income which is not spent on consumption.

Marginal rates of taxation: those paid on any addition to an individual's income.

Market: a notional place where buyers and sellers of goods and services meet.

Market clearing: the process by which changes in the price of a good or service bring about equilibrium between demand and supply.

Market failure: occurs when the market system produces socially unacceptable outcomes.

Merit good: something considered to be socially desirable but which is likely to be under supplied by the market system.

Microeconomics: focuses on how individual markets work and fail.

Missing market: a situation in which there is no mechanism by which the needs of potential buyers and sellers can be reconciled.

Mixed economy: an economy in which decisions are taken by the state, by privately owned companies and by voluntary organisations.

Monetary policy: the use of interest rates, money supply and exchange rates to influence macroeconomic variables.

Money: a means and medium of exchange.

Money supply: the total cash and credit available in an economy.

Monopoly: situation when production of a good or service is in the hands of one supplier.

Movement: in demand, indicates that the price of a good or service has changed.

Multiplier effect: an effect, analysed by the economist John Maynard Keynes, whereby any change in aggregate demand has a proportionally bigger eventual effect on national output.

Nationalisation: the transfer of ownership from the private to the public sector.

Negative externalities: these occur when the production and/or consumption of a good or service imposes additional costs on a third party.

Negative output gap: occurs when actual economic growth is below the trend rate.

Non-excludability: where once something is provided it is not possible to exclude others from benefiting.

Non-rivalry: situation in which consumption by one person does not reduce the amount available for consumption by others.

Normal goods: those for which demand increases as disposable incomes increase and decreases as disposable income decreases.

Normative economics: economics that may include value judgements and lack scientific objectivity.

Normative statement: a statement based on a value judgement or judgements which cannot be proved or refuted.

Open economy: a *circular flow* model that *does* include the effects of foreign trade (imports and exports).

Opportunity cost: the value of what has to be given up in order to produce or consume more of something.

Outputs: actual goods and services produced by firms in an economy.

Parallel markets: illegal markets that often arise when governments try to suppress markets in particular goods.

Pollution permits: permits sold or given to potential polluters in an attempt to limit pollution.

Positive economics: an approach that seeks to be more objective than *normative economics* and to pay much greater attention to adopting a scientific approach.

Positive externalities: these occur when the consumption of a good or service provides additional benefits to a third party.

Positive output gap: occurs when actual economic growth is above the trend rate.

Positive statement: a statement that can be proved or disproved by reference to evidence.

Potential growth: a long-term increase in productive capacity indicated by an outward shift of the PPC.

Price control: the imposition of a maximum and/or minimum price by a government; could be above or below *market equilibrium*.

Price elasticity of demand ($^y\varepsilon_d$): a measurement of the responsiveness of demand to a change in price.

Price elasticity of supply: a measure of responsiveness of supply to changes in price.

Price maker: a firm that has elements of monopoly power that enables it to set the price that consumers pay for its goods or services.

Price mechanism: a means by which scarce resources might be allocated between different and competing uses.

Private costs: costs that have to be paid by the supplier of a good or service.

Private goods: goods whose consumption by one person means that they cannot be consumed by another.

Privatisation: the transfer of ownership from the public to the private sector.

Production: the processes involved in transforming inputs to outputs.

Production possibility curve (PPC): a line showing all the different combinations of two goods that can be produced using all available resources.

Productive efficiency: producing goods and services at the lowest possible average cost.

Productivity: output for a given factor of production over a period of time.

Progressive tax: a tax which takes proportionately more from higher income earners.

Public goods: goods to which the principals of non-rivalry and non-excludability apply.

Public interest: a measure against which an attempt is made to balance up the positive and negative effects of, for example, a monopoly, or other economic factor.

Recession: technically, when economic growth in the economy is negative for more than two or more successive quarters (for six months or more).

Regressive tax: a tax which takes proportionately more from lower income earners.

Retail Price Index (RPI): an index of price changes that includes expenditure of owner occupied housing costs.

Savings: proportion of income not spent on consumption, imports or taken in taxation.

Savings ratio: the proportion of income that is saved.

Seasonal unemployment: unemployment attributable to seasonal variations in demand for particular forms of labour.

Shift: a shift in demand indicates that a variable other than price that affects demand has changed.

Short run: the period of time during which it is only possible to change the input of one factor of production.

Short-termism: choosing options for their likely short-term effect while neglecting their possible long-term effects.

Social costs: private + external costs – the full costs to society involved in the production of a good or service.

'Social housing': housing subsidised by the government, mostly provided by local authorities and housing associations.

Specialisation: the concentration on a particular part of the production process, or on the production of a particular good or service that is likely to lead to an increase in productivity.

Structural unemployment: unemployment associated with a fall in demand for labour related to the long-term decline of particular industries.

Subsidy: payment to a producer to encourage greater production of a good or service.

Subsistence: situation when a society is at best only able to produce enough food and basic products to survive.

Substitute: a good or service that consumers might consider an alternative for another.

Superior goods: goods for which a real increase in income results in a more than proportional increase in demand, and a decrease in a more than proportionate decrease in demand.

Supply curve: this shows the relationship between the price of a good or service and the willingness of a producer to supply that good.

Supply-side factor: a variable that can influence the productive capacity of an economy.

Supply-side policies: government policies designed to increase the productive capacity of the economy.

Supply-side shocks: those which will be first felt on the costs of supplying goods within a given economy.

Tastes: all those other subjective and personal factors that affect the demand for goods and services.

Trade deficit: when the value of exported goods is less than the value of imported goods.

Trade surplus: when the value of exported goods exceeds the value of imported goods.

Trend rate of growth: the averaged-out rate of growth over a period of time.

Trickle-down effect: the suggestion that raising the incomes of the better off can lead to increases in the income of the less well off.

Unemployment: the numbers or proportion of the workforce who are not working in paid employment but would like to do so.

Unitary elasticity: elasticity in which a change in price leads to a change in demand of the same proportion.

Upward multiplier: the mechanism by which growth in an economy stimulates further growth in that economy.

Value judgement: a statement that tends to be subjective and based on our personal values.

Wants: the goods and services which we would like to purchase without taking into account our ability to buy them, which is usually determined by our income.

Withdrawal: income not passed on in the form of consumption in the *circular flow*; sometimes called **leakage**.

Index

Note: page numbers in **bold** indicate definitions; page numbers in *italics* indicate figures and tables.